Foundations
of the
Responsible Society

Foundations
of the
Responsible Society

WALTER G. MUELDER

ABINGDON PRESS

New York *Nashville*

FOUNDATIONS OF THE RESPONSIBLE SOCIETY

Copyright © MCMLIX by Abingdon Press

Library of Congress Catalog Card Number: 59-5212

59 -1793

SET UP, PRINTED, AND BOUND BY THE
PARTHENON PRESS, AT NASHVILLE,
TENNESSEE, UNITED STATES OF AMERICA

THIS BOOK IS DEDICATED TO
Martha
Sonja, Helga, Linda

Introduction

In 1954 I was invited by President Harold C. Case, on nomination of the Board of the Graduate School of Boston University, to deliver one of the University Lectures for the academic year 1954 to 1955. The Lecture prepared for this occasion, "The Idea of the Responsible Society," published by the Boston University Press, comprises the substance of the first chapter of this book. It introduces the theme of the whole volume and anticipates several of its major conclusions. The phrase "the responsible society" has become the major theme in the social ethics of the ecumenical movement. There is a danger that this theme may become only a slogan unless it is developed further. This book attempts to survey the ethical foundations of the responsible society.

The initial discussion traces the development of the idea of the responsible society from the Universal Christian Conference on Life and Work held at Stockholm in 1925 to the Second Assembly of the World Council of Churches at Evanston in 1954. Subsequent chapters do not cover the whole range of social ethics, but they do seek to provide normative discussion of a wider range of issues than are generally treated in a single book in this field. Since cultures and nations are interrelated wholes, it is fruitful to deal synoptically and comprehensively with the basic institutions of mankind, with law, the state, economic life, work and vocation, management, agricultural policy, the family, consumption, the welfare state, social welfare, and the world community.

Such a comprehensive survey provides coherence by showing the cumulative relevance of the principle of social responsibility. The method helps both the critic and the research student to locate areas of study which require major reconstruction and more precise analysis than these exploratory studies have achieved. I have tried to concentrate on aspects of responsibility about which there are persistent theoretical as well as practical differences among competent scholars.

Specialists in theology and philosophy will note, however, the absence of a theoretical analysis of Christian ethics, philosophical ethics, and their interrelationships. In a subsequent volume I hope to deal extensively with the relation of Christ to the moral law showing that theology and philosophy are supplementary disciplines when confronting the problems of social responsibility. Such a study will have to deal critically with antiphilosophical tendencies in Christian ethics, on the one hand, and with the natural law tradition, on the other. It will indicate how a personal and social response to Jesus Christ can be integrated with an empirical and rational analysis of moral principles which are relevant as cross-cultural norms. Space does not permit the inclusion of this aspect of the foundations of the responsible society in this volume.

The reader will note extensive reference to the literature of the field and numerous direct quotations in the text. This method has been employed neither as pedantic show nor as a defense against negative criticism. The device is pedagogical, inviting the readers to meet authors and a literature with which they may be only slightly familiar. Though there is much social interest in American church and seminary circles, there is little knowledge of the rapidly growing discussion of the frontier issues between ethics and the social sciences. In deference to the pedagogical aim of this book I have attempted not to develop original theoretical structures, but to provide a useful introduction to some of the problems of our rapidly changing national and world society.

I have been encouraged by many friends and colleagues to carry this study through to completion. Not least was the earnest commendation of "The Idea of the Responsible Society" in one of the last letters of Albert Einstein. My associates in the faculty of the School of Theology have been a great inspiration to my efforts to combine teaching, writing, and research with my arduous administrative duties. I should acknowledge also that the original outline for the project as a whole was circulated among a number of leading scholars in the field by the publishers. This service to me has also resulted in major changes in design and emphasis. I am especially indebted to Miss Dorothy I. Lord for her valuable contribution in typing the manuscript. Mrs. Donald W. Anderson helped with final revisions.

Since I have drawn heavily and freely on materials from the numerous researches and publications of the Federal Council of the Churches of Christ in America, the National Council of the Churches of Christ in the U.S.A., and the World Council of Churches, I should like to add a final word about the spirit in which the whole study is written. I wish to encourage the ecumenical conversation and to make it more vigorous. I wish to introduce college students, theological students, ministers, teachers, social scientists, philosophers, and colleagues in the ecumenical movement to aspects of social responsibility which they might not encounter except for an analysis of this kind. In some respects my argumentation may appear quite eclectic, but there is an intention to go beyond a mosaic of borrowed concepts to a new level of inter-disciplinary integration. At the same time I wish students especially to be aware of the vast range of specialized literature in many fields which bear on social ethics. I am here writing, as I always work, at the inter-sectional points of theological, philosophical, and social science disciplines, aware of their varied and often conflicting traditions of methodology and conceptions of truth. My concern is for emergent coherence.

WALTER G. MUELDER

Contents

11

CHAPTER I

The Idea of the Responsible Society

A. The Background

The idea of the responsible society is a theme which emerges from the relation of ethics to the fact of world community. Under God mankind is the unit of co-operation. Mankind viewed as community holds the possibility of being a partnership in the good life. The theme of responsibility has roots in Israel's ancient past and in the Christian community's possession of the ethical tension among the norms of equality, freedom, and justice in the idea of the kingdom of God. Responsibility in social relationships is individual and interpersonal, and yet man's membership in economic and political groups poses problems which cannot be disposed of on this level of morality. Responsibility involves group and intergroup decisions in a complex matrix of domestic and international institutions, and yet more than this is involved, for the whole orientation of many institutions rests on cultural realities which tend to predetermine their goals and norms. The late Archbishop Temple perceptively noted this dimension of the human crisis:

> The present plight of our society arises in large part from the breakdown of these natural forms of associations and of a cultural pattern formed to a great extent under Christian influences. New dogmas and assumptions about the nature of reality have taken the place of the old. New rituals of various kinds are giving shape to men's emotional life. The consequence is that while their aims still remain to a large extent Christian, their souls are moulded by alien influences.[1]

[1] *The Christian News-Letter,* No. 198, December 29, 1943, quoted in Amsterdam Assembly, *Man's Disorder and God's Design* (New York: Harper & Bros., 1948), III, 125-26.

William Temple's analysis, directed primarily at the West, is even more relevant when expanded to include the world-wide encounter of cultures today.

To be responsible, men must be aware of goals, values, norms, facts, persons, and needs. To be responsible, men must have an understanding of relationships among these goals, needs, norms, facts, and persons, and of the consequences of possible decisions. To be responsible, persons must be free and willing to confront the hard choices which complex relationships often present. They must also be prepared to accept the consequences and sacrifices which may be involved. These things they cannot do as solitary individuals, but must learn to do according to decision-making processes which often involve many people of diverse backgrounds. Awareness and understanding require virtues of the imagination and mind; choices and sacrifices require virtues of will. Altogether they require moral maturity. They make up free and responsible persons.

The idea of the responsible society may be provisionally defined through an account of co-operative American and more especially of ecumenical social ethics. This theme is an effort within the ecumenical movement to state norms which are adequate in economics, politics, and social relations both domestically and internationally. Responsible society as a norm is still developing, for it is not a deduction from static principles. Like all social standards it is an emergent out of the matrix of ethical principles and concrete situations. As a specific theme it has a history.

On American soil the theme begins with the official formulation of the Social Creed of the Churches in 1908 at the time of the founding of the Federal Council of the Churches of Christ in America. There has been a slow development in the Social Creed in a half century, with slight modification articulated in 1912 and 1932. In 1942 F. Ernest Johnson summarized and evaluated the impact of the creed on American life during the thirty years since 1912. Its significance for the life of business and the role of businessmen has been recounted by the economist Howard R. Bowen in a book entitled *Social Responsibilities of the Businessman*.[2] During and since World War II the Federal Council and its successor, the National Council of Churches, have conducted nationwide study conferences which have contributed to the

[2] New York: Harper & Bros., 1953.

16

idea of social responsibility. These study conferences composed of labor, management, government, trade, and farmers' associations have faced moral issues relating to a just and durable peace, and more especially to the theme of industrial policy and ethics. Such conferences have met in Cleveland, Pittsburgh, Detroit, and Buffalo. In addition the Commission on the Church and Economic Life has prepared memoranda on special problems.

In 1949 under a grant from the Rockefeller Foundation and renewed in 1952, the Federal Council of Churches and subsequently the National Council of Churches have undertaken a series of studies of ethical aspects of economic life. A. Dudley Ward served as Director of Studies from the beginning until the fall of 1953, after which the project was directed by F. Ernest Johnson. These studies have been undertaken in response to the need for a careful and realistic investigation of economic life and its relation to spiritual and moral values in a Christian frame of reference. Both social scientists and theologians, working in close association with persons from many occupations, have worked on the project. The results of the study are available in a series of volumes, and others are still in process.[3]

In the world ecumenical context the idea of a responsible society has been coming to birth in a series of conferences, commissions, movements, and assemblies during the past thirty years. The Universal Christian Council on Life and Work was convened under the leadership of Archbishop Söderblom of Sweden in 1925. It brought together six hundred delegates from thirty-seven countries and was the first world conference to which the churches appointed delegates. During the dark days of the great depression a series of study conferences were convened in such centers as London, Basle, and Geneva. These led in 1937 to one at Oxford on church, community, and state. A large and impressive body of preparatory material running into several volumes dealt with nine main subjects, ranging all the way from the Christian understanding of man to the universal Church in the world of nations.

[3] The following volumes have all been published by Harper & Bros.: A. Dudley Ward, ed., *Goals of Economic Life;* Kenneth E. Boulding, *The Organizational Revolution;* Howard R. Bowen, *Social Responsibilities of the Businessman;* Elizabeth E. Hoyt, Margaret G. Reid, Joseph L. McConnell, and Janet Hooks, *American Income and Its Use;* Howard R. Bowen, John C. Bennett, William Adams Brown, Jr., and G. Bromley Oxnam, *Christian Values and Economic Life;* A. Dudley Ward, et al., *The American Economy—Attitudes and Opinions;* Walter W. Wilcox, *Social Responsibility in Farm Leadership;* John A. Fitch, *Social Responsibility of Organized Labor.*

In 1948 the Life and Work Movement was officially merged in the new World Council of Churches.

Paralleling the development of the Life and Work Movement was the International Missionary Council. Its great conferences at Jerusalem (1928), Tambaram, India (1938), and Whitby (1947) also attended to the social ethics problems of the ecumenical witness of the Church. The International Missionary Council is now in association with the World Council of Churches. The work of the missionary conferences is quite impressive and presents most realistically the need for a world-wide social witness in the midst of revolutionary situations.

The World Council of Churches has formulated its reports and messages through the Amsterdam Assembly of 1948 and the Evanston Assembly of 1954. In addition it has sponsored study conferences in Asia and has expressed itself through its Central Committee and its various commissions. The analysis which follows draws heavily on this whole world-wide conversation as well as on the work of American co-operative Christianity.

B. Definition of the Responsible Society

As a technical term "the responsible society" emerged from the First Assembly of the World Council of Churches, which met in Amsterdam, Holland, in 1948. The context of the emergent idea was the sense of tension between the Communist and non-Communist parts of the world, the desire of some groups and nations to develop a third force politically and economically, and the awareness on the part of Protestant and Orthodox leaders that Christians needed to develop a standard which would be relevant to the needs of their members in all countries. It was further required that the standard would be one which recognizes religious obligation to God and the responsibilities of all men to one another, one that would readily make contact with the sober constructive work of secular agencies such as the United Nations Commission on Human Rights. Moreover, it was essential that the rights and duties of Asians and Africans in the world situation would be as clearly expressed as those of the Europeans and Americans. The Message of the Amsterdam Assembly affirmed the world need as follows:

We have to learn afresh to speak boldly in Christ's name both to those in power and to the people, to oppose terror, cruelty and race discrimina-

18

tion, to stand by the outcast, the prisoner and the refugee. We have to make of the Church in every place a voice for those who have no voice, and a home where every man will be at home. We have to learn afresh together what is the duty of the Christian man or woman in industry, in agriculture, in politics, in the professions and in the home. We have to ask God to teach us together to say "No" and to say "Yes" in truth. "No," to all that flouts the love of Christ, to every system, every programme and every person that treats any man as though he were an irresponsible thing or a means of profit, to the defenders of injustice in the name of order, to those who sow the seeds of war or urge war as inevitable; "Yes," to all that conforms to the love of Christ, to all who seek for justice, to the peacemakers, to all who hope, fight and suffer for the cause of man, to all who—even without knowing it—look for new heavens and a new earth wherein dwelleth righteousness.[4]

Out of this concern and sense of religious obligation emerged the following definition of "the responsible society":

Man is created and called to be a free being, responsible to God and his neighbor. Any tendencies in State and society depriving man of the possibility of acting responsibly are a denial of God's intention for man and his work of salvation. *A responsible society is one where freedom is the freedom of men who acknowledge responsibility to justice and public order, and where those who hold political authority or economic power are responsible for its exercise to God and the people whose welfare is affected by it.*[5]

This definition was supplemented by the following commentary which adds concreteness to the general definition:

Man must never be made a mere means for political or economic ends. Man is not made for the State but the State for man. Man is not made for production, but production for man. For a society to be responsible under modern conditions it is required that the people have freedom to control, to criticize and to change their governments, that power be made responsible by law and tradition, and be distributed as widely as possible through the whole community. It is required that economic justice and provision of equality of opportunity be established for all the members of society.[6]

[4] Amsterdam Assembly, "Message."
[5] Amsterdam Assembly, *The Church and the Disorder of Society,* p. 192. (Italics supplied.)
[6] *Loc. cit.*

19

The components of this composite norm (such as freedom, justice, equality, and control of power) have their respective histories and may even appear somewhat obvious to those reared in the ideals of Judaeo-Christian and democratic social movements. Nevertheless, the idea of the responsible society is a Gestalt or a dynamic moral pattern. On the one hand it rejects the either-or of the East-West stereotype. Those who formulated it rejected both totalitarian Communism and *laissez-faire* capitalism. The negative judgment on Communism was perhaps the more significant since it referred to an organized present reality, a dynamic movement. *Laissez-faire* capitalism, on the other hand, was an anachronistic expression. Present-day capitalism is a complex mixture of many elements, a dynamic international, and by no means simply an American economic system. As the debates since 1948 have illustrated, the responsible society is a developing social standard which brings into unity the world-wide conversation among the church leaders from all continents and from both sides of the Iron Curtain.

Through this idea a number of the most crucial themes in contemporary culture are brought into focus, such as: (1) the role of religious norms in the just and free society; (2) the conception of man, his dignity, rights, and self-realization in community with others; (3) the nature, authority, and scope of the modern state and its functions in relation to the community; (4) the interpenetration of the political, economic, and social spheres of society; (5) the tension of such ideals as equality, freedom, and justice within the general idea of responsible living; (6) the responsibility of persons to domestic and international orders of freedom and justice; (7) the accountability of power groups within nations; and (8) the responsibilities of nations to one another and to the future of responsible international order.

We shall examine a number of these component issues analytically, drawing on the development of some of the leading ideas through the past thirty years.

C. The Religious Component in the Idea

The religious component is the most comprehensive and ultimately the most basic. Before elaborating this dimension of responsibility, however, it is well to note that the churches have been and are aware that the values of the responsible society make contact with and interpenetrate those of culture at large. At the ecumenical Conference of Christian Social Workers in London in 1930 this latter point was frankly stated: "The churches are concerned not only with the preaching of a specifically Christian ethic but also with the furtherance of those broad principles of humanity on which the conscience and reason of the world at large are at one with the conscience and reason of Christianity itself." [7] There are many theologians today who would not agree with such a statement. But most would agree that society's responsibility to God is not a narrow churchly doctrine. Indeed, the Church is answerable to God for its service to every human being in the cause of responsible freedom. As a theologian at Heidelberg, speaking for Christians in the East Zone, puts it, the Church "is the servant of every human being." [8]

Responsibility to God has several ethical fruits such as practical urgency, the majesty of justice, religious freedom, and universal solidarity. It means that the Church is called to represent the principle of responsibility in society without predetermining the cultural content of specific responsibilities. Persons under God have a reference which transcends physical nature and culture. As Joseph Fletcher says: "Responsibility is not a matter of natural and objective fact; it is a moral and spiritual thing. It is a human and personal phenomenon, not to be found 'out there' in the physical world." [9] Persons have rights, "especially the right to say 'yes' or 'no' in response (in being responsible), the right to self-determination, the right to be themselves, to choose; in short, to be a *thou* and not an *it*, a subject and not an object." [10] Being a person is a gift of God recognized by the Church as older and broader than the Church but laying a special vocation upon those who are in the Church.

The religious dimension of the responsible society is an important factor in unmasking the pseudoethical and hypocritical elements in totalitarian regimes. In the totalitarian countries simply to insist on maintaining freedom and integrity in Christian worship is an act which challenges the very heart of the regime in so far as the latter draws its

[7] Report: "The Churches and Present-Day Economic Problems," available in *Ecumenical Documents on Church and Society* (Geneva: World Council of Churches, 1954), p. 21.

[8] W. Schweitzer, "The Church's Freedom and Its Responsibility in Eastern Europe and in the Western Orbit," Memorandum to the Study Department of the World Council of Churches, June, 1950.

[9] *Morals and Medicine* (Princeton, N. J.: Princeton University Press, 1954), pp. 12-13.

[10] *Ibid.*, p. 38.

orientation from materialist presuppositions. The challenge can further be illustrated by the stand taken by Bishop Dibelius, who was elected one of the six presidents of the World Council of Churches. His church unmasked the Communist "World Peace Movement" in December, 1950, in a letter to the minister-president of Saxony as "political fanaticism combined with religious sentimentality." In that same year he had a declaration read in the churches of Brandenburg protesting against all kinds of concentration camps, against the materialistic view of life, against the creation of conflicts of conscience deliberately devised by the authorities, and against propaganda for the so-called National Front among the clergy. In 1950 he declared that there could be no responsibility without responsibility to God—which was equivalent to denying all forms of human autonomy in politics in both their East European and their Western forms.[11]

The transcendent religious reference does not free the religious person from relevant social responsibility, but it does set him free in a twofold sense. Since his responsibility is to God, his basic security is in God, and this frees him from seeking it primarily in the flux of circumstances. In the second place, it frees him from the anxious either-or of social pressures and allows him to transcend the conflict without retreating from it. For example, church members in the East Zone of Germany, who have their security in God, are free to do what can be done without their resistance becoming a front for mere anti-Communism, as is often demanded from them by the West. They can be open for all creative possibilities.

The third way or third force for which the churches seek is therefore a norm of responsibility which is relevant without being restricted to particular forms of public order or the horizontal conflicts of rival power groups. Accountability to God makes human dignity, freedom, and justice ultimate issues. On the one hand it saves personal and social responsibility from the threat of meaninglessness or the sense of cosmic indifference. On the other hand it assures personal worth a stable equilibrium in the churning sea of social relativity.

D. Respect for Persons

There is a current tendency to take human dignity for granted

[11] F. Karrenberg, "Church and Social Questions in Germany," Study Department Document, World Council of Churches, p. 5, n. 6.

without relating it to social responsibility. Moreover, the idea of personal worth is not a monopoly of Western religious groups. One international economist notes that "nowhere is concern over the effects of the prevailing economic system on the quality of human life deeper than in non-Christian countries whose economies are being transformed by the influence of [the American] economic system." [12] In "Persons and Values," Edgar S. Brightman noted that in the Conference on Science, Philosophy, and Religion many creeds and beliefs have been represented, but amid all the differences

there has been one principle on which there has been uniform agreement —the principle of respect for personality. Personality itself is taken to be an intrinsic value; without respect for personality all other values are corrupted. Without personality, no other values exist. Unless personality is valued, all else is devalued.[13]

If there is to be a responsible society, there must be free and responsible persons. They not only make claims, but they also accept their duties. Personal worth not only gives grandeur and depth to the work of the United Nations Commission on Human Rights, but it challenges shallow views of freedom, security, and justice. Persons must develop their capacities for decision making. They do not do this, as the sociologist Cooley pointed out, by having imposed on them complete responsibility for all the decisions that affect their interests. One does not serve the person by giving him more decisions to make than he can rationally attend to.[14] On the other hand, as society looks out for man's welfare, the person must increase his capacity for voluntarily making decisions along with others, or he will fail in some of the greatest challenges to his freedom. Man must learn to do his part in the economic and political order, not automatically but as a moral act.[15] Among other things man's moral loyalty to the community, says John M. Clark, "must be tough-fibered enough to tolerate the amount

[12] W. A. Brown, Jr., in Bennett, *op. cit.*, p. 102. Used by permission of Harper & Bros.

[13] University Lecture, April 16, 1951 (Boston University Press), pp. 17-18. The Conference on Science, Philosophy, and Religion has met annually since 1940. It is composed of leaders from these three fields.

[14] J. M. Clark, "Aims of Economic Life as Seen by Economists," in Ward, *Goals of Economic Life*, p. 48.

[15] *Ibid.*, p. 50.

of inequality that is an inescapable incident of a healthy economy dependent on individual incentives." [16]

The ethic of respect for personality must also be one of personality fulfillment. This ethic of self-realization in community has been a constant theme in the past thirty years of ecumenical social ethics. It has also become part of the humanitarian spirit of the age and perhaps affects economic and political policy more persistently than do economic or political theories. Everywhere in the world one confronts the imperative "to create the environment in which alone man can in fact be free." The drive for personal actualization apportions from time to time a different stress on the values of equality, freedom, and justice. We must accordingly now turn to these norms within responsible society.

E. Meaning of Freedom

Tensions between freedom, justice, and equality are inherent in moral man and moral society. Some see behind the demand for justice the tyrannical dominations of the coercive community; some see in freedom the threat of anarchy or the irresponsibility of individualism; some see in equality the liquidation of personal individuality and the leveling of all creative genius to the plane of dull mediocrity. A healthy dialectic among these values helps man to distinguish "between the social revolution which seeks justice and the totalitarian ideology which interprets and perverts it." [17]

The definition of the responsible society with which we began takes account of this dialectic. In such a society "freedom is the freedom of men who acknowledge responsibility to justice and public order." On the other hand, "those who hold political authority or economic power are responsible for its exercise to God and the people whose welfare is affected by it." Under modern conditions "it is required that the people have freedom to control, to criticize and to change their governments" and that power "be distributed as widely as possible through the whole community." There are times when personal worth demands the struggle for freedom, as in the question of teachers' rights;

[16] Ibid., p. 51. Used by permission of Harper & Bros.
[17] East Asian Christian Conference, "Findings: The Church in Social and Political Life," Statements of the World Council of Churches on Social Questions (Geneva, 1956), p. 27. The conference was convened in December, 1949.

at other times for justice, as in social security; and yet again for equality, as in desegregation.

When one traces the appeal for freedom through the past thirty years of the ecumenical movement, some striking emphases stand out sharply. At Stockholm in 1925 freedom meant the "free and full development of the human personality." [18] In 1928 the emphasis in the Jerusalem Conference was freedom of association for employers and employees alike, especially in the industrially undeveloped area of Asia and Africa.[19] Another type of freedom dominated the Geneva Conference of 1932. The churches there expressed concern that "in the economic and political fields the obstacles be removed which prevent a free exchange of economic forces on a world-wide scale." [20] Yet another form of freedom was lifted up at Rengsdorf the following year. The conference articulated a theology of freedom. "The Church," it said, "is not bound absolutely to any particular social order, and has freedom to judge any social order on its merits." [21] The independence of the Church and freedom to criticize the state and society became an increasingly important element in social pronouncements in the Nazi period and in relation to the totalitarian paganism of Communism and Fascism.

From the time of the great Oxford Conference of 1937 to the present the Church has been alert to all the above forms of freedom. The Oxford Conference rejected the materialism of Communism for deriving all moral and spiritual values from economic needs and economic conditions and in so doing depriving "personal and cultural life of its creative freedom." [22] At the same time Oxford set freedom in opposition to the economic autocracy of capitalism. It looked with favor on voluntary co-operative enterprises and also reinforced the norms of the personal worth of workers, the need for freedom of opportunity, and the ideal of the full development of man's capacities.[23]

[18] "Message of the Universal Christian Conference on Life and Work" (Stockholm, 1925), par. 6.

[19] International Missionary Council (Jerusalem, 1928), "The Christian Mission in Relation to Industrial Problems in Asia and Africa."

[20] "Resolution on Unemployment," The Universal Christian Council for Life and Work (Geneva, 1932).

[21] "Conclusions," Ecumenical Study Conference on the Church and the Problem of Social Order, (Rengsdorf, 1933), par. 5.

[22] "Main Report on Church, Community, and State in Relation to the Economic Order," Pt. II.

[23] *Ibid.,* Pts. III, IV, V.

The question of freedom played a significant role in the discussions in India in 1938. In addition to contrasting real freedom with the individualism and competition in countries dominated by imperialism, the delegates affirmed freedom in contrast to racial discrimination, cultural discrimination, social discrimination, and sex discrimination.[24] Here freedom passes over into what is called "civil rights."

The larger problem of new nationalism gave the issue of freedom a special context as the missionary delegates surveyed what they called "self-satisfied," "self-assertive," and "self-expressive" types of nationalism. Leaders in the missionary movement have been aware for decades that nationalism and the cry for independence are more deeply-lying social forces in Asia than Communism. Consequently it is a pity that the United States has built its policies so much on anti-Communism rather than on the constructive social forces involved in the "self-expressive" forms of national freedom. Asian Christians regard our anti-Communist obsession as an irresponsible support for reaction. Since 1938 they have been articulate in seeking "to create the environment in which alone the whole man can be free." [25]

Since World War II the requirements of freedom over against the growing power of the state have been emphasized. "The increase of state planning, however necessary to provide security, cannot but threaten individual, and sometimes spiritual, liberty; and men often seem ready to purchase security even by the surrender of freedom." [26] This viewpoint seemed to be pushed into the background somewhat at Amsterdam in 1948, when the assembly condemned both Communism and *laissez-faire* capitalism. But Amsterdam, like Whitby, rejected all forms of totalitarianism in the world, whether Fascist, Communist, or religious. Freedom it linked positively to responsibility for justice. At the Evanston Assembly of 1954 there was a shift of emphasis which some reporters have played up as a repudiation of the idea of the responsible society at Amsterdam. *The Chicago Tribune* said of the Evanston report on "The Responsible Society" that it was more similar to the G.O.P. platform of 1952 than to the Amsterdam report. *The New York Times* and *Time* took the line that the churches

[24] International Missionary Council (Tambaram, 1938), findings of Section XIII, "The Church and the Changing Social and Economic Order."

[25] *Ibid.*, "Some Types and Illustrations of Christian Social Action," par. 3.

[26] "Christian Witness in a Revolutionary World," International Missionary Council (Whitby, Canada, 1947), II, par. 3.

upheld "free enterprise." As John Bennett points out, however, this was not the case.[27]

The development between Amsterdam and Evanston is of interest because it became apparent immediately after 1948 that it was a mistake to use "capitalism" as the contrasting symbol to "Communism." "Capitalism" is too ambiguous a phrase. Europeans use it for a spirit and an ideology, Americans use it to describe the present system which is changing rapidly and which is actually a mixed economy, and in Asian minds it is connected with imperialism. Preparatory meetings for Evanston decided not to use so confusing a symbol.[28]

There has also been a development in much socialistic thinking in Western Europe with a greater appreciation of the contribution of free enterprise in economic life. With less stress on doctrinaire arguments the present approach is much more pragmatic, taking for granted a great deal of state action but also giving an important place to private sectors of economic power and to subsidiary groups. So also in the Evanston report a realistic nondoctrinaire approach is taken which recognizes the role of the private power groups in society but also states that "under many circumstances the state is the only instrument which can make freedom possible for large sectors of the population."

F. Justice and Equality

The respect for personality which makes freedom so crucial a norm also requires that freedom be responsible for justice. Between 1925 and 1939 the passion for social justice dominated the discussions of social policy in ecumenical gatherings. Social justice includes distributive justice but is a dynamic idea which embraces also sound goals, social well-being, democratic control of power in industry and business, and the fulfillment of a wide range of needs and rights. Thus the Stockholm Conference of 1925 in the name of the gospel affirmed that "industry should not be based solely on the desire for individual profit, but that it should be conducted for the service of the community." [29] Justice meant co-operation between labor and capital, stewardship, community and individual responsibility in solving problems of overcrowding, unemployment, moral laxity, and crime.

[27] "The Responsible Society," *Social Action*, November, 1954, pp. 5-8.
[28] *Ibid.*, p. 6. Cf. Paul Abrecht, "Social Questions—The Responsible Society in a World Perspective," *The Ecumenical Review*, October, 1953.
[29] "Message," par. 6.

In 1928 the Jerusalem Conference highlighted the concern over injustice in the Far East, such as employing forced labor. It asked specifically that contracts of labor "entered upon by workers of primitive races should be fully understood by them, should be voluntarily entered upon, and should be subject to the approval of the administrative authorities." Taking an active interest in the International Labour Organization, it also advocated satisfactory work conditions and wages, medical and sanitary equipment, elimination of child labor, adequate inspection of work places, various forms of social insurance, the right to organize, and civil liberties.[30] These demands in the mission fields correspond generally to those in the social creeds of the churches in America. Many of these were already matters of legislation in Britain and Europe.

During the great depression questions of justice tended to focus on issues relating to unemployment and to managerial rationalization in industry. Increasingly these led to judgments on the social order as a whole. The present social order, said the London Conference of 1930, "stands condemned as Godless, and as militating against true progress." "Industrial capitalism is at present administered without reference to the will of God." [31] Such judgments reflect the desperate plight of Britain. Constructive solutions were harder to come by, the conference not venturing to state "whether political rather than economic measures or vice-versa" were the key to the solution. However it suggested that "labor's share in the control of industry" might be explored. Perhaps the most important economic judgment was that the problem of the world's prosperity is primarily a problem of distribution. This dominant emphasis on distributive justice recurred at most subsequent conferences.

As opposed primarily to emphasizing distributive justice within the nation, the Basle Conference of 1932 marks a new level in ecumenical thinking by discussing the *integral* character of economic justice, that is, with the principle that justice has to do with the economy as a whole.

Political and economic leaders must strive to keep the idea of the entirety of the economic system always in the foreground and must embody it in

[30] Ecumenical Documents on Church and Society, section on "Protection Against Economic and Social Injustice."

[31] *Ibid.*, "Statement of the Members of the Conference," signed by Miss A. Charles, V. A. Demant, and O. Bauhofer.

economic legislation and the whole structure of industrial life. The lack of insight into the integral character of economic relationships, the failure, especially in recent years, to take into consideration the interest of the whole as above that of individuals and separate groups, has led to gross errors and omissions which have brought about deplorable economic losses.[32]

This level of justice calls for world-wide economic co-operation.

From this point on it becomes increasingly clear that the idea of the responsible society must develop not simply along domestic lines but as a world-wide concept. The responsibility of the United States to maintain a stable and dynamic economy in the world situation becomes more and more evident, though the idea is not emphatically articulated in church statements until World War II. Today writing as a Christian, W. A. Brown, Jr., of Brookings Institution treats stability as an ethical as well as an economic question. He points out that foreign nationals fear the United States because of the danger of marked inflation and deflation in a country which holds such concentrated power in production and consumes so much of the world's production of raw materials and foodstuffs. To fluctuations in American economy are linked the most complex and delicate balances of international exchange. One illustration must suffice. At the time of the 1949 recession American imports were 15 per cent of world imports, but the percentage of the exports of the Philippines, Cuba, Brazil, Chile, Canada, Venezuela, Uruguay, Malaya, and Japan bought by the United States ranged from 72 per cent to 22 per cent.[33] The relatively small recession of 1949 in America released virtual economic warfare abroad in the scramble for a favorable relation to American dollars, with attendant retaliation and bitter feelings.

Along with the international dimension of deflation and inflation the domestic dimension of responsibilities must also be noted. These involve the policies of major economic groups within the nation such as management, labor, and agriculture. In a special study report on inflation the National Council of Churches criticized the tendencies of major economic groups to accept necessary sacrifices only on condition that equal or greater sacrifices are made by other groups. Such

[32] "International Study Conference on Unemployment" (1932), section on "Future Organizations of Economic Life."

[33] Bennett, op. cit., p. 122. Cf. A Trade and Tariff Policy in the National Interest, prepared by the Public Advisory Board for Mutual Security, Washington, February, 1953 (called the Bell Report).

policies only increase inflationary tendencies. The memorandum made two points of special interest in this connection, pointing out

1. That "if every major economic group—whether of workers, farmers, or employers—makes its contribution [to the fight against inflation] contingent on prior action by other groups, and each is continually looking over its shoulder to see what the other is doing, the moral as well as the practical basis for a successful stabilization effort is seriously undermined."

2. That "in an inflationary situation every major economic group strives at least to maintain its real income," and that "if all such major groups are wholly successful in maintaining their command over goods and services while the basic causes of inflation continue to operate," the real burden of inflation will fall on those parts of the community that are least able to defend themselves.[34]

The demand for an integral approach to economic justice involves a judgment on the responsibility of the state as well as the subsidiary groups within the nation. At Geneva (1932) and Oxford (1937) the churches began to formulate their basic position on the modern state. The state, they recognized, is one of the institutions ordained by God, but not any particular form of the state is ordained. Like other values in the social order the political question is generally one of better or worse, a problem of mixed goods and evils. The state derives its authority and its power from God in order to maintain and further justice and peace among men. The source of justice is God; therefore the state is not the lord but the servant of justice. Its sphere is limited. Hence as guarantor and not the ultimate source of law the state may not arbitrarily violate the legal rights of the individual or of associations in society. Neither may it destroy such institutions as family and church. No form of the totalitarian state is just.[35]

Social justice affirms the ideal of the "harmonious relations of life to life" in the face of the "sinful tendency of one life to take advantage of other." Its task is to define the rightful place and privilege which each life must have in the harmony of the whole and to assign the duty

[34] "Christian Responsibility Toward Some Ethical Problems in Inflation," National Council of Churches, 1952.
[35] Oxford Conference, "Report on Church and State" (1937).

of each to each. In such a view justice has both a negative and a positive significance. Negatively justice delineates principles to restrain evil and the evildoer. Positively justice formulates the political and economic skeletal structure of society which carries the organic element of the community. Here justice serves and extends the work of love. As Oxford said: "Forms of production and methods of cooperation may serve the cause of human brotherhood by serving and extending the principle of love beyond the sphere of purely personal relations." [36] Though often the servant of love, the structure of justice must never be identified in any political or economic order with the kingdom of God.

There were additional aspects of justice which clamored for attention. Speaking directly to capitalistic modes and relations of production, Oxford lifted up the danger of treating human labor as a commodity, the loss to the worker of the social meaning of his work, and the hostility engendered among various economic groups. At this time the churches looked forward to the possible abolition of poverty in the world and noted the moral importance of this possibility, saying that this possibility "to an increasing extent . . . makes the persistence of poverty a matter for which men are morally responsible." [37] It is this principle that underlies the imperative for responsible assistance to underdeveloped areas in the world. A Christian society is thus under an obligation to use every means in its power to bring within reach of all its members the material, as well as the ethical, conditions of spiritual growth and vitality. In one form or another the modern state tends to become a "welfare state" operating on the principle that "all men should enjoy the minimum economic conditions and opportunities requisite for a decent and healthy life." [38]

Alongside this we must place a second principle which complements the above demand to abolish poverty: "Economic power must be held continuously in check, so that it does not exploit individuals or groups, exalt private interest against public advantage, restrict access to oppor-

---

[36] Oxford Conference, "Main Report on Church, Community, and State in Relation to the Economic Order," Pt. 1.

[37] *Ibid.*, Pt. 3, "Points at Which the Christian Understanding of Life Is Challenged."

[38] R. M. MacIver in Ward, *Goals of Economic Life*, p. 186.

tunity, suppress the liberty of opinion, or otherwise dominate the creative life of the community." [39]

The ecumenical movement looks back at Oxford as one of the high points in the development of social principles. Yet equally dynamic and quite as telling for the post World War II period was Tambaram, India, in 1938. Revolution was surging in Asia and Africa. "Communism as an economic program for social reconstruction should be distinguished from communism as a philosophy." [40] There are many tasks of justice to be done:

increasing the fruitfulness of the land, raising the level of literacy and intelligence, providing wholesome recreation, turning slums into homes, rescuing people from financial exploitation or trying to prevent such sin, directing the energies and the social instincts of youth into channels of wholesomeness and service.[41]

The missionary leaders looked for a new order of social life in which the sacredness of personality became a working fact; in which the unit of co-operation was the whole human race; in which every person had equality of opportunity for his complete development; in which there was a redistribution of the world's economic goods, that is, a just distribution of the goods which makes equality of opportunity possible among the nations and within each nation; and in which inequality of privilege in respect to access of the world's raw materials had been overcome. Perhaps more than any previous ecumenical conference this one asked the churches to give social justice a powerful spiritual dynamic.[42]

This discussion of justice has inevitably taken account of the problems of equality. In some respects justice is the mean between equality and inequality. Not only is the equalitarian ideal prominent in American life, but it affects the demand for social justice all over the world. Equality and inequality not only are constituent elements of

---

[39] *Ibid.*, p. 189.

[40] International Missionary Council (Tambaram, 1938), "Findings of Section I: The Faith by Which the Church Lives."

[41] *Ibid.*, "Findings of Section XIII, The Church and the Changing Social and Economic Order."

[42] *Ibid.*, "The Social Significance of Christianity."

justice; they are related to freedom. For example, equality of opportunity has to do with personal freedom and with the whole range of group needs at all levels of life. Equality relates to rights, that is, to civil liberties and civil rights. Fundamentally it is not so much a quantitative ideal as a spiritual principle. It is the claim which personal worth makes in every social situation, institution, and condition. The equality which is an absolute claim and a constant in both justice and freedom is the claim of spiritual dignity by the person. Thus in the complex unity of responsible action equality, justice, and freedom are interpenetrating norms and values, but they are also ideas in polar tension with one another. Respect for the equality of personal dignity may require inequality in distributive justice, and freedom of opportunity may have quantitative unequal expressions. Two persons may be spiritually equal, but their gifts and needs may be very unlike and require different treatment. Again, freedom in a competitive economy, as Frank H. Knight points out, does not work for equality in the material sense, but in the opposite direction. On the other hand the liberal sense of justice will not complacently accept extremes of wealth and poverty. As one authority puts it:

On ethical grounds it is hard to see why an individual who has inherited a high I.Q. or a green thumb is more entitled to preserve for himself, as a matter of moral right, a larger share of the product of that capability than the person who has inherited a particularly fertile piece of land.[43]

Taken by themselves equality, freedom, and justice may lead to the most dissimilar consequences.

G. Some Concrete Demands

The idea of the responsible society seeks to find creative solutions "which never allow either justice or freedom to destroy each other." After the Amsterdam Conference where this goal was expressed, efforts were made to build on the norms of responsibility which have been developed in this chapter, notably at Bangkok in 1949 and in Lucknow in 1952. Here the idea of the responsible society was spelled out in terms of Asian and African urgencies. So far as goals and norms for

[43] William Vickrey in Ward, *Goals of Economic Life*, p. 154; cf. p. 228.

underdeveloped countries are concerned, the Evanston Assembly largely incorporated these into its own report.

Five general demands emerge: (1) obedience to God requires an active concern for human freedom and justice; (2) political freedom for hitherto submerged peoples who have awakened to a new sense of dignity and historic mission; (3) a sense of personal worth within the community which rejects an interpretation of man solely in terms of his social and political functions; (4) a fuller participation by the people in the life of society at the level where power is exercised; and (5) a rejection of Communism because it lacks a conception of the independence of moral reality over against power and because it denies consequently the supremacy of the moral law over power-politics.[44] Communism defeats the very purpose of the social revolution and turns the struggle for justice into a new oppression. It is blind to the fact that the most basic freedom is religious liberty. Religion's concern for ultimate values is the foundation for sustained responsible action.

The more socially concrete expressions of the responsible society relate to land reform, planning for production, and raising the standard of living with the assistance of technical know-how and capital from abroad. In East Asia the churches have endorsed basic changes in land tenure and rural development, including abolishing the old feudal landlord system, in some cases without compensation to the landlord.[45] The churches also accept the reality that the "countries of East Asia are committed to . . . the social planning state as a matter of fundamental social justice and concern for human welfare." In actual fact what is supported is a mixed economy conception. Though key industries must be nationalized, due place must be given to private enterprise in the development of both large and small scale industries. East Asian Christians view adequate technical assistance and economic aid from abroad as an expression of world-wide responsibility. Such assistance is a matter of social justice, arising out of concern for human need wherever man lives and as a response to human solidarity. The re-

[44] "Findings of the Eastern Asia Christian Conference, Bangkok, December, 1949. The Church in Social and Political Life."

[45] The Ecumenical Study Conference for East Asia, Lucknow, India, 1952, "Findings of Section II: The Responsible Society in East Asia in Light of the World Situation."

sponsible society is related in Asia to the "welfare state," but Christians view it not as a road to Moscow but rather as a "third force." [46]

In East Asia a summary of social standards may be sharply stated in negative terms. Viewed negatively, a society is *not* judged responsible when human rights and freedoms are *not* effectively promoted for all, when social change and reform are promoted *without* respect for the integrity of the human person, when its people do *not* possess full sovereignty over their own affairs, and when official action *interferes* with voluntary association and religious freedom. Viewed positively, society is judged responsible in East Asia when social justice is actively promoted, the full development of natural resources is pursued, the fullest share possible of the national wealth is guaranteed to all, human rights are effectively guaranteed, the people do have full sovereignty in their own affairs, and the ruling principles of social and political life are in accordance with the concept of man called to responsible existence in community.[47]

H. Emerging Perspectives

The idea of the responsible society which emerges from thirty years of ecumenical discussion, including six years of wrestling specifically with the Amsterdam definition, may be summarized as follows:

1. Theologically speaking society is responsible to God, who is the ultimate source of all true value and its preserver. The responsible society is supported by specifically Christian norms, but it is meaningful also to non-Christians.

2. True justice is a dynamic concept, and its forms must vary to meet changing needs. "Those who seek [justice] should be made sensitive by love to discover such needs where they have been neglected." [48]

3. The conception of the state must be constructive, critical, and realistic with a demand for constant review of its functions and limits. The state is the guarantor but not the source of justice. The state must be "ready if necessary to accept responsibility to counteract depression or inflation and to relieve the impact of unemployment, industrial

---

[46] *Ibid.*, Pts. I-III.
[47] *Ibid.*, Pt. 9.
[48] The quotations in this section are taken from W. A. Visser 't Hooft, *The Evanston Report* (New York: Harper & Bros., 1955), "The Responsible Society in a World Perspective." Used by permission of the publisher.

injury, low wages, and unfavourable working conditions, sickness, and old age. But in doing so the state remains the servant not the lord of social justice." The state is sometimes the enemy of freedom, "but under many circumstances the state is the only instrument which can make freedom possible for large sectors of the population."

4. The nongovernmental sectors in economic life have the task of being guardians of responsible private action in society. "But within the private sector, both employers and employees in all their varied organizations in their turn are the servant, and not the lord, of freedom and welfare."

5. The state alone has the power and the authority under God to act as trustee for society as a whole. This idea of the state is not a static principle embalming the sovereignties of present nation states, but refers to the state as developing in relation to sound world political order as well.

6. The idea of the responsible society, then, has passed beyond the stage of rejecting the ideologies of *laissez-faire* capitalism and totalitarian Communism. It takes account of the new emphasis on state initiative and international organization on the one hand and of the importance of relative freedom in enterprise and the regulating role of the price system on the other. Many socialists both within the church and outside it have in recent years come to appreciate the importance of the private sector of the economy and the need for energetic, enterprising, and expert businessmen. All economies are today mixed economies in one degree or another.

Private enterprise takes many shapes in different countries at different stages and in different parts of one economy and is profoundly affected by the forms of government regulations. The operations of the state in business also take various forms, such as post offices run by government departments, supply of electric power or gas by local authorities, and national or state public corporations. In all types of economy there is to be found a variety of forms; there is no one pattern that is universally valid.

7. State action must do those things for the economy that private industry cannot do properly, such as planning for urban development, stimulating industrial expansion and soil conservation, undertaking

some types of large-scale industrial and agricultural research, and guiding the distribution of industry. But state action needs to be decentralized, limited, and adaptable.

8. In contrast with the almost exclusive emphases of the conferences of the 1930's on justice as equitable distribution within and among nations, the present emphasis notes that "efficient production is important as well as fair distribution." Laziness and waste are evils no less than selfishness and greed. But the emphasis on increased production to meet the world's need does not displace the requirement of equity in distribution. Indeed, "equity in the distribution of wealth and income requires a closer approach to equality."

9. A very special importance resides today in the power of organized groups, such as trade unions and associations of employers, farmers, or professional people. These groups must be responsible to the whole of society and to their members, and their members must learn greater responsible participation within the organization. As in the state, so in these groups power must be controlled through free criticism and instruments of accountability and democratic change.

10. In the conflict with Communism persons who seek the responsible society must beware of the temptation to embrace totalitarian means because there seems in some times and places "no alternative which will bring essential social change quickly enough." Such persons must beware that where Communist methods of social and economic life are introduced, the total Communist scheme will likely come to dominate the minds of men as well as their institutions. On the other hand there exists the tendency in democratic societies to lower standards of civil liberty and sometimes to strengthen reactionary forces in countries abroad. Enemies of essential human freedom appear on both the political right and the political left. The proponent of responsible society must be alert to the subtle danger to community from those who identify as subversive any unpopular opinions or associations. Neither self-righteousness nor obsession with the fear of Communism makes for responsible community. They are in the final analysis self-defeating.

11. Since the unit of co-operation today must be mankind, the norm of the responsible society must be further developed to bring out clearly the relationships of independence and interdependence among nations. This calls for a greater awareness and understanding of human

37

needs and the consequences of economic, political, and social action by one nation or group of nations on all others. It also calls for a willingness to make hard choices and sacrifices in the interest of responsibility. The role of international agencies in the idea of the responsible society is a most urgent problem in ecumenical social ethics.

CHAPTER II

Mankind: The Unit of Co-operation

When we speak of mankind as the unit of co-operation, we are speaking in part of a fact and in part of a goal. For many years social analysts have characterized world society as convulsed, distraught, disintegrated, troubled, and threatened with possible extinction. The world has never been integrated to any significant degree; how then can it be disintegrated? It has never had any purposed unity as an economic, social, or political entity. To formulate an ideal of community which is world wide is, as we have seen, an imperative of moral law. But true unity has yet to be built into the minds of men. No stage other than the world can be the unit for realistic thinking about the responsible society. Eero Saarinen says that in architecture he learned a lesson from his father he never forgot: "Always design a thing by considering it in its next larger context—a chair in a room, a room in a house, a house in an environment, environment in a city plan." [1] Mankind is the earthly context of co-operation. Despite the belligerent attitudes, policies, and programs which divide parts of the world, they are parts of the confluence of modern history and must be approached within a single field of fundamental kinship, interdependence, and human involvement. For better or worse they belong to the one world confronted by one body of ultimate norms. The whole world is developing a common consciousness of a common peril. It must develop a common consciousness of a common fulfillment.

Co-operation highlights the problem of relating purposive change to purposive unity. On the one hand, we have evidence of purposive co-operation promoted by agencies like the United Nations. On the

[1] *Time*, July 2, 1956, p. 51.

other hand, we note the deep penetration of underdeveloped countries by technical assistance and development programs in ways which threaten the cultural integrity of the receiving country. At one level the nations of the world seem eager to cross national boundaries in the quest of resources and know-how to build up agriculture and industry. At another level they are equally eager to express their cultural independence and autonomy.

In relation to one another peoples and nations play a bewildering number of roles, and yet they are caught up in the universal fact that they are an interacting whole. What kind of unity should they seek? What values must be considered? How can the various cultural unities of meaning and value find a common ground for creative interaction? Can rival political and religious faiths be transcended? Are there transcultural themes or cultural universals which provide resources for global unity? Is there such a right as world-wide citizenship? In the interaction of cultures, sovereign nations, and economic systems do science and democratic ideals have a definitive role to play? What constitutes a responsible society?

A. Mankind as Unconscious and Conscious Unit of Co-operation

To be a unit of co-operation does not imply that there is unity in co-operation. When one considers the historic isolation and self-absorption of peoples and nations, when one notes the different and almost contradictory patterns of culture, when one observes the varieties of family life and the competing institutions of property holding, when one confronts the intensity of nationalism and conflicting goals of national policy, or when one finds himself inevitably a partisan in some rival political ideology, it is easy to conclude that there is no unity and hence no functioning unit of co-operation. To the above listed factors might be added the divisive influence of renascent world religions especially in those parts of the world where new nationalisms are stirring the religious heritage of the people into the strong drink of patriotic ideologies. Then, too, there is the rising wave of insistence on the use of national languages and the concurrent tendency to stop reading the literatures of nations written in another tongue. The blocks to communication and community are many and serious. Yet no nation lives unto itself, and no culture dies unto itself alone.

The fact that mankind presents itself as an interdependent whole on quite an unconscious or only semiconscious level is evident from even a cursory survey of economic relationships. Lenin was wont to observe that the Russian peasant was totally unaware of how his labor fitted into the world economic order when he brought the fruit of his harvest into the market. And yet how much his life depended on the dialectics of international trade! During the great depression men were seldom aware that a lockout in a Youngstown, Ohio, rubber plant might be directly related to the pawning of loin cloths in Bali. The economy of Burma was threatened by the "dumping" of American rice on the world market. Tariff changes respecting Swiss watches had a repercussion in the form of Swiss trade commissions going to Moscow. It is commonplace now for children to practice naming all the countries which the food and utensils on an American breakfast or dinner table represent. If one follows through the trade patterns of even some small countries, one is impressed by their global character. In the case of large economic empires one cannot escape the fact of a giant network of units of economic co-operation. The human participants of these cartels may hardly be aware of their global roles.

The common people of Afghanistan may not be aware that their leading exports of karakul skins go mostly to the U.S.A. and that much of their trade, normally carried on through Pakistan, is exported to the U.S.S.R., from which their consumers' goods are derived. Though Afghanistan has no railroads or navigable streams and though much of the trade is carried by camels and horses, yet the life of native farmers is tied to that of the great rival powers of East and West. Albania is still a primitive economy where each family tries to provide most of its own needs. Yet its postwar trade is for the most part limited to the Soviet bloc of nations, whereas once it was tied to Italy. A different cluster of relationships dominates the foreign trade of Argentina. Exports go chiefly to Britain, the U.S.A., and Brazil, and imports come mostly from the U.S.A., Britain, and Germany. The great port of Buenos Aires is second only to New York in the Western hemisphere. Still a different pattern obtains in Indonesia. The leading customers are Singapore, the Netherlands, the U.S.A., and Britain while the principal suppliers are Japan, the U.S.A., the Netherlands, and Britain. In the case of the United Kingdom the prosperity of the nation is directly dependent on its foreign trade. The chief destinies of exports have been to

Australia, South Africa, the United States, Canada, India, and the Netherlands, and the chief sources of imports were the United States, Canada, Australia, New Zealand, Kurwait, and Denmark. Powerful but significantly different combinations of trade relations obtain in the U.S.S.R. and China. The U.S.A. foreign trade, while not a large portion of the total American economy, has become so important for many of the smaller nations from which imports are derived that the maintenance of domestic stability is one of the chief aspects of responsible economic policy.

The above paragraphs are but fractional illustrations of the fact that the world is becoming, however unconsciously, a great unit of economic interdependence. Against the fact of an imperfect multilateral trading system the nations are challenged to pursue *purposefully* an adequate system. Ideally a multilateral trading system would be world wide with all nations entering voluntarily and wholeheartedly into a common and agreed system of nondiscriminating trade.[2]

Other illustrations than those of trade could be used: inventions, ideas of art, principles of social organization, concepts of religion, and philosophy. Not least significant in the present turmoil of human affairs is the international role of ideas such as Marxism, or the scientific method, or the Judaeo-Christian emphasis on the worth of the individual person. In certain respects these may be viewed as parts of the conscious co-operation of men, but in many other respects the effect of such ideas on the interdependence of man is not a product of self-conscious intention.

Turning now to mankind as a conscious unit of co-operation, we may note the role of the major religions of the world. The great living religions are universal in principle, and many are world wide as actual communities. They are a great resource for the integration of mankind as a unity of co-operation as well as for the preservation of a multigroup society. When tied too closely to national cultures and ideologies, they contribute to the promotion of antagonism and hostility. The tendency of religion to give concrete social practices absolute sanctions makes for mass conflict among the respective groups of adherents. Moreover, the conflict among absolute sanctions which are used to defend compet-

[2] N. S. Buchanan and F. A. Lutz, *Rebuilding the World Economy* (New York: Twentieth Century Fund, 1947), p. 295.

42

ing social practices makes for the relativization of ultimate norms. The type of missionary zeal pursued by some world religions accentuates such tensions.

In recent decades there have been many efforts at the political level to bring the life of the nations into positive integration of interests and values. Such efforts are evidenced not only by the League of Nations, the continuing International Labour Organization, and the United Nations general political and judicial organs, but also its specialized agencies. These agencies express the purposive and deliberate effort of nations to accept the whole world as the unit of co-operation and to tackle problems with a view to global human welfare.

The UN agencies have developed an impressive range of goals. It is instructive to note cumulatively their various purposes: (1) FAO: To raise nutrition levels and living standards; to secure improvements in production and distribution of food and agricultural products.[3] (2) IMCO: To promote co-operation among governments in technical problems of international shipping and to encourage removal of discriminating action by governments and of unfair restrictive practices by shipping concerns.[4] (3) BANK: To assist in reconstruction and development of economies of members by making loans directly and promoting private foreign investment; to promote balanced growth of international trade.[5] (4) ICAO: To study problems of international civil aviation and establish international standards and regulations.[6] (5) ILO: To contribute to establishment of lasting peace by promoting social justice; to improve through international action labor conditions and living standards; to promote economic and social stability.[7] (6) FUND: To promote international monetary co-operation and expansion of international trade; to promote exchange stability; to assist in establishment of multilateral system of payments in respect of current transactions between members.[8] (7) ITU: To maintain and extend international co-operation for improvement and rational use of all kinds of telecommunication and to promote development and most

[3] Food and Agricultural Organization, headquarters in Rome.
[4] Inter-Governmental Maritime Consultative Organization, headquarters to be in London.
[5] International Bank for Reconstruction and Development, headquarters in Washington.
[6] International Civil Aviation Organization, headquarters in Montreal.
[7] International Labour Organization, headquarters in Geneva.
[8] International Monetary Fund, headquarters in Washington.

efficient operation of technical facilities.[9] (8) ITO: To promote expansion of world trade and removal of trade barriers.[10] (9) UNESCO: To promote collaboration among nations through education, science, and culture in order to further justice, rule of law and human rights and freedoms without distinction of race, sex, language, or religion.[11] (10) UPU: To assure organization and perfecting of various postal services and to promote development of international collaboration. To this end member countries are united in a single postal territory for reciprocal exchange of mail.[12] (11) WHO: To aid attainment by all peoples of the world of the highest possible level of health.[13] (12) WMO: To facilitate world-wide co-operation and promote standardization in the making of meteorological observations; to further application of meteorology to various human activities.[14]

An International Atomic Energy Agency has been established to promote peaceful uses of atomic energy.

These agencies set in motion long-range forces of technical and cultural change even while providing a global framework of co-operative action. The relations of technical change to the numerous cultural patterns which are deeply rooted in the life of peoples raise significant ethical issues. Among these are the roles of purposive change and purposive concern for persons and the effect of the scientific spirit on the cultures it pervades.

B. Cultural Patterns and Technical Change

This heading is taken from the significant book of the same title edited by Margaret Mead.[15] Many of the agencies noted in the previous section are concerned with the impact of the rapid expansion of technology on all cultures but especially on those least technically developed. There is no doubt about the transforming power of modern scientific technology as it penetrates society. It affects the most basic aspects of social organizations and institutions. Societies must learn to

[9] International Telecommunication Union, headquarters in Geneva.
[10] International Trade Organization (still under provisional organization).
[11] United Nations Educational, Scientific and Cultural Organization, headquarters in Paris.
[12] Universal Postal Union, headquarters in Bern.
[13] World Health Organization, headquarters in Geneva.
[14] World Meteorological Organization, headquarters in Geneva.
[15] UNESCO (New York: Columbia University Press, 1953) and the New American Library of World Literature, Inc.

adapt themselves to technology, for it has profound repercussions on family and kinship relations as well as on man's relation to the land and the systems of property ownership. Science is no superficial or neutral social force when aggressively pursued and applied.

The notion that science is axiologically neutral is still very common. Methodologically it is important to discriminate between descriptive science and normative science, between facts and values, between causal nexus and evaluation of purposes. But as a cultural phenomenon science and the technology built upon it affect all the other aspects of culture. It is useful to distinguish the methodological discipline of science as being rationally objective and factual from the spirit and morals of science, including its social prerequisites. These latter are of tremendous significance in the social ethics of world co-operation. David Bidney notes:

> The scientific pursuit of knowledge is itself a moral good, and the scientist has his own ideal code of professional ethics to obey. Furthermore, the scientist requires a social and cultural environment suitable for the pursuit of his vocation, namely, one which permits him complete freedom of thought and experiment in the pursuit of scientific truth and cultural knowledge. That is why the scientist as scientist must be actively concerned with the preservation of the basic cultural freedoms lest he jeopardize his own enterprise. The unethical pursuit of science leads to ultimate self-destruction, as does the unscientific pursuit of ethics and aesthetics.[16]

As a cultural attitude science has a normative, humanizing function in determining one's entire cultural perspective. It is, therefore, not merely an instrument of technology but an intrinsic value, a "humanity which determines the spirit of a culture." It must be acknowledged, nevertheless, that societies may behave in neurotic ways, embracing conflicting value systems and goals. Moreover, as Louis Wirth has observed, a mature physics can apparently coexist in the same society with an infantile politics.[17]

The most significant aspect, however, of the relation of technical change to cultural patterns is the fact not so much that within mankind

[16] *Theoretical Anthropology* (New York: Columbia University Press, 1953), p. 430. Used by permission of the publisher.

[17] In Lyman Bryson and others, eds., *Perspectives on a Troubled Decade* (New York: Harper & Bros., 1950), p. 269.

as a unit of co-operation the effects of science are to be felt, but that change today is *purposive*. This purposeful activity has the profoundest implications for social responsibility. Margaret Mead highlights this phenomenon in the introduction to the work cited above:

> What is new is the assumption, on an international scale, of responsibility for introducing changes which are needed among peoples in areas of the world which can visibly benefit from the knowledge which the peoples of other areas have—of techniques which will increase production and conserve natural resources; of nutritional practices which will improve the well-being of a people; of public-health practices which will lower the death-rate, the incidence of epidemic and endemic disease, and rescue individuals now doomed to physical and mental illness. New also is the recognition and willingness to deal scientifically with the concomitant effects of such change.[18]

Purposed technical change is thus linked to *purposed* cultural change and to *purposed* mental health of the persons who are undergoing the change.

> In all technical change, even when it seems to be concerned with tools, machines and other impersonal objects, the individual person is both the recipient of change and the mediator or agent of change. His integrity as a person, his stability as a personality, must be kept ever in focus as the living concern of all purposive change.[19]

It is to be hoped that the world-wide emergence of insight into and tender concern for the person will be, despite the awful conflagrations of global wars, the hall mark of the twentieth century. If this tender concern is not only written into the Universal Bill of Human Rights and Freedoms, if it is not only acknowledged by the great religions, if it is not only written into conventions and laws of the member nations of the United Nations—but also written into the methods of social change—a great world-wide coherence of persons-in-community will have taken place. Indeed, unless respect for the dignity of personality and the dignity of human cultures is recognized in the methods of social change, the great goals will not be achieved; for the means one employs determines the ends one will get, whether one intends those effects or not. Means and ends must be coherent.

[18] *Op. cit.*, p. 12.
[19] *Ibid.*, p. 288.

This discussion compels us to face realistically the cultural context of personality and, after considering the wholeness of culture, to ask whether the multitudinous cultures can really be integrated into a unity of co-operation.

C. The Unity of Culture

World society is composed of many cultures. They are, especially in primitive peoples, unities of meaning and value. A culture is a systematic and integrated whole. For the purpose of this discussion we may adopt a definition of culture by Margaret Mead. It

is an abstraction from the body of learned behavior which a group of people who share the same tradition transmit entire to their children, and, in part, to adult immigrants who become members of the society. It covers not only the arts and sciences, religions and philosophies, to which the word "culture" has historically been applied, but also the system of technology, the political practices, the small intimate habits of daily life, such as the way of preparing or eating food, or of hushing a child to sleep, as well as the method of electing a prime minister or changing the constitution. . . . A change in any one part of the culture will be accompanied by changes in other parts, and . . . only by relating any planned detail of change to the central values of the culture is it possible to provide for the repercussions which will occur in other aspects of life. . . . The wholeness of a culture is not a statement that all cultures are integrated in the same way, or that all are equally integrated.[20]

There are several modes in which culture may be integrated, and there are various perspectives from which anthropologists have approached both descriptive and normative problems.[21]

Transformation, which is inevitable, must proceed with due regard for the problems of social cohesion and personal worth. In many primitive societies, for example, a large amount of time and energy are consumed in ritual, magic, and other religious practices which the agricultural expert from America might regard as wasted. But the native farmer does not live by bread alone, and these practices give him faith in his work and save him from the anxieties which so often attend farming. Where agriculture is a total pattern of life rather than

[20] *Ibid.*, pp. 12-13.
[21] See Bidney, *op. cit.*, chs. 13 and 14.

just a way of earning a living, this means that the areas of religion and agriculture are not compartmentalized.

The problem emerges whether a world community is possible when the societies and cultures that make it up live under different political organizations, are regulated and organized under contrary economic systems, are related to rival ideologies or inner religious meanings which are radically diverse, and esteem goals and norms that are quite distinct.[22] Must a world community try to unify all these societies? We cannot answer this question in a simple way.

The several nations and cultures of the world are moving today into a new confluence of history. There are many obstacles to be encountered and overcome. How closely integrated or highly organized a responsible society would be cannot now be envisaged. But one great and basic fact is the essential kinship of the race. Despite cultural conflicts and differences, we must not lose sight of the similarity of fundamental traits among all branches of mankind. Mankind has a unity which transcends the differentiated cultures and the diverse historical paths which the peoples of the world have traveled. It is a temptation to magnify the inflexibility and diversity of historical tradition. As Louis Wirth points out, one should remember that the nation states of the present day have only recently crystallized into the political entities that they are. The same great cultures have at one time or other been shared by diverse peoples, and the same people have been incorporated in and contributed to a variety of cultures.[23] If we were able to ascertain the basic values cherished by the masses of mankind in the various countries of the world, we would probably find that despite local and national idiosyncrasies they have much in common. They share some cultural universals.

D. Transcultural Themes and Norms

The presence of cultural universals is generally recognized in contemporary anthropology.[24] These may be called themes or thematic values. There is continuing debate as to how many such themes or

[22] Quincy Wright, ed., *The World Community* (University of Chicago Press, 1948), p. 30.

[23] Bryson, *op. cit.*, p. 271.

[24] Melville J. Herskovits, *Man and His Works* (New York: Alfred A. Knopf, Inc., 1948), ch. 15; Morris E. Opler, "Themes as Dynamic Forces in Culture," *American Journal of Sociology*, November, 1945, pp. 198-206.

universals there are or how they are to be classified. There is also no final scientific agreement as to how they should be accounted for. But for our present purposes it is important to note that common themes can be recognized in all cultures despite diverse behavior patterns. Linton, like other anthropologists, distinguishes the thematic values from the behavior patterns by which they are instrumented. The latter are inevitably shaped by the practical considerations of materials and skills available and by the conditioning of individuals who compose the society. Among them there is bound to be considerable cultural relativity. Confusion between these two levels of cultural expression is frequent and leads to serious misunderstanding in social sciences and ethics. Two further cautions must also be observed. The universal values (themes) may be used as datum points in developing ethical judgments, but since cultures are wholes, it is important to recognize the effectiveness of instrumental values within the context of the milieu they serve. Moreover, the presence of universal themes does not of itself provide an evaluation of their relative significance in culture or world society.[25] The problems here are both theoretical and practical.

All cultures are internally integrated, but they are differently integrated. Social ethics is interested in how they are integrated and for what ends they are integrated.

It is important to frame an adequate ideal of community and then to note the discrepancies between this norm and the historical realities. This means that cultural relativism has an essential truth in it, namely, that values must be understood in a cultural context, but it also means that the rational criticism of cultural norms and the formulation of adequate universal norms in some order of priority and coherence are also required. At the same time one must not confuse the real value or norm under discussion with the particular mode of cultural expression which it embodies. Cultural relativism is thus relative to coherent reasoning about values. Bidney speaks of the "concept of an absolute value" as a significant regulative norm:

The absolute norm is real insofar as it is conceived as an ideal possibility whose validity is independent of its actual realization in cultural experience.

[25] Ralph Linton in Ward, *Goals of Economic Life*, pp. 308-9.

49

Hence, the absolute ideal may serve as a goal of cultural endeavor which is radically different from the process, the going, whereby it is approximated. The concept of the best is not merely a preference of a given historical society; the normative best is a metacultural ideal which transcends the actually given of historical experience and yet as a regulative norm is a significant factor in molding experience.[26]

The question naturally arises; How does one move from the plurality of present cultures by means of cultural universals to the normative ideal of world integration? Louis Wirth proposed to the Conference on Science, Philosophy and Religion in 1949 some assignments or tasks in this field. These assignments did not presuppose an acceptance of Bidney's theory of regulative ideals, but only of a functional approach based on the assumption of cross-cultural norms. He suggested first that there be integration of knowledge concerning values. This would mean classifying and analyzing the basic objectives or ideals which the various branches of the human family seek to realize, the relative order of priority which each nation or people assigns to particular values, the compatibility or incompatibility of these values, their interdependence, the means available for their satisfaction, their costs in terms of other values, and the probable consequences that would flow from their realization or frustration. The second form of integration of knowledge has to do with the rules or norms governing the striving for the realization of these values, including the analysis of the institutions which affect the formulation and enforcement of rules. The third form of integration of knowledge for which Wirth asked concerns the conditions of life which influence the selection and acceptance of these values and the resources available for their realization.[27]

These forms of integration of knowledge are the tasks which may be laid upon philosophers, scientists, and theologians, but they do not of themselves carry out integration at the point where decisions are made. Nevertheless, such a functional program as has been proposed would be eminently worth while in overcoming the false concepts of cutural relativism that are rife, and would prepare the way for the posing of the most basic alternatives open to man. Meanwhile men are increasingly preoccupied with certain general goals.

[26] *Op. cit.,* p. 428.
[27] "Integrative Tendencies in International Relations," in Bryson, *op. cit.,* pp. 276-77.

One of the emerging transcultural norms which is slowly transforming every culture it pervades is science, which we have briefly noted above. Another such norm which has caught the imagination of the world is "democracy." This term is, of course, not unambiguous. Yet there is more in common among the conflicting groups who adhere to it than may be imagined by one who is a rigid skeptic.

UNESCO made an instructive inquiry of a representative body of scholars on their conception of the specific content they ascribed to democracy. Virtually no one who calls himself civilized today but wishes to be known to cherish democracy, though he places different emphases on its various ingredients. The contrast between "peoples' democracies" and "bourgeois democracies" does not destroy the universal prestige of the word. What is common is not destroyed by party cries of "phony democracy." It is becoming increasingly apparent that the world cultures are converging in the great value stream of the "common man." This concept need not mean that all values are merging in mass mentality. A multigroup society will continue in the foreseeable future. But the "common man" is an image that represents the emergence of personality out of the mass of exploited, downtrodden, colonial, and primitive peoples, out of poverty and ignorance, out of mass impotence, into an imperturbable determination that these evils need no longer be. The conflicting forms of democracy represent different stages and facets of the tensions between freedom, equality, and justice which we noted in connection with the idea of the responsible society.[28] Quincy Wright has said, "Democracy implies in the varied conditions of human environment and society, a proper balance among popular support of, popular participation in, and popular benefit from, government, and a popular balance among liberty, equality, and fraternity." [29]

Democracy and science are but two of many values and norms involved in the global understanding of mankind as the unit of co-operation. Quite as important are the spirit and the methods employed in changes which are purposively induced in the various cultures. This is the great ethical concern of the UNESCO manual by Margaret Mead to which several allusions have already been made. The culture of each people is a living unity. As each human individual embodies the

[28] See Chapter I.
[29] Op. cit., p. 285.

culture through which he lives, the tensions and changes in culture will have their expression in the personality organization of each person. "When the introduction of technical change is purposely initiated, or promoted by individuals or responsible bodies, such purposiveness involves responsibility for the effects not only in improved living-conditions, but also upon the total way of life of the people, for reintegration as well as defense against disintegration." [30] It is not possible to prescribe in advance just how changes should be instituted, for each cultural situation is, despite universal themes, unique. Yet all changes should be introduced with the fullest possible consent and participation of those whose daily lives will be affected by the changes. All the changes that are made occur through the mediation and should be for the benefit of persons.[31] Hence the criteria of the involvement of the whole personality should be used: "Any reliance on a method which is purely intellectual, or purely aesthetic, purely emotional, purely moralistic, purely social or purely individual, will necessarily restrict the area of involvement." [32]

The Western cultural emphasis on the worth of persons is clearly evident in Miss Mead's concern for all men. This emphasis reflects the cultural power of the Judaeo-Christian tradition even when it is not explictly referred to or used as the ultimate sanction. From a Judaeo-Christian standpoint the unity of mankind is that of the family of God's children. In the specific Christian heritage God is held to have identified himself through Jesus Christ with all mankind and to have called out a "People of God," the Church, to express in history the ministry of healing, reconciliation, and service to the world.

---

[30] *Op. cit.*, pp. 288-89.
[31] *Ibid.*, pp. 289-303.
[32] *Ibid.*, p. 302.

CHAPTER III

Basic Institutions of Culture

A. *The Institutional Components of Culture*

Having confronted the fact of mankind as the unit of co-operation and some of the problems of achieving unity in co-operation among cultural wholes, it is necessary to inspect more closely some contemporary crises in the basic institutions of culture. We wish to emphasize as strongly as possible the cultural interdependence of these institutions and the significance of this fact for social ethics. Subsequent chapters will deal more fully with them in relatively autonomous analyses.

In this chapter and the remainder of this book we shall be chiefly concerned with the family, education, political, economic, and religious institutions. Many of the moral problems of other aspects of culture will have to be neglected in the interest of these. The reader should keep this selection and abstraction in mind.

Each culture, as we have seen, has an inner unity. This does not mean that it is completely unified. Karl Marx, for example, showed that class conflict characterized Western society. Complex societies exhibit great inner tensions despite the cohesive forces which define their inner wholeness. To speak of modern cultures as a unity is to use an "ideal-type" expression and must not blind the scientist or moralist to actual historical conflicts.

Modern societies have exhibited great inner strain as they move from patterns described as communal to others described as associative, from social groups based on "status" to those based on "contractual" relations. from homogeneous aggregates to heterogeneous aggregates employing a complex division of labor; from the predominance of "primary groups" to the dominance of "secondary groups," and from "folk culture" to urban industrial civilization. Since cultures are value-oriented, these strains constitute crises for the persons who are undergoing them and who must make the decisions for responsible purposive change.

The tensions and the possibilities are of special concern to religion, for it is not simply one cultural pattern alongside others but expresses, ideally speaking, the ultimate orientation and direction of the whole culture. The meaning of the culture is constituted by the ways the various components are related by the participating persons and groups to this ultimate frame of reference. A crisis in culture occurs when the component elements are torn loose from their common meanings or when the religious orientation is repudiated as in secularism, or when the various aspects and institutions become so specialized, differentiated, or centrifugal in their expressions that the sense of wholeness is lost. Many persons experience the crisis of modern culture when they find conflicting values in their roles as producers, as consumers, as members of families, as church members, as professional people, or as citizens or officers in the state. There is such a deep cultural crisis today in many parts of the world.

B. The Nature and Function of the Family [1]

The crisis of the family is world wide. The family is in transition. Few people wish to dissolve the family, yet it is threatened by dissolution through the convergence of many of the atomizing forces of modern life and the centrifugal forces which rob the family of its cohesion by dissipating its roles. We think of family life as essentially conservative and of the taboos that surround its sexual practices as ancient and fixed. The family cannot be taken for granted. Its cohesive values are as tender and precarious (and as tough) as life and love, and they must be purposed and conserved if the family is to play its part in serving personal fulfillment.

Because a degree of permanence in the relationship of mating partners antedates human culture and civilization, the conjugal family may be said to have deep roots; but the need to conserve the family is only lately challenging the attention of scholars, churchmen, social workers, and statesmen as they see that its stability is no longer guaranteed. With the rapid development and expansion of technologi-

[1] See also Chap. IV.

cal urbanized life, the small conjugal family is displacing the large or joint-family pattern where it still exists. The conjugal family relationship is one in which security in personal relationships, perfected mutual response, and congenial companionship may be achieved but are not given values.

Responsible family planning must provide for diverse personal and social values, such as the complementary functions of men and women, their respective economic roles, the relations of parents to dependent offspring, the long periods of the reproductive cycle, the longer period of childhood and adolescence, the conditions for the optimum development of the personality of the children, the socialization of the siblings, the introduction of the children into the larger patterns of the consanguine group or of the neighborhood and community, and the education of the children for adult roles.

Family life must also continue to nurture the adults in values and norms which conserve emotional maturity and spiritual perspective for daily work.

The consanguine family group has almost completely disappeared in Europe, and its counterpart in Africa and Asia is in a state of transition to the conjugal family type. Many forces are responsible for this. Those that operate so powerfully in America at the present time may be but a herald of the world-wide situation in the foreseeable future. In many ways, despite its historic toughness, the family is highly vulnerable because as an institution it cannot organize much strength to combat its enemies. On the other hand, in its smallness and its plurality lies much of its viability.

To conserve sound family units, a responsible society will need to understand the effect of a number of factors which influence family life either externally or internally. Some of this may be briefly cited as follows: (1) The growing independence or autonomy of women. Women need not be content with second- or third-rate husbands in order to have economic security. (2) The changing economic function of the family as a whole. (3) The increasing role of anonymity in human relationships in the city. This tends to substitute functional roles for organic ties. The diffuse casual social relationships decrease community pressure to maintain family ties when other factors make for separation. (4) The large number of working women. This fact raises the question of the relationship of a man and his wife in the home complementing and not repeating the kinds of relationship found in the work situation. (5) The lessening of religious sanctions and the change in the character, quality, and role of the religious resources employed. (6) The earlier age at which the family nest is empty. (7) As a consequence of all these the interdependence of emotional ties and services within the family is diminished, and the role of satisfying psychological experiences is increased. The need for affection, security, and adequate emotional response becomes much more important. Here, again, purposive action within the family for its preservation and purposive action by the larger community to give the family a favorable environment are indicated. Purposive action within the family does not refer so much to techniques whereby romantic love is kept aflame as disciplined living whereby the roots of responsible love are deepened. Purposive action by the community requires a new appreciation for the personality and character building significance of the family.

The open system of finding marriage partners tends today to a pattern of purely personal choice with minimal parental influence. Social mobility has encouraged this open system and made it dominant in the United States. It is increasingly the case in the great urban areas of Asia and Africa, where formerly arranged marriages were the rule. Subjective sentiment more than objective status and obligations then comes into focus. Talcott Parsons stresses two issues of increasing importance: the changing roles of men in relation to women in the work situation and their bearing on the relationships which obtain within the family. Closely related is the emotional patterns of boys and girls with respect to parents and hence with respect to one another. In early life the mother tends to be *the* emotionally significant adult. This is in some ways more advantageous for the girl than for the boy. The boy in due course develops patterns of defense against feminine identification. We have here at least one clue to a boy's unconscious identification of goodness with femininity so that being a "bad boy" even may become a goal.[2] This relationship also lies at the root of much masculine aggression in society. The girl's entrance into larger

---

[2] "The Social Structure of the Family," in Ruth Nanda Anshen, ed., *The Family: Its Function and Destiny* (New York: Harper & Bros., 1949), p. 187.

society is different from the boy's because she must play a more passive role and cannot simply stand on her own feet. In the occupational world, at the same time, functional achievement is an ideal pattern which is highly institutionalized. Parsons says:

There is no sector of our society where the dominant patterns stand in sharper contrast to those of the occupational world than in the family. The family is a solidary group within which status, rights, and obligations are defined primarily by membership as such and by the ascribed differentiations of age, sex, and biological relatedness. This basis of relationship and status in the group precludes more than a minor emphasis on universalistic standards of functional performance.[3]

The familial and occupational roles of the husband and father are sharply segregated from each other. They tend increasingly to be so for the mother. A problem of delicate balance of roles and non-competitive relationships is inserted into the predominantly psychological character of conjugal life today. The conjugal family is thus basically threatened by uncertainties regarding the roles of men and women.[4]

The above problems are ethical as well as psychological. The relationships of marriage must be lifted to their highest ethical reality if the family is to fulfill its function as one of the ethical foundations of personality and society. Ruth Nanda Anshen has expressed this ideal in a very moving paragraph:

Marriage thus consists in an institution in which passion is shaped not by a code of morals which denies the self but by love in which true morality is grounded and which fulfills the self. For both the man and the woman . . . refuse to separate desire from love. For if desire travels everywhere, is swift and easily spent, love is slow and labored, pledging one for one's life and exacting nothing less in return than this same pledge in order to disclose the real nature of love. In this way the highest experience of the freedom, the inwardness, and the perfection of love is achieved and the consciousness of the man and woman is crystallized beyond its physical and subjective character and elevated to the substantive awareness of the self and thus to the fulfillment of the self's essence. Marriage itself thus constitutes the moral idea in its very immediacy.[5]

[3] *Ibid.*, p. 191. Used by permission of Harper & Bros.
[4] See below, chap. IV, "The Responsible Family."
[5] *Op. cit.*, pp. 430-31.

In responsible family love eros is fulfilled and transformed by agape. This quality made concrete in free personalities becomes an analogue to the understanding of God's own being and character.

C. Educational Institutions

Personality and culture are the direct result of education. Families are not isolated or autonomous groups and reflect as well as help determine the culture of an age or nation. Class and status patterns of society have educative power. Moreover, he who controls educational philosophy and opportunities tends to determine leadership. Leaders cannot take followers far along paths for which they have no readiness. Education is thus a powerful means as well as a value much sought after. It can affect goals as well as effect means.

Education represents the principle of continuity in culture. In the Platonic dialogues Protagoras argued that everybody is educator, and so he is. Education begins with the wedding and ends at the funeral. Traditionally it has been family-centered, but as the roles of the family have been differentiated for one another and assigned elsewhere in society, education has tended to follow these functions away from the unity and coherence of the family into the predominant sphere of formal education outside the home and the influence of other social institutions.

The most fundamental education, nevertheless, still takes place in the home. Here it is that a self really becomes a person. Here the basic personality profile tends to emerge. Here the differentiation of "I" and "you" and of "we" and "they" takes on its myriad of nuances. Here property and the elements of politics are learned. In the family circle emerge, or are educted, those moral and ideal values which are expressed in justice, kindness, fair play, service, quest for loveliness, and the like, or their opposites. Here basic traits are taught not so much by verbalization but by perception of real relationships expressed in attitude and action. Formal instruction is also part of family education, and so is verbalization. The quality of family conversation is fateful for the community, the nation, and the world.

In America, as W. Lloyd Warner and others have pointed out, education is now competing with economic ability as the principal route to success. "Today fewer men rise from the bottom to the top places in industry and business than did a generation ago. More and more, the sons of executives are replacing their fathers in such positions, leaving fewer positions into which the sons of those farther down can climb from the ranks."[6] Research in social class demonstrates that the educational system performs the dual role of aiding social mobility and hindering it. There is still great ignorance of the way social class operates to keep the majority of the "common people" in their place and to let the elite get through. A teacher is himself a product of class status, and this fact enters into his methods and valuations. Today when great numbers of American youth are pressing to get higher education it becomes a major obligation for leaders to approach it with critical understanding of the inner dynamics of the culture and with an appreciation of the sacredness of each personality.

The relationship of authority and freedom is tied to the right functioning of the educational system. Both are indispensable, but the achievement of the right proportion between them, as well as the progressive redefinition of each, depends on the dominant philosophy of society. In the light of the criteria developed earlier in this book, a culture should seek education for the full self-realization of the person, and this should include insight into the relations of freedom to authority. Robert Ulich has used the phrase "dialectical complementation" for the view which goes beyond juxtaposing freedom and authority as hostile forces. This same concept is necessary also for understanding and relating such factors as liberty versus control in national life, change versus stability in history, equality versus differentiation in social structure, and selection and tolerance versus discrimination in the field of conviction.[7]

Formal school education may be viewed as a transitional institution between the family and the adult world or as the preparation of persons to live in secondary groups. The right relationships between the primary groups and the secondary groups are of special concern to educators in a society whose trends are from communal to associative group experiences. Considerable attention must be given to preserving the pluralistic contributions of home, neighborhoods, and other small groups in the face of the educative influences of great organizations and

[6] *Social Class in America* (Chicago: Science Research Associates, 1949), p. 24.
[7] "Freedom and Authority in Education," in Lyman Bryson and others, *Freedom and Authority in Our Time* (New York: Harper & Bros., 1953), pp. 682-83.

powerful institutions. Large groups, properly operated, however, may arrange for the encouragement and corrective influences by small groups. Spontaneous groupings will not be broken up but wisely used. When right principles are embodied in large institutions, people may help protect themselves through these provisions from some of the grosser forms of their own base strivings, jealousies, and hatreds.[8]

It is imperative constantly to review the educational effect of social institutions on persons, as, for example, the value and place of monetary rewards; possessiveness; display; work incentives; attitudes toward manual work; evasion on acceptance of responsibility; attitudes toward government, welfare, pensions, property; co-operation; competitiveness; social taste, the arts, and the like. In societies where the science and technology of the manipulation of psychological mechanisms have been so thoroughly studied as in the U.S.S.R., Germany, and the U.S.A., the ideals which control the total educational apparatus become powerful factors in the culture.

D. *Political Institutions*

Through the idea of government the political order has continuity with the family. The family as an organization has its internal legal or political side in which basic lessons are learned even when they are not formally taught. The political order outside the home is composed of persons who have learned elementary government in the family. Their very personality profiles reflect it. Anticipating a little, we may note that it is difficult to achieve a viable democratic state by trying to impose it through a constitution from the top. There must be holistic education for democratic personalities in the family as the primary matrix of social values. Legal and political education belongs in the home and contributes to the cohesion of the state. For better or for worse it takes place in any case. Karl N. Llewellyn has pointed out some of the specific stakes:

Order backed by authority, fairness in procedure plus decency in result, reasonable compromise of conflicting interests and desires; a hearing in a trial, a voice by petition or by vote in regard to any change; the pledged word kept and to be kept, acquired rights respected, but each of these things limited by recognition of the meaning of materially changed circumstance, each

[8] See Karl Mannheim, *Freedom, Power and Democratic Planning* (New York: Oxford University Press, 1950), p. 186.

(like the action of authority) taking account of the full range of interests within the team and of the felt needs of the whole team as such—these are the legal, governmental, and political lessons to be had from the modern family.[9]

Sound education for family life will integrate the nurture of political virtue in home, school, and state. Too often the family is enemy of sound political education, and the state is enemy of sound politics in the home. Totalitarian states have understood the power of the family and so have tried to manipulate it; democratic states have taken the family for granted or ignored it as irrelevant for citizenship, having turned this function over to the schools. But modern patterns of delinquency show that an unstable equilibrium between the morals of the home and the morals of the school contribute to irresponsibility among both the underprivileged and the overprivileged.

Aristotle said that man is by nature a political animal, and so he is. But we must remember that Aristotle used the idea of nature differently from that current today. He did not mean that man had a political instinct or had inborn knowledge of politics. He meant that political life belonged to man's fulfillment and that it conformed to his nature. For him politics was normative as well as descriptive. Indeed, ethics was a branch of politics. Like Aristotle we must recognize the ubiquity of government. It is deeply rooted in group life. It is not the product primarily of contract or negotiation or subjugation or of class struggle. Government is inherent in the nature of social order. R. M. MacIver says trenchantly: "Wherever man lives on the earth, at whatever level of existence, there is social order, and always permeating it is government of some sort. Government is an aspect of society." [10]

Government is a function, we have noted, of all social groups. The participants learn the kind of governmental ideals which are practiced in them more thoroughly than or even despite the formalized ideals which groups officially espouse. In many high schools and colleges there is often a notorious discrepancy between the civics and political science taught in the classroom and the practical politics of student government, fraternities, and the college administration. The same

[9] "Education and the Family: Certain Unsolved Problems," in Anshen, *op. cit.*, pp. 282-83.

[10] *The Web of Government*, p. 21. Copyright 1947 and used by permission of The Macmillan Co.

dilemma confronts the organization and administration of political power in churches, business associations, professional societies, and trade unions. Since, then, government is ubiquitous, good government depends on a sound moral firmament throughout culture.

Political order is more a matter of integration than of domination. Force alone is never enough to hold a group together. In all constituted government behind any show or organization of force lies authority. Authority always includes the idea of legitimate power, and authority is responsive to the underlying social structure. The force which government exercises, and in the state the monopoly of violence is granted the government, is but an instrument of authority, vindicating the demands of an order that force alone never creates.[11]

But it is not enough to call attention to the moral foundations of political authority. The state has the great task of defining and meting out justice among the individuals and associations that make up the body politic. Assumptions regarding the nature of groups and the end or ends of man enter into the conflicting views on the rationale of rights and obligations. A modern state generally rests on a multigroup society. This means that the state serves a plurality of contending interests and power groups. Since they define values and norms quite differently, the task of integration is complex and difficult.

Efforts to co-ordinate the subsidiary groups in the body politic into one system dominated by a single or limited group of specified values have given rise to the totalitarian state. Complete co-ordination is impossible in modern life, for no one group or association, not even the state, can truly become the sole or inclusive object of man's devotion. Attempts to co-ordinate the frequently antipathetic subgroups in a total system is virtually impossible of full achievement. Such efforts must be made at the cost of human dignity and the sacrifice of the vitality and contributions of the groups at the base of the social pyramid. Here the problem of freedom and authority is acutely joined.

Modern states have combined with their natural functions indicated above the two ideas of sovereignty and nationalism. We shall have occasion to note these more fully below. Suffice it to say that the achievement of world political order is made exceedingly difficult because of the contemporary power of these two ideas, both of which have quite

[11] *Ibid.*, p. 16.

limited ethical validity. Sovereignty has become an especially acute problem because of the nationalistic ideologies which accompany it. Nationalistic sovereignty has become an immoral myth which subordinates the whole range of group and personal values in the nation to itself and then subordinates the interests of other nations, persons, and groups also to itself. National sovereignty makes itself the sole determiner of ultimate interest. This great immorality is being subjected to critical examination in the interest of a responsible world political community. Universal ideals are increasingly acknowledged. Not even totalitarian governments defend totalitarianism as such. What they defend is "people's democracies" and social responsibility versus individualism and colonial domination.

E. Economic Institutions

All peoples have wants and needs that exceed their technical competence to satisfy. Economic institutions are those which deal with the management of the household of culture so that relative "scarce means" may be best used to satisfy needs and wants. Hence in every culture there are methods of production, distribution, consumption, and exchange. Also, there is no society without some expression of economic value, though it may not be in monetary terms. In the great Western systems of capitalism (and their successors) a special relationship has developed between machine technology and pecuniary orientation. The unique focusing of economic effort on production for profit rather than for use has had repercussions on all other aspects of life.[12]

Certain wants are so common to all men that they are called basic needs: the demand for food, clothing, shelter, security, companionship, and sex relations. Wants apparently expand as they are satisfied. As a consequence the demand for a "want scale" or "hierarchy of preferences" arises. In contemporary society the "want scale" seems to be quite unstable, though there are minimal satisfactions without which men cannot live at all. Three basic problems of economic organization emerge which relate to all the other phases of culture in a crucial way: (1) the problem of deciding what "weight" or importance should be given to purely economic values, (2) the problem of deciding what economic satisfactions shall be created and for whom, and (3) the problem of organizing human and natural energies to do the jobs

[12] Herskovits, op. cit., p. 267.

which have been decided on.[13] This last involves a further threefold task including (a) the development of material technology, (b) the development of social technology, and (c) the stimulation and satisfaction of human motivation or the coincidence of the social want scale with the individual want scale. In the final analysis the question of the ideal of personality is paramount, for the whole person goes to work whether he is employer or employee, and the whole person goes to market. The person is the criterion of the want scale.

We have already noted the impact of technology on cultures around the world. The industrial revolution is rapidly becoming global in an intensive degree. All cultures are in transition. The most remarkable aspect of the revolution which is taking place is not the spectacular development in material technology but the revolution in human relationships. The methods of mass production, and the attendant new relationships among people, affect not only the factory system but urban society as a whole, its universities, communication systems, forms of recreation, housing, and all the rest.[14] Since the new patterns of human organization are the products of purposive technical change and set in motion vast human energies and power, a basic ethical issue arises of purposive control of social organization in the interest of persons and valid community life. Political parties and governments have responded to this problem of control under the program banners of capitalism, socialism, Communism, and Fascism.

World public opinion tends to polarize around these symbols of social value and organization. In the flush of tension and the heat of conflict, men and nations find it difficult to be rational or to entertain the possibility that these slogans may carry emphases which cannot be set into a strict pattern of either-or. Indeed, it may be possible to show that diverse economic patterns must simultaneously be at work in a well-ordered society.

There are analogues in the management of any family which has several growing children, as worked out by F. R. Bienenfeld.[15] Bienenfeld argues the case in terms of justice in the family as between brothers.

[13] Arthur Naftalin, and others, *An Introduction to Social Science* (Philadelphia: J. B. Lippincott Co., 1953), Bk. 2, p. 9.
[14] See Kenneth Boulding, *The Organizational Revolution* (New York: Harper & Bros., 1953); and Peter F. Drucker, *The New Society: The Anatomy of the Industrial Order.* (New York: Harper & Bros., 1950).
[15] *Rediscovery of Justice* (New York: Oxford University Press, 1947).

64

In every family there is an element of communism, if by communism is meant the principle "each according to his need." When the children are very small or when there is real want in a family, the need is met without reference to the contractual ethics of the market place. The first-century Christian communism of love was such a family communism of distribution.

As the children grow up, and they begin to make contributions to the family, their contributions require individual recognition, even while the earlier pattern of distribution according to need continues. Bienenfeld calls the recognition of "each according to his contribution" the principle of socialism in the family. It is, of course, not a full conception of democratic socialism any more than a communism of distribution according to need is a full conception of Soviet Communism.

When the children are given something, a present or a privilege, they seek to conserve or preserve it personally, and this too is recognized in the family. This tendency he calls the conservative principle of justice. Children are not expected to share all but may preserve some for their private possession and disposition.

Then there is the principle of liberalism. This recognizes the liberty to take the initiative for oneself and to propose changes, that is, to participate in reforms. A wise family justice includes significant place for the initiative of children and their right to keep a fair share of what they have achieved or earned.

Then there remains the justice of the united front of the family against outsiders. This Bienenfeld calls the root of the idea of nationalism. Such a scheme of distributive justice is only suggestive, but it shows the many-sided relationship of the family, as the primary educational group, to the ruling ideas of the world outside it. The simultaneous operation of several property relationships suggests that economically the family, especially the Western family, nurtures in fact a "mixed economy." Several forms of distributive justice are simultaneously at work in it.

The larger issues of capitalism, socialism, and Communism will engage our attention more fully below. In each of these systems there is an intimate involvement in the political aspects of culture. The anthropological approach which I have taken shows clearly that there are serious limitations to the view commonly called economic determinism. If there is any priority to be given with respect to the relation of the political to the economic realm, a greater influence must be accorded the political. Economic activities are fundamental, but property and its controls are relations which are defined by government, and responsible government speaks for the interests of all, while economic interests tend to be those of interest-limited groups and persons.

In many domestic and international situations economic power has outgrown the existing political order. An interdependent economic world society requires an adequate political instrument to co-ordinate and integrate the various economic claims for justice, freedom, and equality. The perfecting and establishing of such an association of distributive justice is the greatest practical issue of our time.

F. Religious Institutions

Religion is basic in culture because it refers to the ultimate meanings of society. Like government these are ubiquitous either latently or overtly. From a religious perspective modern cultures, even when highly secular, are not so much atheistic as idolatrous. Partial meanings are elevated to a status higher than wholeness or integration of the culture would permit. This idolatrous tendency has been particularly marked with respect to the economic order, in terms of its alleged autonomy for more than a hundred years, and the totalitarian or fascist state which has made man but a means to itself as supreme end. Canon V. A. Demant has brilliantly described the period of the rise and decline of capitalism as one in which the economic sphere claimed an autonomy which, happily, it has not been able to vindicate.[16] This autonomy is assumed ofttimes by the field of science which underlies the technology of the busines system.

Of the various cultural themes science, on which current technology depends, is often set in sharpest opposition to religion. This opposition usually results in a cult of scientism which is not science but a rival faith. The alternative of science *or* religion, observes Clyde Kluckhohn, is fictitious once the functions of religion are properly understood. Every culture must define its ends as well as its means. Religion deals with ultimate meanings. Science cannot furnish the logical and symbolical expressions of the ultimate values of a civilization or state the unifying philosophy behind the way of life of each society at any given

[16] *Religion and the Decline of Capitalism* (New York: Charles Scribner's Sons, 1952).

moment of its development.[17] Science describes and predicts; religion interprets.

In modern culture religious institutions, like other institutions, tend to become specialized and then tend to lead a life of their own. Church life, for example, may become a world apart. Religious institutions by becoming autonomous, and still claiming the total loyalty of persons, may make an idolatrous claim. A church may set itself up as a final authority when ultimacy belongs to the kingdom of God.

Religion has both a conservative and a prophetic function in culture. Persons concerned with the effect of technical change on underdeveloped countries are often quite aware that religious value systems may stand in the way of readiness for change. Such leaders are impressed by reactionary elements in religious institutions. From the standpoint of certain Western standards of human welfare it may seem urgent to respect the unique value of each person whose present life is of great importance, but other religious systems, while affirming the value of human souls, may not think the present life span so important since souls are involved in a wheel of reincarnation. How pervasively conservative religious value systems are becomes apparent when they enter into decisions involving supposedly nonreligious issues like irrigation, immunization, and industrialization. In the West as well as in Asia and Africa religion enters into discussions of population control. A UNESCO report says:

Attempts to resolve such issues, in which the leading political and religious ideologies of the world of the twentieth century are involved, will inevitably colour decisions which are made to build a giant irrigation project in one country, to build factories in some agricultural area, to start the modernization programme with schools or with public-health clinics.[18]

It is in its prophetic function that religion has a special responsibility today. The prophetic function distinguishes the ideal, the ultimately normative, from the historical embodiment. It is able to judge the historical and the cultural by the transcultural and the critically universal. It is able to take a closed society and transform it into an open society, so that it may be enlivened and renewed by fresh contact with scientific knowledge and ultimate meaning. Unfortunately some re-

[17] *Mirror for Man* (New York: McGraw-Hill Book Co., 1949), pp. 202, 248-49.
[18] Mead, *op. cit.,* p. 291.

ligions do not have prophetic traditions. Prophetic religion provides a principle of self-criticism not only for itself, its institutions, and its culture, but for man, the actor, the decider, and mediator of cultural change. Prophetic religion is open about what is good and what is evil in man, being neither pessimistic about his nature nor utopian about his dreams, but responsible to God, who is able with man to do exceedingly beyond all that he may currently think or ask.

No one should underestimate the significance or the difficulty of bringing the great religious systems of the world into a truly creative encounter with one another. The fact that they are all exploited for nationalistic, regional, or ideological purposes only underscores this difficulty. The need for self-criticism and humility by all organized religions can hardly be overstated. Yet the task is by no means hopeless. At least three temptations must be overcome: (1) to bypass religion by a secular approach to culture conflict and (2) to reconcile religions on the superficial basis of verbal doctrinal comparisons. Cultures are living wholes whose dignity ought to be respected. They may grow new forms through the vision of meanings and community life to which they all may contribute. (3) A third temptation must also be resisted, the goal of a monolithic society in which the institutional patterns of one religion will reign supreme over all. There must be rather a cultural open-endedness in the community ideal of each religion which will find a constructive place in the multigroup, even multicultural, society of the coming world community. The creative encounter of the world religious faiths may become one of the greatest of historical educational events before the present century has run its course.

CHAPTER IV

The Responsible Family

There can be no responsible society without responsible family life. The family stands at the beginning, in the midst, and at the end of social life. It is the most basic of all communal forms of organization. Responsible living is always related to it in some way. The ideal community toward which true responsiveness reaches embraces the idea of happy family life both as the root and as the fruit of fulfilled personal existence.

A. Survival Value of the Family

The family has had great survival value and power. But today it is in a peculiarly vulnerable position because so many of its historic functions have been displaced and because its intimate and organic relationships have been so seriously dissolved by individualistic attitudes, by self-centeredness, and by contractual expediency. Instead of being an intimate community of human beings in which its members are related to one another as whole persons, the tendency has been to abandon it to loose associational relations. Family permanence and solidarity tend to be replaced by tentative loyalty and prudential affection. In earlier generations the family unit, together with the values which it generated and conserved, was able to survive war, revolution, and pestilence. Its mores, folkways, and customs persisted despite the fortunes of empire and even the rise and fall of civilizations. While family life differed greatly from culture to culture, it persisted as a generally healthy cell of social life with relatively little change within culture. But today the family is vulnerable as never before, not so much because of war and pestilence but because of industrial and urban life.

Students of family life have asserted that it is decaying. It has become

69

anarchical and atomistic. Baker Brownell argues that the "massive rejection of familism in the twentieth century has had as yet no effective resistance." [1] He speaks of the "vast, anonymous, creeping revolution in family functions, with the widespread disintegration of what once was called the home." Pope Pius XII, like his predecessors Leo XIII and Pius XI, recognized that the family unit is at the focal point of social strains and pressures. "The stress of our time, as well external as internal, material and spiritual alike, and the manifold errors with their countless repercussions are tasted by none so bitterly as by that noble little cell, the family." [2] The stresses of which the pope spoke are not only those which accompany such open attacks on traditional family life as illustrated by the French and Russian revolutions, but also those more basic forces of the industrial and technical revolution.

Modern economic life has created a "cult of homelessness." [3] This cult of homelessness "has become a kind of lethal normalcy of western culture." The social fact is that millions of persons have become rootless with no stable milieu of friends, families, and familiar routines. Workmen and professional people have often substituted occupationally grounded secondary groups for the primary family unit, making of the home only a special interest group. This development is partly the product of the extreme mobility of labor and a wage system which is centered in an individual labor contract and not in the family as a consuming unit. In hard times these economic problems are more acute than at others, but even in prosperity the pattern of industrial life is such as to encourage casual attitudes toward home and family. As only a special interest group the family cannot serve as the vital center of abiding love nor as the wellspring of spiritual concern in the community.

Note must be taken of the present role of the women in the labor force and of the trend toward the two-income family. In increasing numbers women enter the labor force before marriage, after marriage but before children are born, and again after children are in school. For many there is a minimum interruption of their work for the birth of their children. After this the extra income pays for the daytime care of small children. Several basic reasons have been offered by

[1] *The Human Community* (New York: Harper & Bros., 1950), p. 78. Used by permission of the publisher.

[2] *The Function of the State* (1939), par. 58.

[3] Brownell, *op. cit.*, pp. 77-79.

social scientists for this trend.[4] In the first place, during World War II full employment conditions provided jobs for all who wanted them. Since then high level employment has continued. Second, the interaction of several developments relating to food marketing, household appliances, and family size has operated to give women more free time for wage earning. As food preparation time goes down, as automatic equipment becomes more available, the woman in the home is free to earn the second income which makes more possible the purchase of the equipment. There is, then, the satisfaction of owning this modern machinery and the added satisfaction of doing more interesting work outside the home than housework. In the third place, the whole culture is adapting to the working life. One authority writes:

> The husband who would not let his wife work because it reflected unfavorably upon him as a provider is passé. The gleaming porcelain-on-steel automatic electric kitchen which is made possible by the second income seems to substitute adequately for and even undermine the function of the ostentatiously idle wife as a device to indicate economic status. The one-income family is becoming the one which suffers in social status because it is unable to consume at a high rate.[5]

A number of questions emerge from the foregoing considerations. What kind of family will survive in America if these trends continue? Are the problems of American small families the harbingers of family troubles elsewhere in the world as industrialization and urbanism spread? Are women, with or without the full consent of their husbands, contributing as much social value by working as their families and the community are losing by their not being free to contribute so fully of themselves as in the past? Will the habit patterns and the income patterns established by the working wife tend to be controlling even if experience shows that the personalities of the children suffer from these patterns and community activities fail for lack of leadership and support? Can the family successfully fulfill its responsibilities under these modern circumstances?

B. Roles of Men and Women in Work and Family

The changing functions of the family are complicated, as we have just seen, by the changing roles of the wife and mother in the conjugal

[4] E. E. Hoyt, *op. cit.*, pp. 239-41.
[5] *Ibid.*, p. 240.

71

family. These changing roles have widespread repercussions in society and affect the dynamics of relationships of men and women at work and at home. By focusing on the changing role and consequent status of women we are not implying a greater moral obligation for responsible family life on their part. Nevertheless, their roles have changed more radically than have those of the men and accordingly require greater attention.

Because of its mobility the conjugal family is ideal from the standpoint of an industrial society. People can move about from one job opportunity to another. They are not fixed to their ancestral estates. Two parents may thus work in different industrial plants, businesses, or offices, and when the children are eligible to work, they may add to the variety of labor power in the family. This employment situation has meant the potential emancipation of women since they could as individuals enter into the labor market and receive incomes of their own. Not being entirely dependent on a man for their support, they are in a position to influence the initiation of a family and to a large degree control its conduct and management after one is established.

An element of independence and individualism is introduced into family life as a consequence of the new employment situation. The eminent anthropologist Ralph Linton pointed this out at the conclusion of World War II:

The real problem is less that of providing for the sexual and psychological needs of women who cannot find husbands than that of providing for women who will not be satisfied with second- or third-rate husbands. It seems inevitable that the number of the latter group of women will be increased by the development of independence and self-confidence in those whom the war has brought into responsible and well-paid positions ordinarily pre-empted by men.[6]

This individualism and independence have affected the quality of the family bond, especially because the spouses are economically less dependent upon each other. Linton contended further that "in the modern urban community the delicatessen, the steam laundry, ready-made clothes, and above all the opening to women of attractive and well-paid occupations have done more to undermine the sanctity of marriage than has any conceivable loss of faith in its religious sanc-

[6] Anshen, *op. cit.*, p. 30. Used by permission of Harper & Bros.

tions." [7] Such a proposition is, of course, hard to prove. Nevertheless, there is need for Christian thinkers to take note of this revolutionary challenge, as of the correlative fact that for increased millions of new families individual economic requirements are not functionally so important, whereas a major function "is that of satisfying the psychological needs of the individuals who enter the marital relationship." [8]

In a profoundly spiritual sense love may be freer today than heretofore. Men and women may bring to the family more truly autonomous conceptions of themselves, one another, and the community. Yet in their freedom they may lose love or never experience it truly.

The conception of the family as based on truly freed love and the equal rights of the partners went through an almost complete cycle in the Soviet Union, which is worth noting in passing. There the attempted solution, through a particular pattern of equality between men and women, did not have the desired or promised results. The outcome was already a dismal failure in the years from 1917 to 1936 when the basic family law was changed. As Simone de Beauvoir has shown in *The Second Sex,* the family failure of the Soviet policy reversed one of the basic trends of Russia's whole revolution. The Soviet Union visualized women raised and trained exactly like men to work under the same conditions and for the same wages. Since woman was to be obliged to provide herself with other ways of earning a living than entering into marriage, marriage was to be based on a free agreement that the spouses could break at will. This meant that maternity was to be fully voluntary and that all mothers and their children were to have exactly the same rights in or out of marriage; the community as a whole was to pay for the pregnancy periods and would assume charge of the children. It has become quite clear, however, on the basis of the Soviet experience that it is not enough to change laws, institutions, customs, public opinion, and the whole social context if men and women are to become truly equal. Simone de Beauvoir rightly argues that the change in woman's economic condition alone is insufficient to transform her even though this factor has been, and remains, basic in the evolution of her freedom. What is required is a new moral, social, cultural, and religious understanding and achievement.

One of the problems is that the new role of women is conceived too

[7] *Ibid.,* pp. 33-34.
[8] *Ibid.,* p. 35.

much in imitation of man's earlier status of freedom. This conception enters as a factor into men-women relationships in work and family life and invites a re-education of both men and women. Simone de Beauvoir makes this point quite bluntly:

> She appears most often as a "true woman" disguised as a man, and she feels herself as ill at ease in her flesh as in her masculine garb. She must shed her old skin and cut her own new clothes. This she could do only through a social evolution. No single educator could fashion a *female human being* today who would be the exact homologue of the *male human being;* if she is raised like a boy, the young girl feels she is an oddity and thereby she is given a new kind of sex specification. Stendhal understood this when he said: "The forest must be planted all at once." But if we imagine, on the contrary, a society in which the equality of the sexes would be concretely realized, this equality would find new expression in each individual.[9]

In assessing the dynamics of family relationships we must note that there is a fundamental contrast between the essential nature of familiar ties and relationships in the occupational world. Even in the industrialized world, where women have been employed for a long time, there is a sharp contrast in status patterns between the family world and the world of work. The family is a solidarity group within which status, rights, and obligations are defined primarily by membership as such and by the ascribed differentiations of age, sex, and biological relatedness. This basis of relationship and status in the family precludes any major emphasis on standards of functional performance such as are typical in work situations away from home.[10]

In the occupational world status and function are closely correlated. There is a sharp contrast here which is overlooked only at great peril. Mobility on an individual basis is, for example, incompatible with a kinship system where status is stable from generation to generation. Within the conjugal family the solidarity of life must be "protected against the kind of stresses that go with severe competition for prestige between the members."[11] This protection is provided wherever the occupational role and the family roles are segregated from each other.

[9] *The Second Sex*, tr. and ed. H. M. Parshley (New York: Alfred A. Knopf, Inc., 1952), p. 725. Used by permission of the publisher.
[10] T. Parsons in Anshen, *op. cit.*, p. 191.
[11] *Ibid.*, p. 193.

Talcott Parsons notes that the "functional importance of the solidarity of the marriage relationship to our kinship system may therefore be presumed to be a major factor underlying the segregation of the sex roles in American society, since sex is the primary basis of role differentiation for marriage partners." [12]

In the love of true marriage the aggressive tendencies of each partner are reversed, and the "thou" of the other overshadows the "ego" of self.[13] Consequently, when both marriage partners work outside the home, there is a danger that occupational patterns of function and status will undermine the basis of family solidarity. This threat may be all the more acute in homes where the woman's achievement in the occupational world is conspicuously more successful than the man's.

Not much is known about the dynamics of on-the-job relationships between men and women. Still less is known about the impact of these relationships on home life. However, some studies have shown the need of careful attention to these spheres of life. Studies in several types of work situations indicate an almost "generalized cultural resistance by men to action initiated for them by women to whom they are not related emotionally." [14] Thus, for example, men dislike having women as their inspectors. A group of male workers usually oppose the introduction of a woman into their midst. The presence of women is felt to weaken the cohesiveness of the group. Their first appearance alters the environment in a drastic way and is resented accordingly. Adjustments are made in time, but the difficult problem of organizing and overcoming conflict is persistent.

Occupational competition between men and women is complicated by the feelings of guilt aroused in the men, for aggression by males toward females assumes an emotional charge which is quite different from normal competition among men alone. Added to this is the question of the sources of the most permanent satisfactions in men and women. In our culture these seem to require a dimension of affectional relationships for women in occupations which men do not require. A woman's claims to recognition are always checked by the quasi-sacred values attached to the role of the housewife.

[12] *Loc. cit.*

[13] This formulation is suggested by Clemens Benda. See below.

[14] Theodore Caplow, *The Sociology of Work* (Minneapolis: University of Minnesota Press, 1954), p. 242. This portion of the discussion owes a great deal to Caplow's treatment.

One way out of this dilemma is the combination of an occupational role with the role of wife. This solution is seldom fully practicable, for the interruptions occasioned by pregnancy, the care of small children, and innumerable family emergencies create a series of handicaps in competition with male workers. There is the additional complicating factor of competition within the family if both parents work. Moreover, as we have already observed, if the wife achieves a higher occupational status than her husband, she may injure both his self-respect and his formal status, and as a result the emotional support she offers to her husband will be diminished.

We are thus presented with two sets of values involving the twofold resistance of men to the roles of women who try careers outside the home at the expense of homemaking and to those who bring vocational competition into inner family roles. We have noted, in passing, the sources of resistance by men to women in places of initiation. What work and family life need is a set of values which are mutually coherent and which provide dignity and fulfillment for men and women. Contemporary culture, however, often seems to demand that a woman have a source of prestige in the form of a career if she is to be well thought of. At the same time, as Dr. M. F. Farnham says, woman is expected to carry out her biological function through marriage and childbearing. This function involves the further responsibility for adequate upbringing of her children and their protection during the developmental period.

The two roles present a dilemma. "One of these demands requires of the woman a great deal of drive, self-assertion, competitiveness, and aggression, while the other calls for a relaxation of these assertive requirements in favor of those that can be classified as protective or nurturing, passive and receptive." [15] When these two sets of values are not properly resolved in a coherent philosophy of life and interpretation of personality, the consequences can be spiritually serious. Farnham emphasizes several problems which come frequently to the attention of the psychiatrist: "Driven to attempt to harmonize these two requirements, women are of necessity harassed, often psychologically ill, deprived of the ability to enjoy an undisturbed and comfortable ex-

[15] "Women's Opportunities and Responsibilities," *The Annals,* Vol. 251 (May, 1947), p. 119.

istence, hostile and aggressive and perpetually at odds with their environment, constantly seeking some kind of compensation or alleviation." Here, then, is a basic but neglected challenge to responsible family life.

In preparation for marriage men and women must seek to achieve the fullest understanding of their differentiating and complementary roles in the family and outside the family, together with insight into the needs of children for acceptance and emotional security, especially in their early years. It is the same person who is reared at home and who is called on to play his part in the wider world. Deeper understanding of the interaction between family and work situations will contribute greatly to the responsible society.

C. Planning and Family Responsibility

On the basis of the foregoing discussion we can understand why some authorities feel that the conjugal family is decaying. Whether decaying or not the family cannot be taken for granted. Its preservation and improvement must become a matter of intention and planned purpose. Responsible family life calls for intentional living from the outset. This means planning for marriage and parenthood and planning in parenthood. Since family life touches the rest of life so significantly, preparation for marriage must be comprehensive and complete. Its chief themes can be only briefly mentioned here.

Adequate family preparation and planning will accept the following responsibilities: (1) to understand its ethical and spiritual foundations; (2) to take full account of the physical basis of marriage and its relation to personality fulfillment; (3) to seek emotional maturity and the other psychological conditions of satisfactory adjustment; (4) to prepare for the responsible birth and nurture of children so that the time and self-sharing needed for this process can be given with wholeheartedness; (5) to know the psychological and other needs of children as they grow up; (6) to prepare for the social, moral, and religious growth of children; and (7) to appreciate the role of the family in the life of the church, the school, and the community and to participate in these responsibilities.[16]

[16] For excellent practical suggestions see Donald M. Maynard, *Your Home Can Be Christian* (Nashville: Abingdon Press, 1952).

77

Planning for responsible family life must have adequate moral and spiritual foundations. Remnants of false asceticism in the church may undermine these foundations.[17] A false asceticism tends to depreciate marriage and sex life. A healthy Christian ethic of family life regards sex as good and marriage as the normal state for men and women. At the other extreme from a false asceticism is a naturalistic conception of sex which views man as simply a highly developed animal. In practice this view misunderstands the meaning of love as developed earlier in this book and interprets it as simply sexual desire, the loved one being simply an object of desire to be possessed. Consequently sexual practices are regarded simply as ends in themselves. The relation of sex to the whole fulfillment of personality and responsible partnership in the family is either overlooked or explicitly denied. This extreme naturalism lacks not only an adequate ideal of person and community, but also an empirical understanding of personal love in relation to sexuality.

In a sound Christian view of sex there is no shame attached to the sexual impulse as such. It is God-given. Man is both physical and spiritual. When adequately related to God, man's biological and psychological life is enriched by the values which come from shared experiences. Sex involves men and women at very deep levels of personality. Their life together in responsible mutuality marks the difference between lust and love. Today, with the relative independence from economic compulsion which modern life makes possible, marriage depends for its permanence on that which Jesus emphasized, a free, monogamous, faithful, and permanent relationship. Men and women are incomplete in themselves. They need each other for fulfillment, but they are not truly fulfilled unless the family is blessed with children whom they care for in the right way. The crisis of modern family life will not be met until men and women intend responsible marriage, adequately prepare for it, and carry it out in good faith. Christian marriage is a permanent partnership in moral development and the joyous sharing of love and companionship between the parents and with the children who are brought into the family.

A responsible family life requires an adequately conceived attitude toward children. Some hold that the moral connection between sexual

[17] See G. F. Thomas, *Christian Ethics and Moral Philosophy* (New York: Charles Scribner's Sons, 1955), pp. 222-23.

intercourse and procreation is so obvious that the bearing of children is the only purpose of marriage. Many Protestants and Catholics take contrary positions on the question of birth control and planned parenthood. Protestants generally will agree with the view taken by the General Conference of The Methodist Church: "Planned parenthood, practiced in Christian conscience, may fulfill rather than violate the will of God." [18] Such planning is part of the larger responsibilities of the life of love between marriage partners and between parents and children. Failure to plan may actually involve a lack of moral and emotional maturity.

Emotional maturity presupposes an understanding of and an experience of love. Clemens Benda has thrown significant light on the presuppositions of the love relationship in a study growing out of many years of psychiatric observation.[19] In order truly to love, one must have experienced real love. But in modern society, increasingly in modern family life, this experience is on the decline. Many are incapable of loving, despite freer sexual expression, because they do not know what it means to be loved. In the family, as in the New Testament community, we love because we have been loved. But if the dynamics of daily life are such that the children do not grow up in love, we cannot expect that the children will become adult persons who know what love is or how to love.

The kind of person for whom the responsible family finds its *raison d'être* is the product of a group and a community in which love is regarded as the central value of all human relationships. It is precisely for this reason that the fragmentation and disintegration of family life in present urban and industrial society is so perilous. Love in the emotionally mature and spiritually significant sense is not sexuality *plus* marriage and family relations; love is an attitude of the whole person which transforms sex feelings and drives to a new level of consciousness. Parents make a serious error in supposing that their children will naturally evolve into this level of maturity. Plenty of vitamins, a shiny kitchen, and progressive public schools cannot compensate for love as the full-time vocation of the marriage partners. The greatest thing in life not even the two-income family can buy.

[18] *Doctrines and Discipline of The Methodist Church* (1956), par. 2021.
[19] *Der Mensch im Zeitalter der Lieblosigkeit* (Stuttgart: Steingrüben Verlag, 1956), Kap. 1, "Liebe und Sexualität."

Men and women who deliberately make of family life only a marginal interest or a matter of convenience or an adjunct to high rates of consumption have failed to perceive the role of the home as a creator and preserver of personality. This function of the family is an aspect of its face-to-face character and its ongoing educational process. The interpersonal educative process not only creates whatever character is produced in the children but is as significant for the growth of meaning and value in the adults as well. Although it is difficult to overemphasize the early experiences of childhood and their importance for later personality adjustment, it has been characteristic of family studies and popular opinion alike to underestimate the creative function of sound family relations for the middle-aged and older persons.

In many ways the family is a more basic educational institution than the school. Therefore parents should understand both their teaching roles as conscious teachers and their often unrecognized modes of relating to their children. Table conversation controls valuations on innumerable subjects outside the home. The attitude of the father and mother on most topics, domestic and international, often carries more weight in the responses of the children to life situations than formal instruction in the school.

The religious education of children in the home includes, of course, conceptual instruction on the family's faith and induction into its prayers, customs, knowledge of the Scriptures, and participation in institutions, but it also includes the way in which world issues and needs are presented, the interpretation of races, ideologies, policies, other than those of one's nation, the degree of sensitivity to the efforts of organizations like the United Nations, and the things which have to do with the abundant life of all peoples. The public school or college has a difficult time to overcome the self-centered, bigoted, or prejudicial attitudes which a child has received at home. The family is the educator basically also on such matters as the use of beverage alcohol and narcotics, gambling, personal indulgence, and self-discipline. In the family may be learned the fine art of evaluating propaganda, the numerous ideas which are communicated over the radio and by means of television, and the news and opinions expressed in newspapers and at the movies. The home should be a key institution to disciplined and kindly criticism, to independent thought and appreciation.

This educational function of the home, as we noted in earlier chapters, deeply affects the economic and political aspects of culture. The home is a basic institution for types of economic participation; it is a "mixed economy." Some aspects of it are strictly on the basis of "to each according to his need." Other phases of it are "from each according to his ability." Some of its activities are fully co-operative. Other actions respect the individual property rights of the various members. Yet others depend on learning to share what is one's own. On the one hand, the rights and limitations of individual initiative must be respected. On the other hand, there are times that call for complete solidarity. A thorough understanding of the various modes and stages of property acquisition, distribution, control, and use within a family can contribute much to understanding the relevance of these modes to the larger life outside the home.

In a similar way the family is a basic institution of law and government. All the rudiments of civil and criminal law are found there. Theocracy, absolutism, monarchy, paternalism, matriarchy, democracy, and the rest have their embryonic counterparts in the structure and process of daily life in a family. Arbitrary punishment, reasonable review of evidence, consideration of circumstances, accountability, contempt for constituted authority, the second chance, stable law and discipline, and much else form the agenda of the basic political education of parents and children alike. Democratic societies can hardly be built on autocratic family governments. Neither can responsible democratic society be built on families that know no order or where freedom is merely license and permissive chaos. Families must provide stable orders of responsible love if community life is to be wholesome. Fathers and mothers must have stable and dependable roles in relationships that are understood by all. Perhaps the confusion and instability of so many youth today can be traced, at least in part, to the need for more decisions by more parents to make of the family unit a responsible society.

CHAPTER V

The Social Foundation of Civil Law

A. The Ethical Crisis of Law

Like the family the institution of law has been a conserving force in the development of culture and national life. Law shares in the ethical crises of contemporary history. The ethical crisis in the legal aspect of culture is found in the relation of civil law to moral law. Some contemporary social movements like Fascism, Nazism, and Marxism have sought to separate civil law from objective moral foundations. They have interpreted the law as the function of state, nation, or class apart from universal principles of justice or responsibility. The ethical crisis of law is reflected, furthermore, in such theoretical tendencies as legal positivism, Kelsen's attempt to formulate a purely rational legal theory, Freud's theory of civilization and force, and the historical and sociological schools of thought.

In analyzing the ethical component of law this chapter will deal with the relation of law to justice, the authority of law as grounded in moral authority, and the meaning of penal justice in its function to redeem offenders and restore community order.

Contemporary life has encouraged an exaggerated emphasis on the idea that law rests primarily on physical coercion and violence and should be defined in these terms. MacIver rightly observes that the "notion that force is the creator of government is one of those part-truths that beget total errors." [1] Government emerges within the context of historical social life and is, as we have seen, inherent in the nature of social order. In this sense it is much greater in extent and complexity than the political association of the state. "Every society, at every stage

[1] *Op. cit.,* p. 15. Used by permission of The Macmillan Co.

of civilization, rests on a firmament of law that is vastly greater and much more intricate than any ever devised by any government, one that is too great and too intricate to be completely overturned even by the most revolutionary of governments." [2] This sociological approach to law is sometimes expressed as follows: "Law is only social order enforced by government." [3]

The dramatic role of violence in the twentieth century has tended to exaggerate the idea of force in connection with law. The fascist philosophy and the Nazi state which placed state and *Volk* above law have tended to obscure the social and ethical foundation and understanding of law.

The spread of Marxist revolutions has also lifted up the idea of conflict and force. Lenin said in *State and Revolution:* "No, democracy is a *State* which recognizes the subjection of the minority to the majority, that is, an organization for the systematic use of *violence* by one class against the other, by one part of the population against another." As I tried to show in another work,[4] the implicit moral nihilism in the Leninist attack on the state includes the concept of law as well as of government. This amoralism was reflected in Stalin's conception of the dictatorship of the proletariat as the "domination of the proletariat over the bourgeoisie, untrammeled by law and based on violence and enjoying the sympathy and support of the toiling and exploited masses."[5] He described the New Constitution in 1936 as a "summary of the gains already achieved, . . . the registration and legislative consolidation of what has already been achieved and won in actual fact." [6]

A similar perspective is evident in the People's Republic of China. The aim of democracy is to facilitate the full realization of the will of the people. The "will of the people" is not what the actual living people themselves happen to want, but what the Communist Party experts think that the people ought to want if they know what is in Communist terms good for them. Lenin earlier called such a view of law

[2] *Ibid.*, p. 65.

[3] Frank E. Horock, Jr., "The Role of Law in a Democracy," in Lyman Bryson and Louis Finkelstein, *Science, Philosophy and Religion: Second Symposium* (New York: Harper & Bros., 1942).

[4] *Religion and Economic Responsibility* (New York: Charles Scribner's Sons, 1953).

[5] *Foundations of Leninism*, I, 47. A lecture delivered at Sverdlov University, April, 1924. quoted in M. R. Werner, ed., *Stalin's Kampf* (New York: Howell, Suskin & Co., 1940).

[6] *Ibid.*, "Report to the Eighth Congress of Soviets," November 25, 1936.

and government "democratic centralism." [7] No standpoint could be much further from the classical conceptions of the natural law which have undergirded so much of European and American politics, for Lenin revolted against every spiritual and moral ontology.

In British and American jurisprudence the rejection of natural law is found in the positivistic and analytical approach of John Austin. He begins with Hobbes's concept of a human sovereign of unlimited authority. Law is simply the aggregate of the commands which the sovereign power promulgated to his or its subjects. Austin separated the theory of sovereignty from its ethical and historical background and by a process of abstraction built up a theory of positive law. He rejected the social contract, holding instead that men are bound together in political society not by formal consent but by the habit of obedience. He denied that government rests upon the consent of the governed and argued instead that only a small proportion of highly enlightened men give conscious attention to such matters. The majority of persons support authority and obey law through habit and sentiment. Accordingly, law for Austin is a command given by a superior to an inferior and is binding by reason of the power of the superior to enforce penalties. All other human commands set by indeterminate or nonsovereign superiors he called positive morality. Such would be custom, laws of fashion and of honor, the mass of understandings and conventions that form international law, and the principles and precedents of constitutional law. [8]

Another view which has commanded attention in America is that of Hans Kelsen. [9] He attempts a theory of pure law and seeks to overcome Austin's rather static conceptions inasmuch as they offered so little aid in legal growth or law making. Kelsen rejected both legal positivism (including the pluralism of L. Duguit) [10] and the theory of social interests (Roscoe Pound). Accepting the Kantian formal approach

[7] See Paul M. A. Linebarger and others, *Far Eastern Governments and Politics* (Princeton, N.J.: D. Van Nostrand Co., 1954), ch. 9.

[8] John Austin's most important treatise was *The Province of Jurisprudence Determined* (1832). See E. M. Sait, *Political Institutions* (New York: Appleton-Century-Crofts, Inc., 1938), ch. ix, and R. G. Gettell, *History of Political Thought* (New York: Appleton-Century-Crofts' Inc., 1953), for brief treatments.

[9] *General Theory of Law and State* (Cambridge, Harvard University Press, 1945).

[10] L. Duguit denied the existence of right as distinguished from law, holding that men's position and activity in society are sufficiently defined by the duties imposed upon them by social solidarity. See *Law in the Modern State*, tr. Frida and Harold Laski, 1919.

to law, he sought vigorously to separate the "*is*" and the "ought-to-be." Pure legal theory is the study of the ought-to-be. It is normative, not descriptive. Kelsen thus eliminated all axiological factors such as morality, religion, politics, and economics. He strove for a theory which would be logically normative without being axiologically normative. It is "directed at a structural analysis of positive law rather than at a psychological or economic explanation of its conditions, or a moral or political evaluation of its ends." His theory is interested as a "science" only in the "cognition of law, not its formation." Critics have pointed out that in the end he is forced to a position which becomes a new kind of natural law.[11]

Freud's essay on *Civilization and Its Discontents* has also had some influence on legal thinking. He says:

Human life in communities only becomes possible when a number of men unite together in strength superior to any single individual and remain united against all single individuals. The strength of this united body is then opposed as "Right" against the strength of any individual, which is condemned as "brute force." . . . The first requisite of culture, therefore, is justice—that is, the assurance that a law once made will not be broken in favor of any individual. This implies nothing about the ethical value of any such law.

There is considerable doubt about the anthropological soundness of his view of social cohesion since he stresses the negative role of force. Psychiatrists have generally been brought into relation to legal system through the deviant behavior of patients, and this lifts up their orientation especially to questions of conformity and nonconformity. Lawrence Z. Freedman, therefore, notes that the function of law "seems to have been the enforcement of community values through governmental action. Group attitudes, crystallized in legislation and judicial decision, were buttressed by tradition." [12]

The historical and sociological theories of law, developed in the nineteenth and twentieth centuries, saw law as something which reflected the essence or spirit of a people. Some of its proponents were

[11] A. L. Harding, *Religion, Morality, and Law* (Dallas, Tex.: S.M.U. Press, 1956), pp. 39-41.

[12] "Conformity and Nonconformity," in Paul H. Hoch and Joseph Zubin, eds., *Psychiatry and the Law* (New York: Grune Stratton, Inc., 1955), p. 43.

so impressed by the power of the spirit of a people to project itself in law that they seem to have failed to recognize the capacity of men to create law. Gustav Hugo, Friedrich Karl Savigny, Sir Henry Maine, and J. C. Carter have been outstanding representatives of the historical school. The sociological school has seen law as a social institution. Its theorists stress the *sources* of law whereas most of the schools of thought mentioned above stress the *nature* of law.[13] The two must, of course, be considered together. Sumner's work *Folkways* has been influential. "Acts of legislation," he said, "come out of the mores. . . . Legislation, to be strong, must be consistent with the mores. . . . The regulations must conform to the mores, so that the public will not think them too lax or too strict." However, laws are to be sharply distinguished from mores. "The element of sentiment and faith inheres in the mores. Laws and institutions have a rational and practical character and are more mechanical and utilitarian." The mores, he argued, come into operation where laws and tribunals fail. Sumner is here stressing a point which MacIver has made basic, that is, that a firmament of law in society undergirds the formalized law of political government.

When one approaches the making of law, the sanctions of law, the judicial process, and the administration of law, it becomes clear that morality is a part of law. This does not mean that legal rules may at times not be established primarily on grounds of expediency. Moreover, there are patterns of order which do not in every case require the authority of ethical norms. But what is apparent is that the sanction of law which inheres in the idea of enforcement (1) goes beyond simple moral approval or disapproval on the one hand and (2) does not operate entirely or even principally apart from it. I shall deal with this issue below in discussing authority. Max Weber went too far when he said that the concept of law turns on the presence of a group of men engaged in enforcement.[14]

B. Social Foundations of Law

Present law itself springs from many origins, from customs and experience, the long record of decided cases in common law, earlier

[13] See Sait, *op. cit.*, pp. 162-75.
[14] See his *The Theory of Social and Economic Organization* (New York: The Free Press, 1957), pp. 128, 130.

legal systems, the influence of alleged revelations and religious authorities, the constitution, and the acts of legislatures. Differing societies present various infused elements with contrasting patterns. Generally, with rare exceptions the law is conceived as the law of the community to which the ruler is himself also subject. Political government is the formal machinery for making, enforcing, and deciding the laws. Legislators, executives, administrators, and judges provide the army of officials who make law work. The operation is government; the result is law. During the process of legislation law is but a social datum, but after it is enacted, it is cloaked with the sovereign authority of the people. Law, like the moral life in general, is largely a matter of making agreements, keeping agreements, and improving agreements.

The complexity of modern law grows in large part out of the division of labor which calls for some kind of integration on the part of experts in conciliation and human relations. Formal law is an instrument of integration. Some anthropologists give the impression that law is a bad thing, that is, that it is only a second best when real common culture breaks down. Louis Wirth has observed: "It has long been a truism in our field that, when we introduce formal specifications of conduct, we sometimes destroy the very vitality of the informal relations that previously existed." [15] Law is thus a function of the scale of complexity of organizations, but it is important in this regard not to think of law as solely or even primarily concerned with the settlement of disputes or conflicts. The functions of law in defining situations, defining rights and expectations and obligations, are just as important as the question of conflict itself.[16] Emil Brunner sees actual law as the sum of all the regulations in force in a state, no matter whether they agree with the requirements of justice or not. State law is regarded by him as above all the product of the struggle for power among the various groups in the state.[17] This must be regarded as a one-sided perspective. Law is much more than making explicit a portion of the agreements that are tacit in the social experience of a people. Formal laws and ordinances may be said to define the *minimum* standard of conduct; they never define the *maximum* standard. For example, we do not pass a law that the ice man shall be a generous man. What we do is pass a law that he shall

[15] In Wright, *op. cit.*, p. 40.
[16] Talcott Parsons in *ibid.*, p. 27.
[17] *Justice and the Social Order* (New York: Harper & Bros., 1945), pp. 208-9.

not give forty-nine pounds of ice when he charges us for fifty pounds.[18] This specific type of minimum definition is not quite like custom and informal regulations which define the whole range of human conduct.

Formal law is rooted in culture and pervades the community. But good rootage for formal law does not depend on *how much* culture we have but on the *kind* of culture we have. Democracy, for example, cannot be maintained by law or fiat. It can result only from the desire of people for the freedoms and processes implicit in democracy. Democratic government must draw on a democratic ethos. In the midst of changing conditions, if the people have a general apathy toward the new situation, the formal law can do little. It cannot outrun a cautious, diffident, or resisting society.

The relation of law to the quality of cultural foundations is significantly illustrated in the relation of Supreme Court decisions to the structure of community attitudes, prejudices, and institutions. E. F. Waite studied the Negro cases according to the kind of right claimed by that minority, classifying his data from cases decided between 1868 and 1936 on that basis. His results show a surprising correspondence to the rank order of discrimination scheme of Gunnar Myrdal.[19] This scheme shows greatest prejudice on intimate personal relations and least on economic relations. (1) Negroes won only two of fourteen cases involving courtesies and respect in the use of the same public facilities as whites. (2) Negroes won six of sixteen cases that involved political equality. (3) Negroes won twelve of twenty-one cases in which they questioned the factor of legal discrimination. (4) Negroes won all three cases in which they fought for the lowering of the bars of economic discrimination. The changed world social conditions since World War II have had a definite bearing on the Supreme Court decision on segregation in public education.

The relation of formal law to society is a complex one, for the various strata and institutions of society have varying relations to it. Public opinion has a close relationship to the enactment of certain kinds of legislation, but less so to matters affecting the Constitution. The courts often conserve the values of historical achievements though public feeling may be at a pitch so as to overthrow the values. For example,

[18] *Ibid.*, p. 41.
[19] *An American Dilemma* (New York: Harper & Bros., 1944). See E. F. Waite, "The Negro in the Supreme Court," *Minnesota Law Review*, XXX (1946), I, 106-7; cited in S. H. Smith, *Freedom to Work* (New York: Vantage Press, 1955), p. 5.

the first amendment to the Federal Constitution is based in part on the moral value of the freedom of the mind, including the freedom to speak and publish. Logically this would carry with it the responsibility of truth and sincerity plus tolerance for those who hold differing views. Yet many abuse the right or evade their responsibilities. Some use the freedom to destroy the privilege or its effective use by others. Nevertheless, it is still important to protect the First Amendment for the sake of democratic values.

Democracy is based not upon a single value but upon a subtle and intricate texture of many values. Its strength lies in the realistic balance of social interests and institutions along with a healthy respect for individuals. Thus our modern law has become a highly differentiated structure of rights and duties, growing out of the differentiated roles which various persons and groups play in our complexly specialized society.[20]

We are constantly driven back to the fact that law as a principle of social control requires an intelligent understanding of the character, tendencies, virtues, and limitations of the stable (or unstable) substratum of law which is the point of departure in new legislation. This substratum not only is the point of departure for making law but pervades the legislation itself (especially in the processes of interpretation) and shows at times a great resistance to change by legislation. Legislative revolutions are often in fact not as revolutionary as they seem to be.

Enacted law, we must agree with MacIver, is the outer framework of the great firmament of order in society.[21] Positive law enters also into the firmament often as a positive influence. Moreover, the attitudes of the people toward government are part of the total dynamic situation. John Stuart Mill pointed out in his essay "On Liberty" that in England there was considerable jealousy of direct interference by the legislative or the executive power, with private conduct not so much from any just regard for the independence of the individual as from the still subsisting habit of looking on the government as representing an opposite interest to the public. The majority, he said, had not learned to feel the power of the government as their power or its opinions as

[20] John M. Clark, *The Ethical Basis of Economic Freedom* (Westport, Conn.: The Kazanjian Foundation, 1955), p. 13. See Kluckhohn, *op. cit.*, p. 241. See John M. Clark, *Social Control of Business* (New York: McGraw-Hill Book Co., 1939), p. 13.

[21] *Op. cit.*, p. 73.

their opinions. This attitude shows how much of their common lives men feel to be rightly regulated by nongovernmental sources. In other words, the laws of custom, tradition, religious ordinance, family training, the rules of the various associations to which they belong, and the spirit of the age all play significant roles. We shall note these roles again in connection with the problem of authority.

Many sociologists are impressed by the fact that people generally obey the law not merely because they recognize the legitimacy of its source, nor principally because it seems reasonable in content, nor because of fear of consequences and the sanctions of the law, but on account of the habit of law-abidingness.[22] The habit of law-abidingness is unequally directed, for men ignore some laws, evade others, and show a margin of indifference and tolerance to yet others. But habit is their responsiveness to the totality of social conditions. That is, men are socialized beings and hence trained and indoctrinated in the normative ways of their society. "Law-abidingness is the pragmatic condition of and response to the whole firmament of social order." [23]

C. The Function of Law

The function of law is to articulate justice and to be its instrument. What then is justice? It may be given an inclusive definition such as "Justice consists of all the moral virtues in their social aspect. The moral virtues are habits of acting rightly, and justice is the habit of acting rightly in society." [24] It may be defined as that which is in accordance with positive law. It may be defined in terms of the natural law as when Emil Brunner says that "justice consists in rendering to each man his due," thus combining Aristotle's view with later concepts.[25] Any actual law is just, he says, which allows the rights of man and the claims of the community established by creation to assert themselves.[26] In saying this he recognizes that there is no timeless system of just law on the basis of the law of nature. Justice may also be defined in terms of several interrelating factors including the "right organization of men's common labor, the equalization of their social power, regula-

---

[22] *Ibid.*, p. 76.

[23] *Ibid.*, p. 77.

[24] Robert M. Hutchins, "The Bar and Legal Education" (address, St. Louis, September 29, 1937).

[25] *Op. cit.*, p. 86.

[26] *Ibid.*, p. 210.

tion of their common interests, and adequate restraint upon the inevitable conflict of competing interests." [27]

Some interpret justice in such a way as to refer to the minimum conditions of the social and personal good and others as the fullest expression of the social and personal good, making it virtually akin to righteous love. Nicolai Hartmann takes the first of these positions when he says that through law, with its objective order and equality, justice

makes room in the sphere of actuality for the higher values. The more diversified moral life cannot begin, till the simple conditions are supplied. Justice is the moral tendency to supply these conditions. It is the prerequisite of all further realizations of value. At the same time it is the pioneer among the virtues. Justice is the minimum of morality that paves the way for all the higher forms.[28]

The second is seen in those blendings of doctrine that unite the Platonic view of harmony in man and the state with Christian views of love and righteousness. On the basis of an ontology of love, Tillich asserts that love is the principle of justice. Love presses justice to make its form adequate to the content of love. It also embraces spiritual equality before God, or the principle of personality, and the principle of liberty within community. Tillich distinguishes levels of justice, the intrinsic claim of being and tributive or proportional justice. The latter deals with calculative justice, of granting or withholding what is claimed, but points to transforming or dynamic justice.[29]

There are other significant distinctions within the general definition of justice. Corrective or retributive justice refers to administration to enforce obedience to law. Distributive justice refers to the rights of a person to his share in whatever values there are to distribute at a particular time within a given social order. In both cases one may distinguish between the legal expression of justice and the moral evaluation of the legal expression of justice. Then, again, justice may be approached both negatively and positively depending on whether a person is being punished for noncompliance or fulfillment or whether one is positively doing that which is demanded or expected. In the

[27] Reinhold Niebuhr, *An Interpretation of Christian Ethics* (New York: Harper & Bros., 1935), pp. 181-82.
[28] *Ethics*, tr. Stanton Coit (New York: The Macmillan Co., 1932), II, 231-32.
[29] *Love, Power, and Justice* (New York: Oxford University Press, 1954).

case of corrective justice it has become customary to distinguish between the function of law to vindicate the principle of justice (or retribution), to deter by setting an example, or to reform the wrong-doer. In the case of distributive justice a number of complex questions arises as to what standard should be applied in the distribution of scarce values.[30] Wilbur M. Urban emphasizes in this connection the "feeling for moral symmetry."[31]

Moral symmetry relates to what many authorities regard as the essential spirit of justice and just law—objectivity or impartiality. This refers in the case of citizens to equal or impartial standing before the law. It also refers more normatively to respect for personality in relation to what the social order or community ought to become. Positive law is seldom, if ever, able to do more than approximate full justice in a roughest sort of way. A law must be universal in form and hence tends to define the distribution of goods and penalties in terms that do not meet the ultimate requirements of justice in what love requires in individual cases. However, the skillful administration of law often makes a fuller approximation to justice possible than is the case in a wooden or mechanical application of a statute or regulation. Impartiality is popularly taken to mean equal application. Strictly applied equality in law may be in fact unjust, yet many persons feel less unjustly treated if all are treated materially alike than if allowances are made for individual cases. The full personalistic norm of love is the final standard for justice in both moral and legal formulations.

The problem of justice in the family illuminates the problem of legal justice. In Chapter III Bienenfeld's discriminating analysis of justice among children in the family indicated some important tendencies: (1) If in need the child leans to Communism; (2) if efficient, to socialism; (3) if attacked, to conservatism; (4) if attacking, to liberalism; and (5) if all are threatened from outside, to nationalism. Bienenfeld generalizes the family situation as follows:

The five contradictory claims for justice, presented to parents in every nursery, represent those of humanity in general. Instead of the parents, the State, embodied in the king, in Parliament or in a judge, has to dispense

[30] See D. S. Robinson, *The Principles of Conduct* (New York: Appleton-Century-Crofts, Inc., 1948), ch. xxiii.

[31] *Fundamentals of Ethics* (New York: Henry Holt & Co., 1930), p. 211. This is also the inclusive idea of Aristotle's *Nicomachean Ethics*.

justice; the legislative and judicial authorities, besought by entreaties and sometimes shaken by revolts of the discontented, have to seek for the least dangerous path to order/ The subjects are divided into five main groups which aim at the preservation of privileges, at just rewards, at freedom, at equality, and at the display of national superiority respectively.[32]

From this perspective justice is neither a system of ideal rules or immutable decrees (as in some forms of natural law), nor a temporal principle inferior to positive law, but a method. It is the method of giving reasons for every order, persuading claimants to forego satisfaction of desires for the sake of their fellows in the community, providing for the urgent needs of the helpless or defenseless, and resorting to force unwillingly as a last resort.

Bienenfeld's approach has certain affinities to the famous theory of Roscoe Pound which is oriented in the fact of differing and competing interests. Pound defines an interest as a "demand or desire which human beings, either individually or through groups or associations, or in relations, seek to satisfy." [33] Pound's concern here is primarily with distributive justice. Human beings have desire for more things than the world can provide. Consequently some way must be found to apportion scarce "satisfactions" and to arrive at a balance among them. In this context a legal system attains the end of the legal order or at least strives to (1) by recognizing certain of these interests, (2) by defining the limits within which those interests shall be recognized and given effect through legal precepts, (3) by developing and applying the judicial and administrative process according to an authoritative technique, and (4) by endeavoring to secure the interests so recognized within defined limits. Interests, of course, do not organize themselves, and balance is not to be had by fiat or arbitrary arrangement. "Ultimately," says Pound, "recognition or denial of recognition of interests and delimitations of those recognized is done in accordance with an established measure of values." At this point the legal problem becomes one with the moral criterion of justice.

Pound's theory has been criticized for its failure to recognize that law may "create" interests as well as discover and express them. Law has indeed a positive function; it does more than order and balance

---

[32] *Op. cit.*, p. 24.
[33] *Social Control Through Law* (New Haven, Conn.: Yale University Press, 1942), pp. 63-80.

the personal and corporate interests which contend with each other in modern society. It may embody a spirit and participate in creating a new social reality. Government then through law plays a creative and an educative role. It shapes the future and guides the formulation of social goals.

D. Authority of Law

Law cannot work in a free society or endure long in any society unless it has the common morality of the people behind it. We have already noted that this comes about quite naturally as people internalize community standards in the slow evolution of common law.[34] Special problems arise when law is changed rapidly in the milieu of modern division of labor and fragmented interests. Margaret Mead has shown how in several contemporary cultures the shattering of authority patterns has resulted in serious social disintegration. In Burma, for example, the rationally superimposed system of British administration clashed with the concept of personal authority which was part of the customary power pattern of the villages and had malevolent consequences. The groups of villages thought of themselves as having always belonged together and their chief as having been born to them. Their laws also belonged to them and were part of village life and structure. These laws were followed as inherent to a way of life and not through imposed obedience to authority.[35] The new order was disintegrative.

It is important to recognize, of course, the difference between the social psychological fact of authority and a critical or normative analysis of authority. Students of social ethics ought never forget that law roots in what is normative for the people. Those who are concerned for the establishment of a responsible society will be sensitive to community readiness for purposive change. Harold D. Lasswell, dealing with legislative policy in relationship to conformity and psychiatry, suggests that when *new* legislative proposals are under consideration, the following questions are pertinent: "1. What degree of compliance will probably occur immediately on the announcement of a prescribed norm with its accompanying sanctions? 2. What degree of compliance will be reached as a result of a given level of enforcement activity?" When it is a matter of revising statutes, the following additional questions are

[34] See Clark, *The Ethical Basis of Economic Freedom*, p. 37.
[35] *Op. cit.* The relation of community to authority is constantly reiterated in this book: pp. 31-35, 157-59, 171-73.

relevant: "1. What trends have there been in the degree of compliance (and non-compliance)? 2. How has compliance been affected by the activities of enforcement authorities? 3. What factors other than enforcement have influenced the degree of compliance to date?"[36]

The authority of law has a significant relation to its social foundation. S. H. Smith showed in his study of Fair Employment Practice laws how a number of social factors operated in both enactment and administration. There was first of all, the matter of the *effectiveness* of the interaction between proponents of legislation and the legislation. This interaction included the *manner* in which the legislators were convinced that it was in their interest to vote for such legislation. If there was a suspicion that FEP legislation was the objective of groups in the community who were obnoxious to the majority, such as Communists, the legislative process was inhibited at many points no matter how worthy a bill may have been intrinsically. Those who supported such legislation had to be broadly representative of the community and provide a sense of political security to those who were to vote for the bills. Fears had to be overcome.

Just as the level of community morality expresses itself in the enactment of law, so it must be equally concerned with success in the administration of law. Here the questions by H. D. Lasswell cited above are especially relevant. In administration of such laws emphasis must be placed on getting the voluntary co-operation of persons concerned in the community rather than resorting to force. This may generally be accomplished through the judicious use of the methods of mediation, education, and conciliation. Direct force is a last and often dubious resort. The procuring and appointing of the right type of personnel and adequate appropriations for the wise and effective administration of law are indicated. The authority of law is dependent on all the factors (tradition, reason, personal leadership) making for the moral rightness of it and the ethos to support it.[37]

Authority must be distinguished from power. Power may be defined as the capacity to oblige obedience from others. In the felicitous phrase of Jacques Maritain, "authority requests power." It is the right to direct, command, to be listened to, and to be obeyed. Authority, then, refers to *legitimate* social power. It involves the moral capacity to com-

[36] "Legislative Policy, Conformity and Psychiatry," in Hoch and Zubin, *op. cit.,* p. 13.
[37] Smith, *op. cit.,* pp. 199-201.

mand service or compliance from others. It means established *right* to do such things as make policy, pronounce judgments, settle controversies, and the like. By itself power has no office, no mandate, and no legitimacy. The accent in authority is not on power but on moral right. An authority does not act, strictly speaking, in his private capacity, but always by virtue of a right which the community has conferred upon him for this purpose.[38] The authority of government rests in an authority wider and deeper than itself. That authority is the actual moral consensus of the community and the ultimate theonomous context of man and God. Civil authority is not ultimate moral sovereignty. This belongs only to God. Civil authority is derived.

Because it is socially derived, it follows that civil authority is generally conservative and hence is likely to be in conflict with the demands of the few who wish social change. The authority of the new generally comes with that of some personality who is respected (Weber called it *charismatic* authority) like Jesus, or with the authority of reason, or with a persuasive reinterpretation of an earlier accepted moral ideal, or with an ideal that expresses the felt need or goal of the community. It has been argued that in an ideal moral community freedom, coercion, and authority will be related somewhat as follows: (1) law will state clearly what are in fact the ethically legitimate purposes to be achieved by the group; (2) authority will be administered in nonarbitrary ways; (3) authority will so define group decisions that coercion by groups and individuals alike will be minimal; (4) conflicts will be resolved by discussion, negotiation, and reformulation of principles rather than by coercion; (5) leaders will be kept effectively responsible to the group; and (6) minority opinion will be free and encouraged to express itself.[39] In the rough and tumble of actual social situations in a society composed of many powerful competing groups this community ideal cannot be simply applied. Nevertheless it states principles and norms clearly. It defines the spirit which is needed to pervade the ethos of a democratic society.

E. Law and Penal Justice

The maintenance of the order of justice and authority is essential to the life of moral community. Emil Brunner states that the primordial

[38] See MacIver, *op. cit.*, pp. 82-87.
[39] See Naftalin, *op. cit.*, p. 17.

function of the state is criminal justice.[40] When the judge pronounces a sentence, it is essentially a process of *restoration* of just order.[41] The injury cannot always be equalized in fact, so a representative or symbolic restoration is ordered. This shows that the primary concept of justice in punishment is seen to be equivalence, the balance of guilt or injury with symbolic restitution or punishment. Punishment is just retribution for the disturbance of the social order.[42] This punishment definitely, he says, is not revenge. Retribution is not subjective but objective in character. In saying that it is objective Brunner does not rule out the idea of proportional equality which takes account of the subjective involvement or intention of the wrongdoer. The intention and the injury are taken together as part of the objective judgment. What Brunner does rule out along with revenge is the idea that reform or improvement can ever be the determining principle of punishment. "The sole and exclusive principle of punishment is and remains atonement, that is, the restoration of order by symbolic restitution." [43]

By separating the idea of reform from the idea of restoration Brunner contributes more to the idea of revenge and aggression against the offender than he may realize. The prevalent punishment of criminals is more effective in releasing the aggressive tendencies of society to get even and have revenge by giving them what they deserve than it is in changing criminals into good citizens.[44] As Paul E. Johnson points out, the most subtle aggression of all is to withdraw emotional support and to isolate the offender. And this is precisely what Brunner makes central in his view. This idea roots in his radical separation of love from justice and of ethical principles from the interpersonal context of community, both divine and human. Except within the context of supportive love, judgment and punishment are restorative neither of social order nor of the person who has made an offense. Since the ultimate situation is a cosmic society of persons, the principle of restoration must include the love of which justice is a constituent element.

Punishment can never be an end in itself. Its function is found within a larger context of interpersonal responsibility and reconcilia-

[40] *Op. cit.*, p. 220.
[41] *Ibid.*, p. 221.
[42] *Ibid.*, p. 222.
[43] *Ibid.*, p. 224.
[44] Paul E. Johnson, *Christian Love* (Nashville: Abingdon-Cokesbury Press, 1951), p. 114.

tion. The psychological dynamics of the situation cannot and must not be separated from the ethical principles employed. The analogy of the family to the larger community is useful here. Unless punishment in a family takes place in a prior inclusive security of love, it can produce only a sense of alienation and rejection leading to bitterness, rebellion, and further offenses. To deal adequately with wrongdoing is a complex and challenging task, for persons are the mediators of action and the ends involved.

Functions of retributive justice which have not yet been discussed are social protection and deterrence. These are values which may not be denied. They must not be separated from a serious inquiry into the ways in which society is best protected and the actual function of specific treatment in relation to deterrence. Both protection and deterrence tend to be limited by the negative goals at which they aim.

Much has been made in recent years of the findings of depth psychology and sociology to the effect that the freedom of any person is much more circumscribed and conditional than was formerly assumed to be the case. Some theorists go so far as to dismiss the idea of personal responsibility and moral guilt entirely on the ground of psychological or social determinism and tend to shift the "guilt" or the "blame" to society. Depth psychology and sociology may be both useful and limited in their contributions for this reason.

Dynamic psychology has shown that the drama of litigation and punishment is profoundly linked to the demands of conscience. Many who fall foul of the law are driven to make clumsy errors which lead to their detection, owing to unconscious self-punishment reactions in their own consciences. They demand punishment to relieve the inner discomforts of living. On the other hand, the inner dynamics of non-offenders must also be understood. The average man is viewed as one who has learned to repress a part of his basic drives and to find socially acceptable outlets for the others. Dr. Franz Alexander calls this a kind of "contract between the powers which restrict our instinctual expression and the instinctual demands of the individual."[45] The equilibrium is precarious and is held in check only with the help of the social threat of punishment. On this theory the appearance of crime disturbs the inner equilibrium of law-abiding citizens and activates

[45] See Wilber G. Katz, "Christian Morality and the Criminal Law," in Harding, *op. cit.*, p. 57.

their repressed impulses. Anxiety ensues which is relieved by a dramatization of the adage that crime does not pay. Here the Freudian view cited earlier in this discussion is supported by Alexander's theory that an "individual's sense of justice is his feeling that he may be fairly asked to maintain his renunciation only if like sacrifices are forced upon others also." Penalties thus have a deterrent effect. Criminals are used to keep others in line.

Such a view is set in opposition to the one which says that retribution is morally defensible only if acts are freely chosen. W. G. Katz supports the idea that the "new theology" with its "realistic" insights of human nature are closer to the findings of dynamic psychology than was the earlier freedomistic view. Character tendencies become relatively fixed at an age so young as to make it inappropriate to speak of personal responsibility. Katz argues that to the extent that criminal behavior is conditioned by early family influences and by later environment, to that extent the responsibility imposed upon the criminal is "responsibility without fault—vicarious responsibility for the acts of those who determined his character and conduct." This, he says, is no stumbling block for the Christian view of law which he accepts.[46] The largely vicarious character of criminal responsibility is a clue to the deeper meaning of responsibility.

Unfortunately Katz does not make clear what the moral role of the margin of freedom is which he apparently still allows the individual person. When the margin of freedom has been reduced to zero, it is doubtful whether we can speak meaningfully of responsibility at all. Moreover, in the Christian sense vicarious suffering has dignity only if it is self-imposed or accepted, and this presupposes that very freedom which Katz so approvingly has delivered over to a deterministic depth psychology.

There is another function of law which Katz lifts up—this is its "call to repentance." Here he is on sounder ground. He accepts the modern terms of reformation or rehabilitation as meaning much the same as repentance. But he also recognizes that the law alone is powerless to accomplish this end. Indeed, it often impedes it by the nature of the

[46] *Ibid.*, pp. 58-60. There seems to be general agreement among theologians today that personal behavior is conditioned by many internal and external factors. But there still remain significant differences on the degree, quality, and nature of freedom in conduct.

penalties and the modes of its administration.[47] "The process of reformation is a process of moral development, of growth in responsibility." It can take place only in a favorable environment and in a process of personal relationships which hold out to the offender understanding forgiveness. Yet the environment does not make the reformation inevitable. Here a dimension of personal freedom must be appealed to which is not provided for in the discussion of vicarious responsibility. Man's capacity for self-transcendence and insight are parts of his freedom. All men have this power to some extent. There is wide variation among persons as to their effective freedom. Nevertheless Katz is correct in saying:

There must be free and painful acceptance by the offender of the help extended to him; he must take upon himself full responsibility for his acts. He must forego any attempt to shift responsibility to others who have determined his conduct. He must be willing to accept freely and vicariously the responsibility for their acts which is inextricably intertwined with his own.[48]

At this point we must return to the figure of the judge who represents the community. He must blend ideally the authority and the impartiality of justice with the insight of the psychiatrist, the science of the sociologist, the vision of the philosopher, and the love of the redeemer. As judge he can do something, but the court needs all the co-operative resources of the community to fulfill the demands of love within the instruments of justice.[49]

[47] *Ibid.*, pp. 60-61.
[48] *Ibid.*, p. 63.
[49] On this last point see Albert Morris, "Wanted: A Core of Basic Knowledge for the Prevention and Control of Crime," *Federal Probation.*

CHAPTER VI

The Ethical Reality of the State

The state for some writers of Christian ethics is an ethical enigma,[1] an enigma consisting in the problem of the relation of power to justice. The state needs power in order to fulfill its function of justice, but justice cannot be fulfilled without mercy and humility. What kind of dialectic holds justice, power, mercy, and humility together? Mercy and humility are often ascribed to the Church and not expected of the state. Is it the function of the Church to keep justice in the state free from pride and the cruelty of pride? This view of the relation of religion and the state approves the aphorism of Reinhold Niebuhr: "Nothing short of the knowledge of the true God will save (men) from the impiety of making themselves God and the cruelty of seeing their fellow-men as devils because they are involved in the same pretension." [2] Undoubtedly the problem of the state is one of the central issues in Christian social ethics, for in the statements of both its nature and its functions there are involved doctrines of man, community, civil law, welfare, culture, history, and ultimate moral principles.

A. The State and Law

Government is ubiquitous. It is a dimension of all social groups. These have their customs, mores, rules, regulations, and sanctions which are lock-stitched at many points with the fabric of culture as a whole. We have interpreted law as deeply rooted in culture as well as responsible for reordering culture. The differing theories of the nature, source, function, and authority of law are reflected in varying theories

[1] Sydney Cave, *The Christian Way* (New York: Philosophical Library, 1951), pp. 233, 258-59.
[2] *Op. cit.,* p. 237.

of the state. The converse is also true. For example, a sociologist like Max Weber argues that the concept of law turns on the presence of a group of men engaged in enforcement. Accordingly, the state is defined in terms of the use of physical force. The state, he says, cannot be defined in terms of its ends, but only in terms of its means. This implies that the state is a human community that successfully claims the monopoly of the legitimate use of physical force within a given territory.[3] In such a conception politics is viewed as a striving to share power or to influence the distribution of power within a state or among states.[4]

Because government and law are ubiquitous, there is much confusion about the basic idea of the state. Some of the sources of confusion in the idea of the state and law grow out of failure to distinguish (1) a normative theory of the moral foundation and nature of the state, (2) legislative processes in all kinds of governments, (3) the historical development of actual codes of law and the historical differences of state power, (4) the relation of the state to government in culture, (5) the state and various forms of government, and (6) the state distinguished from community or society in general. The reader should keep these distinctions in mind in the subsequent discussions.

Three closely related theses of this whole book are (1) that responsible states can be developed (and do exist to a degree), (2) that the state properly understood is an association which can be made responsible to God and the people, and (3) that the people need to learn how to use the state and all other forms of political organization to express social responsibility. No one design of political organization of the state is historically sacrosanct. In order to use the state responsibly, one must respect political life and its functions, and one must understand its intimate relationships to culture as a whole and to the myriad of communities and associations which make up the plurality of subsidiary institutions in national and world society. We are not assuming that the modern form of the state is a permanent historical institution. There are, for example, evidences of significant change in national European political structures today.

---

[3] "Politics as Vocation," in Hans Gerth and C. Wright Mills, *From Max Weber* (New York: Oxford University Press, 1946), pp. 77, 78.

[4] See Sait, *op. cit.*, chs. 5-9.

B. Conflicting Theories of the State

There is no end to the lexicon of definitions of the state. A few are of special relevance for this discussion. Hegel regarded the state as the realization of the moral idea, as the incorporation of the objective spirit of right, and as the actualization of freedom. The state included in its comprehensive historical concreteness subjective ethical right, the family, and civil society generally as well as the *Volk*. On the contrary Marx, consistently with his view of law, conceived of the state both as a reflection of class struggle and relation of production in any period of history and as an instrument of social change. He viewed it as a transitional institution which would "wither away" in a classless society and be replaced by a more humane form of political organization. The state, he argued, is the product and the manifestation of the irreconcilability of class antagonisms. When, where, and to what extent the state arises depends directly on when, where, and to what extent the class antagonisms of a given society cannot be objectively reconciled. Conversely, the existence of the state proves that the class antagonisms are irreconcilable.[5] Like the anarchists the Marxists have contended that the abolition of the state is their final aim. But this goal does not prevent the temporary use of the state to wipe out the oppressing class. Marx's view has the merit of approaching the state historically and sociologically, but his view of history does not have the merit of understanding the dynamics of power or the nature of political responsibility. By repudiating Hegel's and Christian moral ontology completely he failed to provide for the dignity of the individual proletarian.[6]

In Roman Catholic theory the state is viewed (1) as a "perfect" society, (2) as an order embracing and respecting a hierarchy of ends under the common good, and (3) as a moral organism. Being a "perfect" society refers to the fact that the political community, its order, and the decisions of the authority administering it are legally self-sufficient, that is, sovereign. The idea of self-sufficiency is co-ordinated with the idea of the Church as a "perfect" society. The Church moves at the side of the state emphasizing the idea of Christian personality, the belief that one must obey God rather than man, that the things of Caesar are different from those of God, that the ultimate end of man

[5] See Lenin's commentary on Engels in *The State and Revolution*.
[6] Muelder, *op. cit.,* ch. vi.

103

is the salvation of his soul which is beyond the reach of the state, and that the states themselves, though self-sufficient and sovereign, exist as co-ordinated equal members of a community of nations. The Church itself is independent of the state, related to the citizens of all states, to the members of all cultures, races, and civilizations.

As a servant of a hierarchy of ends the state is not absolutely sovereign but gives to each intermediary organization between the family and itself its proper place. The ends of the many intermediary organizations such as economic enterprises, professional groups, institutions of learning, and those for the promotion of particular interests are in their nature self-governing, but they are partial and represent partial ends, not the common good. The state relates them to the common good which is its own proper end.

The state is a moral organism. This means that it is more than a system of legal norms. It is a concrete order wrestling with the tensions and seeking to unite such antithetical concepts as freedom and subordination, authority and autonomy, nature and spirit, reason and will, state and the individual, power and law, and economics and ethics.[7]

Within this Roman Catholic conception the state has certain protective functions and certain promotive functions. Among the *protective* functions are: (1) keeping order and providing for the protection of persons and property from violence and robbery; (2) fixing legal relations between man and wife and between parents and children; (3) regulating the holding, transmission, and interchange of property, and determining its liabilities for debt or for crime; (4) determining the contract rights between individuals; (5) defining and punishing crime; (6) administering justice in civil cases; (7) determining political duties, privileges, and relations of citizens; and (8) dealing with foreign powers, preserving the state from external danger and advancing its international interests.[8] Among the *promotive* functions of the state are (1) physical welfare such as life, health, home life, and property and (2) nonphysical welfare such as (*a*) religion, (*b*) truth, (*c*) good name and social approval, (*d*) liberty, (*e*) government, (*f*) mental development, (*g*) arts, and (*h*) the self-assertion of the person.[9]

[7] Heinrich Rommen, *The State in Catholic Thought* (St. Louis: B. Herder Book Co., 1945) , chs. x, xi, xii.
[8] F. J. Haas, *Man and Society* (New York: Appleton-Century-Crofts, Inc., 1952) , p. 398.
[9] *Ibid.*, pp. 409-10.

In contrast to the Hegelian, Marxist, and Roman Catholic theory of the state was the earlier liberal conception which separated sharply the roles of the political and the economic spheres of social life. It was generally symbolized by the term *laissez faire*.[10] Some of these early liberal theories were essentially individualistic and utilitarian. John Stuart Mill rebelled against the selfish idea of each individual devoting himself to deliberate attempts at satisfying his own happiness and stressed the essential social nature of morality. Social well-being was the end of government, and the fostering of virtue and intelligence was the test of its success. His emphasis was strongly on liberty and democracy, though in economic matters he was fearful of governmental interference. A more mature form of liberalism is found in the personalism of T. H. Green. He added to liberal theory the notion that collective well-being is a precondition of individual freedom and responsibility. His revision closed the gap which *laissez faire* had placed between politics and economics and put on government the duty of regulating the economic system when it fails to produce humanly satisfying results.[11]

The responsibility of the state to intervene in the social order to assure the minimum of human welfare is now generally recognized, though great differences emerge when particular issues are under discussion. In a sense all states are today welfare states. In a separate chapter I shall discuss the limitations that Christian theorists have urged should be placed on the "welfare state." In the United States there is no commonly recognized or consistent theory about this matter due to the mélange of older individualistic conceptions, the acceleration of social change, the low state of political morality, the positivistic attitudes toward legislation, and the pragmatism and pressure of contending power groups.

There is a moral and religious foundation in American political theory, but it is undermined and threatened by the amoralism of economic institutions, the corruption of government officials, the liquidation of representative government, the rejection of responsibility, and the sense of political impotence on the part of the people.[12]

[10] The echoes of this early liberalism are heard in the thesis that the state is a necessary evil. See E. A. Opitz, *The Powers That Be* (Los Angeles: Foundation for Social Research, 1956); and Gerald A. Heard and E. A. Opitz, *The Kingdom Without God* (Los Angeles: Foundation for Social Research, 1956), pp. 161-62.

[11] G. H. Sabine, *A History of Political Theory* (New York: Henry Holt & Co., 1937), p. 676.

[12] See G. A. Graham, *Morality in American Politics* (New York: Random House, 1952).

One of the crying needs of the nation is for a return to the understanding of the moral and social foundations of law and politics, the strengthening of its roots by moral renewal in all social groups from the family to the state, and a rebirth of the sense of the vocation of politics as a sacred religious and moral duty on the part of churchmen and others.

In the ecumenical movement there is a lack of consensus but a growing practical unity on the nature and function of the state. Nils Ehrenström has pointed out in *Christian Faith and the Modern State* that the conceptions of the state among continental Protestants range all the way from the idealist's depreciation of the state or the anarchist's absolute denial up to the most extreme form of the conservative deification of the state—all in the name of Protestant principles.[13] This lack of consensus grows out of conflicting theological conceptions of God's dealings with men. When a pessimistic view of human nature is taken, the state tends to be interpreted in negative terms as a dike against anarchy, as an instrument to protect man from the grosser consequences of his own selfishness, and as an essentially coercive coordinator whereby a tolerable existence for sinful man in a sinful world is made possible.[14] Practical commitments do not always correspond to the implications of theological positions, however. Theoretically speaking, a theological outlook, like that of Karl Barth, which condemns all human aspirations, activities, and organizations as spiritually insignificant cannot be expected to concern itself seriously with attempts to ameliorate man's lot by political and economic means. Yet the practical fact is that Barth is a socialist. Like Barth's view the theory and practice of the ecumenical movement has yet to achieve coherence.

Despite great variations in theology and theoretical Christian ethics the representatives of the churches at the great ecumenical conferences like Oxford, Amsterdam, and Evanston have developed significant pronouncements on the function and authority of the state. The "Message" of the Oxford Conference (1937) said: "We recognize the State as being in its own sphere the highest authority. It has the God-given aim in that

[13] Tr. Denzil Patrick and Olive Wyon (New York: Willett, Clark & Co., 1937), p. 98.
[14] Edward Duff, *The Social Thought of the World Council of Churches* (New York: Association Press, 1956), p. 121.

sphere to uphold law and order and to minister to the life of its people. But as all authority is from God, the State stands under His judgment. God is Himself the source of justice, of which the State is not lord but servant." The state itself is not an ultimate political unit but a member of a family of nations. The ecumenical conference at Tambaram (1938) called upon the Church to take an attitude toward the state which was positive and constructive, not merely negative and critical. "The Church should acknowledge with gratitude the function of the State as the preserver of law and order, without which society would disintegrate, and also as an instrument for the promotion of a better and fuller common life." [15] At Amsterdam (1948) when the phrase "the responsible society" was introduced, the following application was made: "For a society to be responsible under modern conditions it is required that the people have the freedom to control, to criticize and to change their governments, that power be made responsible by law and tradition, and be distributed as widely as possible through the whole community." [16] In 1952 the Ecumenical Study Conference for East Asia at Lucknow accepted the idea that the countries of East Asia are committed to the idea of the social planning state as a matter of fundamental social justice and concern for human welfare. In 1956 an Ecumenical Christian Conference was held in Bombay on the Socialistic Pattern of Society.[17]

At the Second Assembly of the World Council in Evanston (1954) many of the Oxford and Amsterdam perspectives on the state were endorsed. It was recognized, on the one hand, that no one form of government has a universal claim on Christians but also, on the other hand, that the state has a positive function in the field of social justice. Moreover, the ecumenical conceptions insist that the state is not coextensive with society. However, despite these arguments it is evident that within the concept of the responsible society there is not yet a comprehensively designed theory of the state. That theory, we believe, should stress both constitutional stability and responsiveness to the community.

[15] Findings of Section XV of the International Missionary Council on "The Church and the State" (1938).

[16] Report of Section III of the First Assembly of the World Council of Churches, Amsterdam, 1948.

[17] Report: *A Socialistic Pattern of Society* (1956).

C. Power and Responsible Political Order

Too much thinking about the state today is rooted in fear—fear of power and fear of the historical fact of the totalitarian states. This judgment does not mean that the fear is not related to reality, but a generalized fear reinforces certain tendencies toward misanthropy. Fear of power may increase the power of fear. An overemphasis on the idea of power and the negative function of the state in using physical force inhibits creative thought on how the state, conceived as a limited but responsible association, can be constructively developed as a servant of justice and freedom, perhaps even of love. At the same time, Christian social ethics must not underestimate the real nature of the social bond or ignore the nonviolent power of the moral cement within and underlying political institutions. Excessive concentration on the role of power reflects a view of man in which the nonrational, egocentric, and lustful deviations from responsible personal experience are given major attention. The state might more profitably be understood as the responsible association which the political community uses and adapts to meet its needs and which it constantly reforms.

Power is an ambiguous term. Like the Greek word *dynamis* it may mean moving, determining energy, as in the natural sciences. It may refer to the actual ability of a person to determine a course of action from among various alternatives. Being is power. Ultimately being is divinely personal power. Abstractly considered power is morally neutral, but it enters as a constituent into every moral situation. No one can be morally obligated to do what he cannot do. Duty implies ability. The ethical is always the possible. On the other hand, power also refers to the actual ability of a person or persons to determine the will of another person either through persuasion, or response to love and the good, or through manipulation. Here ethical issues of respect for personality are deeply involved. Power also may refer to the ability of a person to require obedience to his imperative demands by threat or fear. The fact of obedience by others constitutes power.[18] In concrete historical situations physical, political, and moral meanings of power interfuse.

The moral and legitimately political use of power always refers to a norm, never simply to private wish or the interests of a power group. Political power properly defined rests on obedience by free rational

[18] Rommen, *op. cit.*, p. 380.

beings and refers to the ends for which the group exists and the law under which power is controlled and criticized. Political power in this sense is responsible to rightful authority and presupposes the communitarian interdependence of its members, their mutual duties and rights. True political power is the contradictory of power politics.

Normatively speaking Augustine was right when he said in *The City of God,* "Without justice what are realms but great robber bands?" This is a statement in political ethics, not in anthropology. C. H. McIlwain's commentary on Augustine's passage is admirable: "Justice and justice alone is the only possible bond that can unite men as a true *populus* in a real *res publica.*" [19] The state is a great social emergent which when functioning rightly serves to bring man to self-realization. Plato, Aristotle, Hegel, and the Roman Catholics are right in conceiving it as a moral reality, though they may be in error in their specific interpretations of it. Man ought to be willing to obey the moral order which is made historically concrete through the institutions and laws of the state. Since man is communitarian by nature, his subordination to the social group cannot be regarded as evil in principle. To subordinate the private interest to the public good does not necessarily interfere with human dignity, for there is no rightful definition of public good which does not respect individual personality.

Because man realizes himself only in community, his rational nature requires that he acknowledge the proper political authorities which exercise dominion over him. On the other hand, since the state is an association established to be the servant of justice, conscientious obedience to moral law may require disobedience to the positive law of the state. Indeed, the right of revolution is inherent in the dignity of man and the system of moral law.

Because it serves the common good, the political order is comprehensive. The state is the most synoptic form of societal organization. Therefore it is given the monopoly of ultimate forms of coercion. As the people come to greater and more inclusive awareness of their whole problems and the fruitfulness of co-operation on a large scale, they are no longer satisfied with merely negative state functions like police power or with the state as the instrument of repression for the few

[19] *The Growth of Political Thought in the West* (New York: The Macmillan Co., 1932), p. 158.

whose privileges are embalmed in laws whose ancient good is now uncouth. Everywhere in the world the common good requires a reassessment of public and private property claims, comprehensive programs dealing with natural resources, population growth, employment, race relations, minority groups, technical change, urban development, health and educational services.

Because of its comprehensive character as the embodiment of ultimate political authority (not to be confused with absolute sovereignty) in a given territory, the state takes logical and ethical precedence over the economic order. Economic welfare is only one aspect of the general welfare. The extreme Marxist view must be set aside in favor of a view more socially coherent with the way cultures actually function and human beings are fulfilled. Indeed, in those states where Marxist views of power have been most emphasized, the state has become excessively comprehensive and has assumed functions which were better left to subsidiary groups and to others independent of the state. On the other hand, the attack on the state as only a necessary evil may under modern conditions weaken the only comprehensive protection which the individual person has against the powerful private governments organized in business and industry. Rightly used the state can be an effective instrument for increasing freedom in the nonpolitical associations and institutions.

The state cannot evade the question How shall unjust economic institutions be reformed and conditions improved? When all private measures have been exhausted, the power that is able to define property rights, the state, must be employed. Heinrich Rommen has stated the correct ethical position on this problem:

If the economic system renders either the fulfillment of . . . duties or the realization of . . . rights more difficult, or if the system deprives the worker of these rights, then the order of the common good is gravely violated. When this violation is caused, not by merely individual incidents but by the institutional inadequacy of the existing order, of its institutions and group relations, there arises for the state a binding duty to reform the order so that it can more perfectly promote the common good. For everyone has a right to participate in the use and enjoyment of the good life, of the common good, as a member in proportion to his contribution to the realization of the common good. The state exists for man's sake and not for any class or simply for the production of wealth. And this improvement, this

110

reform of the economic order on the part of the state, is a duty arising from distributive justice.[20]

Modern economies have demonstrated that it is impossible to trust an "invisible hand" to turn crude self-interest into a servant of general personal good. Men need to be aware of what the real social needs are, what economic institutions are doing about them, and then with conscious purpose set the economy to work to meet these needs. Such objectives require political action.[21]

A state should be as powerful as its responsibilities for the general welfare indicate. Comprehensive concern for the general welfare will include the conservation of the values of small groups and the plurality of decentralized institutions of many kinds. A just state will not be omnicompetent. But justice, nurtured in every expression of group life, will develop a citizenry capable of controlling a strong state. Human nature, as J. E. Boodin and others persuasively argue, generally functions at its best in small groups.[22] To these the ethicist should accordingly give special attention: the family, the church, the professional association, the school, the consumers' co-operative, the small business, the trade union local, the municipality, the welfare agency, the public corporation, the fraternal orders, the service and discussion clubs, the civil liberties committees, and the like. Critical, creative, and responsible participation in these on the part of the common people and at the local level make for responsiveness by the state to enlightened and aroused public opinion. By emphasizing local group life we do not mean to restrict the outlook of citizens to provincial proportions, but to stress the habits of daily democratic responsibility in local situations. We need not fear the strong state if a sense of responsible concern is effective in person-to-person and person-to-group relationships.

This conclusion leads to a realistic facing of the problem of organization of political life and its current dilemmas. Democracy must be made stronger in its pattern, atmosphere, techniques, and understanding of group dynamics. Democracy must be rescued from simple identification with majority rule and the mere façades of parliamentary

[20] *Op. cit.*, p. 349. Used by permission of B. Herder Book Co.
[21] Clark, *The Ethical Basis of Economic Freedom*, p. 14.
[22] *The Social Mind* (New York: The Macmillan Co., 1939) ; A. E. Morgan, *The Small Community* (New York: Harper & Bros., 1942) ; Brownell *op. cit.*

governments. As government is a partnership in the good life, so democratic government requires critical, imaginative, and responsible participation on the part of a free citizenry in all levels of political expression.

One of the crucial problems of state power is the perfecting and preservation of the principle of representation in harmony with respect for law and the common good. Since the state is a public institution, what it does must be kept open to view by the people whom it serves. It must show rationally that its acts are those of the public good in the comprehensive sense indicated above. Public servants who should represent all the people are constantly under pressure from powerful special interests to serve limited interests. The Douglas Committee of the Senate on Ethical Standards in Government noted that the problem of corruption is highly focused:

> The forces that would drive public servants from the straight and narrow path of virtue center chiefly upon a limited area, the area in which Government is heavily "action-laden." This is the area in which there are big economic stakes, where the decisions of legislators and administrators directly affect the business, or the property, or the income of particular groups or individuals. The abuses of discretion or the exploitation of power are most serious chiefly where the Government is dispensing valuable rights and privileges, constructing extensive public works, spending vast sums for military supplies and equipment, making loans, granting direct or indirect subsidies, levying taxes, and regulating the activities of privileged monopolies or economic practices in which there is a public interest.[23]

The problem is not merely corruption, however, but legislation which is passed on behalf of special interests, though often in a way that is technically legal. This same committee notes:

> We should also realize that morality is violated not merely by politicians and by the weak, but also frequently by the strong and powerful, who sometimes are able to have their antisocial acts approved by legislation or court action. The medieval English quatrain about the way in which the common lands were enclosed and taken over by the nobility of England has also real meaning for our times:

> > The law locks up both man and woman
> > Who steals the goose from off the common,

[23] *Ethical Standards in Government*, p. 10; quoted in Graham, *op. cit.*, p. 29.

> But lets the greater felon loose
> Who steals the common from the goose.[24]

Breakdown in representative government can often be traced to moral apathy. An attitude which contributes to moral apathy on the part of the citizens is what Graham calls the "automatic system of representative government."[25] This conception is partly the product of mechanisms set up to be realistic in matters of human nature and power. It was a morally realistic view of human nature, its weaknesses and possibilities, which gave rise to the American system. This political system developed historic emphases on constitutionalism, federalism, delegated powers, limitations on power, division of powers, checks and balances, and extensive elections as a mechanism to secure both democratic procedures, stability, and progress. The present tendency, however, is to regard this ingenious governmental mechanism as automatically effective. The result has been to hold officials responsible for its operation while freeing everyone else from a sense of responsibility. The American democratic system was devised to promote and distribute responsibility; it has been used and is frequently used to encourage irresponsibility. Special interests have taken advantage of popular apathy.

If one sought to note the many influences in American life which contribute to the weakening of representative government and to the lowering of the moral tone of political life, one would have to include at least the following: legalism (giving moral consent if something "gets by" legally); mores of tax evasion; crime as organized big business; infiltration by criminals into legitimate businesses and trade unions; gambling; impersonality and bigness (the amorality of size and oligarchy); the extreme division of labor and specialization; anonymity of urban life; the concentration of economic control both in rural and in urban industrial areas; the mores of ruthless competition; the nàiveté of the average citizen concerning matters outside his immediate concerns or area of specialization; lack of preparation for synoptic or integral thinking in the educational system; individualism in religious outlook; double standards (conflicting codes of conduct); the multiplication of rules and regulations; and the expectation of poor performance in public life. These problems cannot be solved by govern-

[24] *Ibid.,* pp. 32-33. Copyright 1952 and used by permission of Random House.
[25] *Ibid.,* p. 37.

113

ment alone; they are an assignment for the whole culture. They challenge the churches to improve the ethos of American society in the local communities as well as to protest at the federal level.

In summarizing some of the moral problems at the heart of representative government, G. A. Graham notes that American legislative bodies are not at present known either for their courage or for their leadership in tackling tough questions.

The great forum, potentially the greatest in the world, which Congress provides for debating the great issues of national policy that are of deep concern to the country and to the entire world, has given way to 150 side shows—the thirty-four standing committees, the special and select committees, and the hundred-and-thirty-odd subcommittees. This "greatest show on earth" has almost completely lost its big top, and the important decisions are largely determined before action reaches the center ring. The state legislatures are much the same. American legislative bodies do not exercise legislative leadership on great questions of national or state policy, and they seldom clarify basic issues or educate the public by their debates. They have great legal power; but they lack moral force and functional effectiveness.[26]

In order to correct these defects in the life of the state, the legislative machinery must be redesigned or modified to accord with the demands of the present situation. Practical proposals for doing so fall outside the scope of the present discussion. Certain moral issues should, nevertheless, be acknowledged. A persistent moral problem is that legislative members are so absorbed in trying to be representatives that they have too little time or energy to be representative. They tend to become popular errand boys instead of statesmen.[27] Their absorption in committee work may make them incapable of taking an integral and comprehensive view of the common good. Administrative departments are also plagued by such particularism.[28] An equally, if not more serious, problem in our representative government is the distortion of power which results from the bicameral system and which accords each Senator to Congress equal power no matter how many constituents he has. In the Senate New York with 15,000,000 population

[26] *Ibid.*, p. 71. Cf. G. B. Galloway, "The Operation of the Legislative Reorganization Act of 1946," *American Political Science Review*, March, 1951.
[27] *Ibid.*, p. 79. See proposal by Representative Robert Ramspeck for a drastic remedy.
[28] *Ibid.*, p. 105.

has the same number of Senators as Nevada with 158,000. In 1949 Senator Paul Douglas pointed out that a majority of the Senate is now elected by 19 per cent of the nation's population, while the remaining 81 per cent of the population are represented by a minority. This has meant the development of a machinery of legislative power which plays into the hands of special interest blocs and sectional prejudices. Analogous issues in the ethics of representation obtain in many state legislatures. "The power of representatives of a minority of a state's population to pass legislation, or to block it, is the most dangerous sort of irresponsible power." [29]

To exercise genuine responsibility to the people who are affected by those in political authority is, on the basis of the above examples, a problem of personal integrity, of political motivation, of understanding of the common good, of insight into political priorities, and of designing the instruments and procedures appropriate to the discharge of the responsibility. Responsibility requires a sense of political action as the citizen's vocation under God. This vocation rests also on a Christian appraisal of democratic political participation.

D. Christian Foundations of Democracy

A generation ago many Christian social liberals in America practically identified Christian political ethics with democracy. Today almost everyone makes it a point to say that Christianity cannot be identified with any one form of government. At the same time a more sober ethical determination seems to underlie the present desire to make democracy a responsible expression of Christian evaluations of man, of valid social goals, and of the means to their realization. The "powers that be" are ordained of God, but they are instrumented by man.

1. Many writers today combine a "realistic" view of human nature with a profound sense of its personal dignity. Niebuhr's aphorism is often quoted: "Man's capacity for justice makes democracy possible; but his inclination to injustice makes democracy necessary." [30] This is an interesting formulation of a natural law doctrine. W. A. Visser 't Hooft presents an unrelieved "realism" in the following argument for

[29] Loc. cit.
[30] The Children of Light and the Children of Darkness (New York: Charles Scribner's Sons, 1944), p. xi.

free speech: "We need free speech, not because men are so wise that by discussion they necessarily find the truth, but because men are so wicked and so stupid that unless contradicted they will take their own voices for the voice of God." [31] Bishop Berggrav of Norway also puts a realistic view of man to the service of arguments for democratic institutions:

We are all used to appeals to "men of good will": the phrase is meaningless if there is no realisation that human nature contains also ill will . . . The Church's task . . . must be to proclaim that there can be no eradication of aggressiveness and egotism from the human mind, and that the obligation to strive after God's good will rests upon nations as well as individuals . . . The call of Christ was, Repent ye! . . . The Church can only issue such a call if it is itself conscious of its solidarity, even in sin, with this world of men under the judgment of God. On the other hand, there was never a prophet of God who was himself without sin, and the Church is not forced to keep silence by the fact that it is a part of a world bearing its burden of evil.[32]

There are basic values undergirding these references to sin and evil in men and groups, though it is probably the case that a positive conviction for democracy would never be generated out of a purely negative approach to man and the state. Visser 't Hooft is well known for his insistence on conserving the possibility of free discussion, the independence of truth, the possibility of responsible choices, and a sense of proportion in social life.[33] When people say negatively that "no person or group of persons is either wise enough or good enough to control others, except as specifically delegated to do so," [34] they are presupposing the positive value that persons are intrinsically valuable and all persons have a rightful power to assert themselves. Theologically they are appealing to the faith that God has some truth or other value to express through the least man in society which on pain of disloyalty to God must not be ignored.

2. The positive valuation of the least man in society is in harmony

[31] *Bulletin of the Ecumenical Commission on European Cooperation,* No. 1, February 18, 1953.

[32] "The Task of the Church in the Field of International Affairs," *The Ecumenical Review,* II No. 4 (Summer, 1950), 333-41. Used by permission of the United States Conference for the World Council of Churches.

[33] *European Issues,* Vol. 1.

[34] F. E. Johnson in Bowen, *op. cit.,* pp. 248-49. Used by permission of Harper & Bros.

with moral law in general and with the point of view of Jesus in particular. When Jesus said, "I thank thee, Father, Lord of heaven and earth, that thou hast hidden these things from the wise and understanding and revealed them to babes" (Matt. 11:25), he was appealing to a theme which runs throughout the Bible. God has concern for the experience of the humblest member of the community, who may discern truth which has escaped the notice of the powerful and sophisticated.[35] The spirit of democracy is an eager sensitivity to let the people "play the music" which God has put in their natures and to devise the institutions which make possible its effective utterance.

3. Because man is by nature social and hence in need of his fellows who have an equal claim in spiritual worth with all others, because in their fallibility and proneness to self-centered decisions each must be corrected by all, and because they have personalities to actualize—both Christianity and democracy stress the fundamental importance of free discussion. To take discussion seriously means (a) to devise machinery which will represent differences; (b) to provide for and even encourage an official opposition, as well as other forms of criticism; (c) to encourage positive tolerance; and (d) to express the democratic spirit in other forms of social life as well as in politics. The method of discussion puts a high value on objective truth as well as on differences of opinion and interests.[36] Tolerance is ultimately based not on skepticism (the view that no one is wholly right and all may be finally wrong) but on love and respect for the person. Much Catholic thought is determined by the idea that error has no rights. Protestant thought focuses on the right of the person to express his conscience. Christianity requires responsible participation in the common life. Hence it is quite consistent for John C. Bennett to argue that Christian political action requires working for, preserving, and improving government that is based on consent and participation of the people and the setting up of constitutional protection for the rights of minorities to organize politically and to express their convictions.[37] This is no mere American enthusiasm. In *Against the Stream*, Karl Barth states: "The Church always stands for the constitutional State, for the maximum validity and application of the twofold rule (no exemption from and full pro-

[35] Cf. Mannheim, *op. cit.*, p. 204.
[36] See A. D. Lindsay, *The Essentials of Democracy* (London: Oxford University Press, 1935).
[37] *The Christian as Citizen* (New York: Association Press, 1955), p. 55.

tection by the law) , and therefore it will be against any degeneration of the constitutional State into tyranny or anarchy." [38]

4. The developing political and religious insights of the West, following many years of bitter and bloody religious warfare, perceived that religious faith cannot be coerced. In practical terms this meant that persons who may be in error have rights of participation that must be guaranteed. Consequently, force may never be directed against opinion as such. Since God does not coerce the will of man, but has given the gift of faith and obedience in a freed decision of man, no lesser authority may set up a more ultimate coercion over his conscience. This applies to both church and state and is the basis for the claim that religious liberty is the most basic of all human rights.

The Evanston Assembly emphasized four essential criteria of political institutions which ought to characterize the responsible society:

(a) Every person should be protected against arbitrary arrest or other interference with elementary human rights. (b) Every person should have the right to express his religious, moral, and political convictions. This is especially important for those who belong to minorities. (c) Channels of political action must be developed by which the people can without recourse to violence change their governments. (d) Forms of association within society which have their own foundations and principles should be respected, and not controlled in their inner life, by the state. Churches, families, and universities are dissimilar examples of this non-political type of association.

5. Rights of participation and freedom of expression are but one side of a shield whose reverse side is the duty to contribute and the responsibility to use freedom for the enlargement of justice. The state as appreciated by democratically minded Christians has a twofold relation to the community. On the one hand, it presupposes that many institutional and community practices are already imbued with the spirit of democracy. On the other hand the state provides a secure foundation for the development of cultural life. The state's function in this regard is so to deal with and undergird the institutions of education, culture, and social welfare as will allow voluntary effort and activity to operate to an optimum degree.

---

[38] (New York: Philosophical Library, 1954) , p. 35; quoted in *ibid.*, p. 56. This argument has an implicit acknowledgment of the moral natural law.

6. The Christian's relation to politics is direct since in a democracy he is a citizen, but as a member of the church he has also an indirect responsibility to deepen and enrich the ethos underlying the state in the community. This is an application of all that has been emphasized in the previous two chapters. A people cannot suddenly turn democratic by a quick change in attitude. No borrowed scheme of government can be functional for a people that does not possess its concepts nor appreciate its community ways of life.[39] Real democracy is not a formal mechanical or imposed parliamentary scheme; it is a whole cultural way of life. It must grow in family, school, and neighborhood and become the "second nature" of leaders of the community. This spirit, and the Christian ethos which makes it a religious vocation, must challenge all entrenched social hierarchies which place people at higher and lower levels in communities. The Judaeo-Christian dogma that all men are precious in the sight of God because he is the Father of all and we are brothers because we are his children, reinforced by the moral law which universalizes the principle of the intrinsic worth of persons, is a powerful influence in the daily life of the American nation. But democracy is no easy achievement; it must not be taken for granted.

7. It follows from the previous points that politics is indeed a vocation, but it is not an isolated one. A democratic way of life requires a broadly based nurture associated with personal and group advancement both economic and cultural. Where the population is kept or remains illiterate, poverty-striken, and remote from the seats of power, it is easier to rule by dictatorship. Democratic goals require democratic means. It is important that the population be politically active, have education, be conscious of social problems, have a conscious sense of unity and an ethical conviction about freedom, justice, and equality. Authoritarian institutions, customs, and manners make the realization of democracy more difficult and constantly threaten its continuance.

E. Separation of Church and State

Church and state are intimately related through participation in common culture and ethos in a nation. Generally speaking their goals are ideally formed by mutually compatible values. Despite social

[39] MacIver, *op. cit.*, ch. viii.

compatibility they should be legally independent societies and constitutionally so defined. This generalization, which reflects the history of the friendly relations between church and state in America, runs counter to patterns elsewhere in the world. There is a rigid church-state plan in force in Spain and in many Latin countries. In a number of nations where Eastern Orthodoxy is dominant, there is no such separation as in the U.S.A. This is quite clear from the current situation in Cyprus, for example. A tolerant constitutional church-state plan obtains in England. In the Soviet Union the pattern is that of opposition to religion within a constitution which pledges religious liberty and separation of Church and state.[40] From a practical perspective the views of this relationship on the part of churchmen and statesmen alike are bound to be influenced not only by theoretical considerations but by the modalities of historical circumstances.

The historic position of the church has been to assert the primacy of the spiritual over the political order. Roman Catholics view this primacy in terms of the two hierarchies of church and state which they relate to one another in a positive way. Protestants generally assert the primacy of the spiritual over the political but do not interpret the relation, by and large, in hierarchical terms. Both Roman Catholics, Protestants, and Anglicans vigorously combat the idea of the incorporation of the church into any political monism. The actual definition of proper relationships requires continuous restatement, however. The term "separation," being negative, gives no creative norm on how the positive relations should be stated.

Both Roman Catholic and Protestant churches in recent decades have been aggressive in political action. The churches have been protagonists for man and for truth, but with contrasting emphases on freedom and authoritarian dogmatism. This involves them in tensions regarding family life, education, and social welfare. Roman Catholics are not as likely as Protestants to affirm democracy as a political expression of religious faith (though Protestants are more realistically circumspect here than formerly), but many Roman Catholics are quite insistent that "today the spiritual freedom of the Church seems every-

[40] Anson Phelps Stokes, "The Church and the State," in J. R. Spann, ed., *The Church and Social Responsibility* (Nashville: Abingdon Press, 1953). See Stokes's definite work *Church and State in the United States* (New York: Harper & Bros., 1950), 3 vols.

where linked to the political freedom of the people and to that limitation of governmental power by the right of the human person which is of the essence of the liberal tradition, entrenched in it by its long alliance with the Christian tradition." [41] For the Roman Catholic Church the focus of its historical strategy is not so much diplomatic vis-à-vis government as in terms of relating the church to all the institutions of human society.[42]

There is, of course, no one conviction or doctrine of the "separation" of church and state among American Protestants. Some who are members of denominations which were at one time established churches are today very critical of any effort to break down the wall of separation. Others are adamant on "separation" in principle but blur the lines of demarcation on practical issues for pragmatic and expedient reasons.

Church and state influence each other and involve each other not only morally but institutionally. Anson Phelps Stokes has shown some of these areas quite plainly in his monumental treatise. There is church interest and influence regarding marriage and divorce laws and legislation covering birth control. Many churches have used all types of political action to pass or modify social legislation on such subjects as child labor, old age pensions, social security, woman's protection, and the like. Civil liberties, the courts, and prison reform have received much attention. The status of government chaplaincies and religious services in the armed forces have elicited conflicting philosophies of policy and relationships. Some churches have carried cases to the Supreme Court on the question of required oaths and blasphemy laws. Then there are such matters as Sunday observance laws, the government recognition of religious holidays and occasions, the various rights of the Bill of Rights, and the claim of the churches to protection by government of time, privilege, and freedom in programs involving mass communications. The aggressive social concerns of the churches have led to many social-legislative adjustments that are not self-evident in the phrase "separation of church and state." [43]

[41] John Courtney Murray, "On the Structure of the Church-State Problem," in W. Gurian and M. A. Fitzsimons, eds., *The Catholic Church in World Affairs* (Notre Dame, Ind.: University of Notre Dame Press, 1954), p. 26. Used by permission.
[42] *Ibid.*, p. 27.
[43] Stokes, *op. cit.*, III, 1-251.

In a pluralistic nation like the United States the development of a common body of ideals and values has probably been more rapid because there was no established and, therefore, coercively controlled body of norms in society. The context of political freedom has invited all groups to be aggressive and to seek to influence the social order. In so doing they have discovered many themes and values which are common to most religious groups having a Judaeo-Christian heritage. There is a remarkable practical ecumenical ethos in many parts of the nation. The churches have been encouraged to emphasize the universal democratic elements in their ethics. Separation of church and state has kept them largely free from political manipulation and has given them more power to criticize the state and society.

The variety of American denominations and faiths may contribute to weakness as well as strength. If they are to be effective, they must present a common ethical front to the state. Max Lerner argues that Protestant, Roman Catholic, and Jewish lines are hardening in the second half of the twentieth century since they are becoming increasingly self-contained.[44] There is greater mobility within the class system than among the three religious groupings as reflected in marriage practices. He notes, furthermore, that in American politics the trend toward a three-religion society is most clearly reflected. Should the differences among these groups harden ideologically, it will become increasingly necessary to calculate the religious affiliations of candidates in designing a slate of candidates. Religious dissent and political dissent have complex interactions in church-state relationships.

In J. C. Murray's Roman Catholic formulation of the structure of the relation of church and state there are affinities to that taken historically by some American Protestant denominations:

The relation does not somehow draw the state into the Church as part of its structure, as aspect of itself, an instrument for its specific purposes; this was the defect in the mediaeval idea. Nor does the relation somehow draw the Church into the state as part of its legal order, a constituent of its political unity, a support of its government; this was the erroneous idea of absolutism, in both its royal and its popular forms. The relation of Church and State is not constitutive of the being of either or of a third being some-

[44] *America as a Civilization* (New York: Simon & Schuster, 1957), p. 714. Lerner here follows Will Herberg.

122

how distinct from both. The relation is in the order of action. It implies a dynamic relatedness of distinct purposes and of distinct lines of action toward these purposes, under respect of their proper hierarchy.[45]

This means a harmony of actions, a co-operation that respects the integrity of both independent institutions and operations but "collineates" them toward "one common, complex, hierarchically structured end and good, which is the perfection of man in the distinct but related orders of nature and grace." This reformulation is significant.

Just as the position of the Roman Catholic Church is being reformulated, without change in fundamental principles, in the light of changing historical circumstances, so also the Protestant position continues to emphasize "separation" for reasons of principle *and* the historical situation. A theological difference separates Protestantism from the authoritarianism and hierarchical structure of Roman Catholicism, and the fear that these will distort and pervert the ethos underlying democratic government adds to the current Protestant determination to keep the wall between church and state high in matters of education, welfare, and government.

A statement on church and state approved by the National Council of the Churches of Christ in the United States of America dealt specifically with opposition to sending an ambassador to the Vatican. Its introductory paragraphs contain a representative Protestant point of view:

Separation of Church and state was established as a distinguishing and characteristic principle of American democracy by our Constitution. It has become an essential feature of the structure of our society, the cornerstone of our religious liberty, which is the most basic of all liberties. Guaranteeing equality of rights to the various sects, with discrimination against none, it has been an essential feature of our way of life, which has been blest with tolerance and unity. Our people, though gathered from many nations, with different cultural and religious backgrounds, have been singularly free from religious strife. As Christians believing in the freedom of conscience and as Americans believing in our national traditions, we are deeply and resolutely committed to the separation of Church and state as a sound principle amply verified by our experience.[46]

[45] Gurian and Fitzsimons, *op. cit.,* p. 31.
[46] January 17, 1951. *Reference Manual on U.S. Diplomatic Representation at the Vatican.*

The inadequate conservation of religious liberties in certain predominantly Roman Catholic countries has tended to confirm Protestant positions on the basic issues. In a subsequent chapter I shall deal more specifically with the relation of church and state in the field of social welfare.

CHAPTER VII

Economic Aspects of the Responsible Society: Property and the State

A. The Interplay of Economic and Political Forces

The economic and political forces of a culture or nation interpenetrate; they tend mutually to determine the forms that each other assumes. In technically well-developed nations they take on highly institutionalized and specialized expressions that seem at times to act almost with complete autonomy. Some writers have given to the economic relations of society the primary role, regarding the political as a superstructure built on the powers and the relations of production. Other writers conceive of liberty as meaning the noninterference of the political in the realm of the economic and measure freedom by the degree or amount of involvement of state action in economic affairs.

Economic institutions are never, in fact, as autonomous in relation to the authority patterns of society as might appear at first sight to be the case. There is much truth in the thesis developed by Canon V. A. Demant that the twentieth century is witnessing on a widespread scale the disappearance of the economic autonomy of the capitalist era. Many writers have noted that the so-called "eternal" laws of classical economics were valid only under certain social and political conditions. Only so long as its economic "freedom" did not occupy the whole field was the *laissez faire* of capitalism possible. Its formative power depended in part on the fact that it was related to and rested on a "solid layer of non-economic relationships which it proceeded to obliterate." [1] The fate of various types of economic systems in the

[1] *Op. cit.*, p. 29.

world today is dependent in large part on the way in which they are being integrated into larger cultural goals and institutions.

Though economic activities are not autonomous, most political discussion deals with economic problems and interests. Dean Roscoe Pound, as we noted in the discussion of the nature of law, defined its function in relation to interests. The power of these interests is a challenge to representative government, and the willingness of financial interests to pay for favors and privilege is a major source of corruption in politics. Giant corporations and cartels maintain vigorous lobbies and a professional staff who are in constant communication with legislative bodies, departments of state, and the foreign offices of the executive branch of national governments. Government is partly shaped by this economic setting and by the economic tasks it is called on to undertake. Government is challenged to take command as a determining force in economic life. As government becomes an instrument through which groups may promote their particular interests, the strains on political and administrative machinery enormously increase, often compromising seriously the democratic character of government.[2]

When I discuss the goals of economic life, it will become even more evident that economic life is an aspect of the responsible society as a whole, not of a separable realm.

B. The Political Framework of Economic Life

The major goals of economic life are primarily determined today within the framework of the political sphere of culture. This is apparent from even the most casual survey of international and domestic affairs. The famous "five year plans" of the U.S.S.R., the development of the petroleum industry in the Middle East, the future control of the Suez Canal or the Panama Canal, the European Coal-Steel Community, and the nationalization of English industry illustrate the fact that political decisions determine the ultimate economic decisions in the international field. Domestic governmental policy regulates and defines "free" enterprise, the fiscal policy, taxation, patents, transportation, utility rates, the endorsement of contracts, the power of trade unions and trade associations, urban development and redevelopment, and

[2] See John M. Clark, "America's Changing Capitalism," in Morroe Berger, and others, eds., *Freedom and Control in Modern Society* (Princeton, N.J.: D. Van Nostrand Co., 1954), pp. 192-205.

the relation of military expenditures to the balance of the economy. An economy is always in part the economy of some nation, for it is within the legal framework of some political entity that basic policies are determined.

Because government inevitably interacts with economic life, conflicting attitudes of their proper relationships naturally arise. Some hold that government is best which governs least and hence should not compete with private business. Others hold that government should assist private enterprise in indirect ways providing a favorable climate for its development and encouraging the entrance of new business into the established production and exchange system. Still others hold that resources controlled by the government may be treated as a "come-one come-all barbecue." This view relates to the "spoils" concept that revels in waste and the conservative protest that government participation in business inherently means a wastrel administration. Many have advocated that the state might temporarily "take over" in grave emergencies like war or strikes in basic industries or communications. This concept is related to the view that government is directly responsible for economic welfare only in crucial areas where private industries and agencies have broken down, failed, or been found otherwise inadequate as in prolonged and serious depressions. Two other ideas are often urged: that government's role is one of over-all planning and co-ordination and that government should take the initiative in new fields like nuclear energy, leaving subsequent development to private enterprise. Finally, there are advocates of the government as a general welfare institution, having a flexible pragmatic role with respect to such matters as providing subsidies, controlling price levels, managing credit, and the like.

In the U.S.A. there are still many persons who vigorously advocate a libertarian theory of government based on the definition that the latter "is only an arrangement which sets aside a small group of people and gives them the power to coerce all the rest of people." [3] On this view the "essence of government is power—the power of a few men over many men." Since freedom is the natural birthright of man, "all that government can do in behalf of freedom is to let the individual alone." It is then asserted that the role of government is to protect the voluntary associations which men, acting freely, form to further

[3] Heard and Opitz, *op. cit.*, p. 161.

127

their private ends. Government has no mandate to interfere unless some other man's equal claim to freedom is being impaired. Applied to the present social situation the implications of these views would seem to be to eliminate all operations of the state from interference on behalf of or against any persons or groups of persons in society except, of course, obvious criminals. The main application of this theory seems to be against those functions of government which are devoted to welfare, more particularly economic security. Those defending this theory assert that it is sheer fraud for the government to be active in this field because no person has a right to give away what he does not possess, and government does not produce the economic goods it promises to dispense in the welfare field. Government, it is argued, is not a factor in economic production, the real factors being land, labor, and capital. Hence before the government can give anyone anything, it must first unjustly take it away from others.

There are several basic errors of fact and valuation in this position. It rests on an individualistic conception of the foundations of society which is contrary to anthropological evidence for the organic character of culture. It neglects both the sociological fact and the Christian valuation that we are members one of another. It makes the state a servant of voluntary economic associations without positive criteria for the limitation of the rights or duties of such associations. In other words, it lacks a basic conception of the grounds of personal or communal good other than the general idea of freedom. It emphasizes only the coercive aspects of government and thereby is committed to a half-truth that begets total error. It fails to see that government is deeply involved in land, labor, and capital because as economic factors these entities are aspects of property, and government provides the legal definition of property, that is, its rights and limitations. Without government land, labor, and capital have no property status in organized society. Finally, this point of view sees power only as a problem of the state's threat to personal liberty and not as a pervasive problem of all human life, both individual and organized, which government brings into some provisional state of equilibrium in the interest of the common good. The practical effect of the theory would seem to be the removal of state restraint on the voluntary associations of the powerful.

The role of government can, of course, be overemphasized. Yet the economic realm must rely on it to provide the legal framework of the organization of production, the business system, and the income-spending activities of the people. Government must also furnish certain vital services; it must correct antisocial tendencies, and it must supply a balancing factor in promoting economic stability and growth. These minimal functions of government are supplemented by others when economic life is understood as integral to the whole of abundant living.[4]

A fruitful approach to the problems of the political-economic order is through a review of basic functions and goals. Many of the ends of a social order are not strictly economic, for they have to do with the dominant values of the culture or society. Such goals may be military power, or religious domination, or security, or peace, or democracy, or the optimum realization of personality, and so on. It is not in the sphere of the economist to determine what social ends should be pursued, but rather the allocation and use of the scarce resources which are means to these ends. This larger sphere includes also the social relations involved in production and distribution of the goods and services.

Professor Frank H. Knight has usefully divided the main functions of an economic system into five categories: (1) fixing standards, (2) organizing production, (3) distribution, (4) maintenance and progress, and (5) adjusting consumption to production.

The five [5] main functions of an economic system are significantly limited for practical purposes by the political policies and legal structure of the countries where the system is located. The *first* function is that of fixing standards. There has to be a social decision in a complex society as to the relative importance of different uses of productive power, as to which wants are to be satisfied and which left unsatisfied, or to what extent any one is to be satisfied at the expense of another. Whose wants and which wants are to be satisfied and in what degree? The state may decide to stress capital goods at the expense of con-

---

[4] See Carl L. Becker, *Freedom and Responsibility in the American Way of Life* (New York: Alfred A. Knopf, Inc., 1945), ch. v, "Private Economic Enterprise."

[5] Following the outline as developed by Professor Knight in *The Economic Organization* (1951) published by Augustus M. Kelley (College of the University of Chicago). The names of the functions are those of Professor Knight. The commentary relating these to the state is mine.

sumers' goods or a heavy military establishment, or to protect certain industries or a group of farmers, or it may decide to let the market play a relatively more autonomous role. In any case the decision for more or less individual or corporation "freedom" is partly a political decision.

The *second* function of an economy is that of organizing production. This has to do with the *allocation* of available productive forces and materials and the effective *co-ordination* of the various means of production into such groupings as will produce the greatest result. The second of these is a technological as well as an economic question. Both issues depend on the social goals of the nation as a whole and relate, for example, to governmental policy regarding natural resources, regional development, centralization or decentralization of industry, interracial policies, monopoly control, and the like.

The *third* function of an economy is distribution. There is a close relationship between distribution and the control of production. The decision as to what to produce is closely bound up with the decision for whom to produce. Where traditions of "private property," "free competition," and "contract" prevail, the emphasis is different from what it is where the stress is on sharing production as widely as possible. Here the questions of incentives enter in. Governmental policy in response to the ethos of people tends to design the pattern of distribution. Even when the government does *not* decide to equalize distribution, that decision is a political one. In the basic sense employed here low income taxes for people with large incomes constitute political intervention in the economic sphere quite as truly as high taxes for the rich and low taxes for the less fortunate.

The *fourth* function of an economy is economic maintenance and progress. This is the question of how much development society can afford or cares to have at the cost of sacrificing present values and what forms it shall take. How much shall be consumed now? How much shall be used to develop the economy? Who shall carry the burdens? Who will get the benefits? Governments have increasingly concerned themselves with these questions. They relate to the decision as to how responsible the economy wishes to be with respect to the value of productivity and progress.

The *fifth* function of an economy is to adjust consumption to production within very short periods. Production cannot always be adjusted quickly to meet consumption demands. For example, the crop of a given year has to last until next year's crop is produced except as it is affected by the world trade situation. Even in manufacturing, production cannot always change rapidly, and decisions in the area of consumption must be made. Here, again, governmental policies of various kinds will influence the economy significantly.

The conclusion we wish to draw from thus relating governmental policy to the five functions of an economy is a proposal not to increase the power of the governmental sector in economic life, but to emphasize the need to have a positive theory of the political framework of economic processes. Every system of government sustains a corresponding system of property. Change in one involves a change in the other.[6] Consequently a Christian criticism of the state must be co-ordinate with and coherent with the Christian criticism of the economy. As the Christian criticism of the state rests on a Christian criticism of law and authority of government, and on an affirmation of personality and the duties of love and brotherhood, so a Christian criticism of the economic order rests on an affirmation of the primacy of personal and social rights and duties under the sovereign ownership of God, man being but a steward of the kingdom of God. The conflict between "free enterprise" and "collectivism" is not primarily economic but requires an analysis of varying constellations of freedom and order under varying historical circumstances. It involves a functional understanding of property.

C. The Nature of Property

Today when Americans are evincing a great interest in becoming homeowners, many persons think of property in terms of something material which they possess. The term property, they spontaneously feel, refers to land, houses, furnishings, cars, factories, and the like. A little reflection will add such immaterial items as ideas, credit, time, privilege, one's skill, reputation, or almost any scarce value. But no matter how gross or refined, material or nonmaterial the value may be, property is not basically one's relation to any of these things. Property has to do with the rightful claims of persons on one another and with the reciprocal claims of the group and its members with respect

[6] MacIver, *op. cit.*, p. 125.

to some scarce value.[7] My property right does not consist of my physical possession of a piece of land, for example. It consists of my moral claim to certain privileges, uses, and relations to that land—claims which are consistent with moral law. My legal property right consists of the community's political recognition of my moral claim and its willingness to put its authority and sanction behind that recognition. What is essential in the idea of property is the social relationship of claims within which a scarce value is placed. Property rights, then, have to do with moral and legal claims of members of a community on one another, or of groups of persons on other groups, with respect to such scarce means. A private legal property right cannot be absolute, for the political community defines the legal right, and the authority (legitimated power) which performs this function is clearly more ultimate than the private interest making the claim.

Property constitutes a complex problem of morals and law because the historical disposition of scarce values is diverse in its development and expression. Philosophers, theologians, social scientists, and political administrators have developed a vast literature on the subject. Much of it suffers from a failure to observe the relativity of property with respect to cultural values and the political order. Property has to do with the relations of people to one another. Hence it has to do not only with personal or group *use* but also with the *power* of one person or group over others, with status, prestige, emulation, competition, privilege, family inheritance, the continuity of institutions, and the instruments of the political order.

In dealing with property issues it is important to face afresh a number of the moral laws. What are the consequences of a particular form of property right? What is the best possible order of restraint and liberty with respect to private property? What is the relation of this value to all the other values at stake in culture? What should the most inclusive end be? What kind of personality should we be trying to develop in relation to the law of co-operation, of individualism, of social devotion? What kind of community ideal should dominate present decisions regarding the power of property-holding groups?

Idealistic philosophers and many theologians have held that private property is necessary for human freedom. There must be freedom over

---

[7] See Muelder, *op. cit.*, ch. v, "Religious Conception of Property," for an extended statement of the view presented here.

one's most immediate "natural" property, his body. Dignity requires that no one be a slave. If a person has no private possessions, he is completely at the mercy of others, for he has no means to express himself. It seems reasonable, then, to assume that free men need a minimum of property. If the people have economic means at their disposal, they have independence. It is difficult to deny the force of this and similar considerations. This consideration is but one component in a complex pattern of cultural variables. What economic means and how much constitute freedom? Moreover, freedom not only is an expression of personality affirmation, but it affects other persons. What relations of persons to one another with respect to property make for real enhancement of personality?

There is thus a basic spiritual principle involved in the idea of property. James Madison, in elaborating the meaning of property, argued as follows:

A man has property in his opinions, and the free communication of them. He has property of peculiar values in religious opinions. He has property very dear to him in the safety and liberty of his person. He has equal property in the free use of his faculties. In a word, as a man is said to have a right to his property he may equally be said to have a property in his rights.[8]

Here the doctrine of property merges into the general doctrine of human rights. Yet, as T. V. Smith observes, "it is veritably not the privacy of property which characterizes the genius of democratic capitalism; it is the property of privacy." Property thus relates both the subjective and the objective aspects of personal claims to the collectivity of such claims in the community.

When one thinks of property in terms of home ownership, for example, one has a major social policy to deal with. Do all have a right to own their own homes? Do all have an equal claim? Who accepts responsibility for providing decent and adequate housing for all? What are the minimal standards? Where does the economics of basic human needs end and the economics of emulation and competitive status begin (and end)?

[8] Quoted in T. V. Smith, "The Happiness of Pursuit," *Western World*, No. 1, May, 1957, p. 57.

Those who own land and factories, or other means of production, have a power over other persons. All property which represents social power stands always in need of moral scrutiny, for power to determine the lives of others is the crucial problem in dynamic systems of justice. Concentration of power must be brought under adequate social control. The worker, in struggling against corporate industrial power, sets the organized strength of his union and his political franchise against that of the power of great ownership. The victory of the masses in gaining the political franchise is one of the greatest historical steps toward economic freedom, for it places the workers in a more effective position to control the government, which defines the rules of the game with respect to property relationships. How far the political control over corporate wealth goes in a nation of culture depends in large part on the value scale of that society.

D. The Goals of Economic Life

The instrumental character of economic values has been frequently recognized by students of ethics. Economics has to do with the management of scarce means. As a specialized discipline economics should not be confused with economic life. Economic life refers to the total involvement of persons in economic processes. Therefore intrinsic personal values are as truly involved in economic life as in any of its aspects.

The eminent economist Frank H. Knight has eloquently stated some larger goals of life which economic-activity serves or should more efficiently seek to serve:

Civilization should look forward to a day when the material product of industrial activity shall become rather its by-product, and its primary significance shall be that of a sphere for creative self-expression and the development of a higher type of individual and of human fellowship. It ought to be the first aim of economic policy to reduce the importance of economic policy in life as a whole. So it ought to be the highest objective in the study of economics to hasten the day when the study and the practice of economy will recede into the background of men's thoughts, when food and shelter, and all provision for physical needs, can be taken for granted without serious thought, when production and consumption and distribution shall cease from troubling and pass below the threshold of consciousness and the effort

134

and planning of the mass of mankind may be mainly devoted to problems of beauty, truth, right human relations and cultural growth.[9]

It would be difficult to express the means-function of economic life more beautifully, truthfully, and with more promise of cultural growth and good human relations.

These general goals of economic life have elicited great interest in religious circles for more than half a century. With the prospect of the achievement of an economy of abundance, purposive action has become more and more specific. As explored in recent ecumenical research in the U.S.A., the following goals may be summarized under eleven subheadings: [10]

1. *Survival and Physical Well-being (Productivity)*. Each person should have access to the conditions necessary for health, safety, comfort, and reasonable longevity. This goal requires an economic emphasis on productivity or efficiency. The right conditions of production give the additional goals of safe, healthful, pleasant working conditions and adequate leisure.

2. *Fellowship*. Each individual should have a variety of satisfying human relationships. Economic life can offer the individual a sense of belonging, of participation in matters affecting him, of friendship, sociability, and of co-operative endeavor. Yet the formation of economic classes and conflicts among classes may divide the community and generate hostility. The right ordering of economic life should have fellowship as a goal. One of the criteria of judging the industrial and agricultural orders of society has been the principle of brotherhood.

3. *Dignity and Humility*. Each individual should have the opportunity to earn a position in society of dignity and self-respect. This value is challenged by social processes which inflate the passions for prestige and power and tempt men to take advantage of their positions over other men. Power is a trust which should be worn with humility and which needs social control in the interests of all. Social status is achieved through both the operations of production and the mode of

---

[9] *Op. cit.* Used by permission of the author. Quoted in Naftalin, *op. cit.*, Part 2, pp. 58-59.

[10] Bennett, *Christian Values and Economic Life*, ch. 4. This chapter summarizes the findings of five other volumes published by Harper & Bros. in 1953 and 1954 as follows: Ward, *Goals of Economic Life*; Boulding, *The Organizational Revolution*; Bowen, *Social Responsibilities of the Businessman*; Hoyt, *American Income and Its Use*; and Ward, *The American Economy—Attitudes and Opinions*.

consumption. Dignity and humility are required moral goals in both these aspects of economic life.

4. *Enlightenment.* Individuals need to satisfy their intellectual curiosity and must be as informed as possible if they are to fulfill the moral law. This becomes the more imperative as we understand the interrelatedness of the different phases of culture. Persons require the skills and knowledge of intelligent citizenship and family life as well as of efficient workmanship and discriminating judgments in consumption if they are to make responsible economic decisions. All work comes morally under the measurement of the degree to which it contributes to moral and social enlightenment.

5. *Aesthetic Enjoyment.* All men have aesthetic needs. More and more of both production and consumption can be brought under the control not only of the ideal of efficiency but also of beauty. Work may be conducted in ugly or beautiful surroundings. Industry may be designed to produce a slum and a polluted river, or it may be designed as part of an industrial park. Human relationships may be conducted with a view to refinement or crassness. Artifacts may be pleasing or crudely utilitarian.

6. *Creativity.* I have repeatedly emphasized the value of creative participation in social life. Hence one criterion of economic activities is the degree to which they provide for the expression of creative imagination. Many cultural factors, political, educational, and religious, enter into a social setting which provides encouragement for freedom in creation. Freedom is the precondition of creativity.

7. *New Experience.* One of the great social problems is to provide constructive and peaceful ways of attaining this significant goal. Persons need problems to solve, variety, and novelty as over against what is routine and boring. If an economy is to be productive and efficient in realizing the goals already mentioned, there must be progress and change. Persons need to have faith to experiment with new possibilities. Yet much ordinary work is plagued with monotony and lacks challenge and stimulation for new ideas. Many persons move restlessly from one occupation to another because the work fails to satisfy the desire for new experience.

8. *Security.* Each individual needs the assurance that the objective conditions necessary for the attainment of legitimate values will be accessible to him. Indeed, responsible society means in large part the

establishing and improving of social institutions in and through which man can be truly free. Security includes many values beyond assurance of income; it includes an expectation that persons will keep their word, tell the truth, follow the rules of the game, and abstain from unethical coercion or take unfair advantage. Economically speaking, security requires a basic stability in economic activity, social insurance, and other protections against life's contingencies, and a sound distribution of power with acceptable procedures for negotiating differences.

9. *Freedom*. Freedom is a high goal in Western society. It is undergirded by the Christian doctrine that man has freedom of choice, that he can significantly direct his own life when not externally coerced by undue restraints. Even in the midst of intolerable circumstances he has freedom to determine what his ultimate attitude toward life will be when he has the means for appraising his situation.

Out of the inherent capacity of the freedom of self-transcendence, the freedom to choose among alternatives, and the power of contrary choice many applied freedoms may emerge. Important applied freedoms include freedom to select and rank what goals should be sought and to select the means to achieve them. This involves the right to dissent within the framework of responsibility. We have already noted that the fundamental social freedoms include thought, speech, and association. These should be protected in the economic realm as well as in politics and education.

Within the economic sphere freedom takes the form of demands for freedom of enterprise, of consumer choice, of occupational and job choice, of investment, of property, of market-price determination, and of organization. The competing claims of these freedoms do not automatically adjudicate themselves. It is, therefore, necessary for the whole community to participate through voluntary associations and government in deciding the weight to be given to each. The failure to practice voluntary responsibility in economic affairs invites external controls from political sources. It is becoming increasingly apparent, however, that the notion that political government is a necessary evil rests on too skeptical and negative a view. A wise use of governmental control enhances the total quality of freedom in society. Government is not inherently repressive. Hence Christian freedom includes accepting the responsibilities of political justice.

10. *Justice.* Justice means that all men shall be treated with equal consideration and be afforded the same opportunities. Justice is thus closely related to equality in the sense of spiritual dignity. It is also the social demand that freedom be respected, for this too is a spiritual expression of personal worth. In practice justice means finding the right way among the competing claims of persons and groups. Justice means compromise. It is therefore the principle of relative right and value in a community of persons who present both fundamentally equal claims and also individual and culturally unequal ones. The tendency of each person to favor his own interests above those of others makes the application of justice a sober and realistic appraisal of claims in the light of the ideals of personality and community. As an inclusive principle of responsibility justice means wrestling with power, property, opportunity, security, present needs and wants, persons, groups, the claims of future generations, and the conservation of both material and immaterial values. Justice is not a static value but a dynamic goal. It must take account not only of present inequities but also of man's ultimate end; it sees not only the individual person but also the solidarity of mankind as the unit of co-operation.

11. *Personality.* Personality is the climactic intrinsic moral value. The goals considered above indicate the qualities of personal experience which communities ought to seek in economic life.

The greatest tests of economic activities are the kinds of persons they tend to produce, the kinds of communities they tend to develop, and the quality of ultimate meanings which they encourage their participants to embrace.

E. Capitalism and Communism

Discussions of economic life tend to polarize around the slogans of "free enterprise" and "collectivism." The conflict between "East" and "West," between "democracy" and "dictatorship," between the "free world" and the "Communist" world, tends to confuse the discussion of the social systems that are contending for supremacy. This conflict is, of course, no longer one between *"laissez faire* capitalism" and "socialism." Responsible students of contemporary society generally insist that no progress in understanding and the resolution of basic issues is possible by stating the issue in this way. The question is not whether government should meddle in the economic order but how, when, where, and for what ends.

Many Americans have held that that government is best which governs least, but no class of Americans has greatly objected to governmental meddling if it appeared to benefit them. The Federal Government has regularly enacted tariff laws to help industries, to keep up labor standards, and to sustain agricultural prices. It has constructed highways, given public land to railroads, subsidized railroads and other transportation companies, given away public land to persons and corporations, maintained free schools, and rendered innumerable services. From the beginning of the life of the nation American governments have contravened the theory and practice of *laissez faire*. They have operated on the assumption that it was appropriate for the government to limit the private initiative of some persons and to encourage the initiative of others. To some extent the economy has always been a managed economy.[11] The method by which this was done is most significant. It is the method of public discussion, hearings, debates, compromise, legislation, and court review. The assumption was the desirability of preserving the capitalist system of private enterprise and the belief that the evils of the system could be corrected by democratic methods of procedure.

Freedom of enterprise is not explicitly provided for in the American Bill of Rights, but it is taken for granted there in the clauses which deal with property. Economic freedom in this tradition is in practice one of the many freedoms which should be conserved in some kind of equilibrium. This tradition has withstood the contention that the capitalist system of private enterprise for private profit is the major source of injustice and hence must be abolished. In Europe the Communist contention and method have been to abolish the alleged root cause of injustice—the private ownership of capital and capitalistic production —by violent revolution, dictatorship, and the forcible liquidation of the capitalist classes. In Britain and America the holders of the democratic faith have resisted the contention that the intellectual and political freedoms could be temporarily suspended in the interest of more ultimate freedom.

The growth of social democracy in the United States has increasingly taken a pragmatic attitude toward economic institutions and methods.

[11] See Becker, *op. cit.*, pp. 108-9.

This attitude has refused to make of economic theory and practice a doctrinaire credo. Consequently, the national economy has embraced many aspects of a managed society and is, in fact, today a "mixed economy."

Despite their own accommodations to governmental regulation the representatives of what is sometimes called the "people's capitalism" constantly attack the state-planned economy of socialist and communist countries. Among the alleged benefits of long-range private planning as opposed to state planning, they urge the following points: (1) Because of America's political freedoms planning by government is subject to considerations not necessarily related to the economic or social problems to be solved. (2) The long-range needs of the public are often made a secondary consideration to the immediate political needs of a party or candidate. (3) Governmental planning is subject to change as control shifts from one party to another in the political power struggle. (4) No single person can be held accountable for the plans adopted. (5) Political maneuvering often delays decision for years while the economic crisis, for example, in transportation or agriculture, continues. (6) There is a tendency for state planning to be too small and too rigid. (7) Bureaucratic control fails to provide either the information or the productivity that is provided by the incentives and competition of a substantially free market. This point means, in the words of Ralph J. Cordiner of General Electric, that "no amount of planning downward or outward by governments or corporations or individuals will ever produce the demand information or the right production of goods as to type or output, which is provided every day by the two-way communications process of the free market." [12]

Tension between government operation and regulation, on the one hand, and private economic power, on the other, can never be resolved on any a priori basis. The conflict is so embedded in the total value crisis of modern life that it can be struggled with successfully only as part of man's integral involvement in society as a whole. Only proximate and provisional answers can be given to the shifting focuses of personal and group desires and power alignments. But through provisional and proximate social decisions they may become more re-

[12] By permission from *New Frontiers for Professional Managers*, p. 90, by Ralph J. Cordiner. Copyright, 1956. McGraw-Hill Book Company, Inc.

sponsible as they are guided by acceptable goals of economic and political life.

The prosecution of economic activity within the political context of freedom makes possible the vigorous criticism of economic life by all types of groups. "Free enterprise" is, therefore, not a closed or total ideology. It does not prejudge in a doctrinaire manner the ultimate status of ideals or values, the nature of man, moral agency, ideas of class and power, the metaphysics of science, the function of religion, the place of the economic order in culture, the foundations of law and politics, the character of evil, and the philosophy of history. While many economic groups seek to determine public opinion on all such subjects, the political organization of democratic society makes possible the holding of the widest possible range of convictions and the monopoly of none of them. The Oxford Conference in 1937 pointed out that the dominant economic order makes for the enhancement of acquisitiveness, that its production is distributed with great and often shocking inequality, that economic power is often in the possession of irresponsible groups, and that the kinds of work many persons do frustrates the sense of Christian vocation.[13] Within the context of freedom such ethical criticism may become a social force making for change. In Communist-dominated countries the effective relation of Christian criticism to social process is markedly and even radically different.

Since the goals of economic life ought to be coherent with the true goals of life, the criticisms of Communism must be in terms of its total outlook on man and society. The chief differences between capitalism and Communism are not to be found within the purely technical sphere. At this level both are reared on the same scientific foundations. In the same way a Christian social criticism of these two social ways of life takes into account the goals we have listed in an earlier section of this chapter. Because the Communist philosophy of life pervades its whole organization of economic activity, it is important to be inclusive in a criticism which can be briefly schematized under ten points:

1. The dominant Communist philosophy rules out every moral ontology and every theistic outlook on life. Its view of matter is that it is eternal and creative and self-explanatory. It is not grounded in a distinct spiritual principle.

[13] *Official Report* (Chicago: Willett, Clark & Co., 1937), pp. 87-91.

2. Communism has a faulty view of the nature of man. Because of its materialistic metaphysics it denies man basic security in a loving God and rejects ultimate spiritual goals for men. Atheistic Communism rejects the existence of eternal truths and ideal values which transcend the individual.

3. Communism has an inadequate view of freedom with the result that the individual person is not fully respected. There is no conception of a free moral agent responsible to God for all his actions. Character is but a function of social conditioning.

4. The sense of personal worth tends to be suppressed under the power and requirements of the group. Communism, following Marx's analysis, is right in recognizing the reality and power struggle of groups and classes in society, but it fails to appreciate the integrity and rights of persons as persons.

5. Communism has a distorted view of science since it elevates it to a metaphysic which supposedly has all the answers to the problem of human life. Moreover, in social science it lacks a sound principle of self-criticism. For this reason it tends to be dogmatic and authoritarian. Authoritarianism in all its forms violates the right of freedom, conscience, personal worth, and ideals which transcend all institutions.

6. Communism has a false view of religion. Marx's followers have been so obsessed with historical reaction in the church and with the historical failures of the church to meet its social responsibilities to the workers that they have failed to grasp the prophetic principle in religion and have been blind to its creative and redemptive functions. They have failed to see that Communism is itself a crude secular version of some of the truth and power of Christianity and Judaism.

7. Communism has an exaggerated understanding of the place of economic forces in society. Economic determinism, as we have repeatedly noted above, is defective social science. This defect means also that the role of cultural interaction as a whole and of the political order in particular is distorted and even perverted.

8. Because of its economic determinism, its attitude toward law, and its theory of the state the political doctrine of Communism exaggerates (a) the role of physical coercion, (b) the function of class interests, and leads to (c) totalitarian collectivism. It is one of the best illustrations of the maxim of R. M. MacIver that the "notion that force is the

creator of government is one of those part truths that begets total error."

9. As a consequence of these several factors Communism has a false conception of the sources of corruption in man and society and accordingly a false view as to how corruption and evil are overcome.

10. Finally, by its practical policy that the end justifies the means, Communism has undercut faith in the pledged word and confidence in voluntary co-operative activities for worthy social goals. It turns the struggle for justice into a new oppression.

CHAPTER VIII

Christian Criticisms of the Welfare State

A. Social Welfare and the Welfare State

Social welfare is today a complex phenomenon. Roscoe Pound has pointed out that the whole legal order has for centuries been adapting itself to changing ideas as to man's well-being. The basic goals of society have changed since ancient and medieval times. In the Middle Ages there was profound concern for tradition, that is, for stable social control. Then for several hundred years the emphasis shifted from basic social order and stability to the individual person. We have noted in previous chapters how the spirit of law and the idea of the state were profoundly altered in the interest of individual freedom. This individualistic emphasis probably reached its high point in the nineteenth century and is now being superseded by more communitarian goals. At one extreme social welfare is defined in terms of an intense collectivism or totalitarianism. On the other hand social welfare is being defined in terms more compatible with pluralistic democratic goals. In this latter conception the state is seen as the legal instrument of the politically organized community, but not as the total community, a legal association which is the instrument, not the master, of the community. The problem of the relation of social welfare to the welfare state is that of learning how to use the state for the true good of the community of persons.

The welfare state is not, then, primarily a socialist or Communist conception. There is, as Charles H. Seaver points out, a capitalist welfare state.[1] In a democratic state welfare may and should include the

[1] "The Capitalist Welfare State" (Ecumenical Study Documents of the World Council of Churches, July, 1953, No. 53E/353) Social Questions: Responsible Society in a World Perspective.

idea of freedom. This concern for freedom may require positive community action to assure equitable distribution of opportunity. Freedom may be conserved through both public and private agencies in the fields of education, recreation, information about employment, slum clearance, and low rent housing, for example. Freedom may also be conserved by government through protection of the freedom of speech, of assembly, of public action. This means that the instruments of government may be used to protect freedom from governmental repression.

But welfare in a democratic capitalist state may also include the idea of security. In America such security has included the patent laws and copyright laws, veterans' benefits, bankruptcy laws, banking laws, food and drug laws, property protection, and public health. Beyond these there are other welfare measures such as laws to protect security of employment, guarantees of bank deposits, farm price security, old age pensions and insurance, unemployment insurance, child-welfare grants, low cost housing, and many others. The state also provides the framework within which a vast array of voluntary welfare is organized and administered, such as industrial pension plans and Blue Cross and Blue Shield health insurance plans. In the United States the "welfare state" is very much a mixed economy, with "free enterprise" a component of welfare.

In the present chapter we shall critically examine some Christian bases of the welfare state, reserving for a later chapter a consideration of the role of the church in social welfare and some church and state issues which emerge in the effort to define and redefine roles and relationships. The focus of the church's place is on the responsibility of the religiously oriented voluntary association. Before I analyze the issues precipitated by the relation of private to public welfare agencies, I shall undertake to assess the Christian estimate of the large responsibility which the state is accepting in almost every part of the world.

Today every state is to some extent a welfare state. In many nations capitalistic methods of production are highly developed and a large share of the direction of economic life is left to individuals and private groups, and yet these nations assign major economic responsibilities to government in order to maintain economic stability, to prevent large-scale unemployment, or to provide basic forms of social security. These countries may differ widely on such issues as economic planning, their selection of industries and services for public ownership, or their use of taxation to promote equitable distribution of property and income. They reflect in many cases the fact of a revolutionary transition in the social and economic goals of their respective societies.

An important force in the shift of social goals and personal values in the present century has been the Christian Church. Its ethic has undergirded humanitarian concern. Even when the Church has acted conservatively as an institution, its ethic has penetrated the culture through many facets of Christian concern and through unofficial movements. It has affected the doctrines of law and government, the philosophy of work, the attitudes toward the class structure, and the theories of property.

The roots of the social welfare state go back to the various efforts in the nineteenth century to alleviate by governmental action the worst effects of the industrial revolution in England, the European continent, and the United States. Some would trace social welfare legislation to the earliest of the "Poor Laws." There is considerable evidence that the evangelical revival in eighteenth-century Britain bore fruit in much of the social reform of the next century. The story of Roman Catholic and Protestant influence is too complex and rich to be recounted here and has been fully documented elsewhere.[2] Its influence in the twentieth century has been both indirect and direct. Because of the dramatic emergence of the welfare state in Britain following World War II, it is useful to note the perspectives of certain leaders there whose work immediately preceded the expanded governmental activity. In England and on the continent the role of the modern state precipitated much explicit discussion of the responsibility and limits of state action. English writers found many readers in the United States. For the American situation the reader is referred to such writers as Reinhold Niebuhr, John Bennett, A. C. Knudson, F. E. Johnson, Walter

[2] C. H. Hopkins, *The Rise of the Social Gospel in American Protestantism, 1865-1914* (New Haven, Conn.: Yale University Press, 1940) ; R. H. Gabriel, *The Course of American Democratic Thought;* J. N. Hughley, *Trends in Protestant Social Idealism* (New York: Columbia University Press, 1948) ; F. E. Johnson, *The Social Gospel Re-examined* (New York: Harper & Bros., 1940) ; M. J. Williams, *Catholic Social Thought* (New York: Ronald Press, 1950) ; Stokes, *op. cit.;* J. A. Hutchison, *We Are Not Divided* (New York: Round Table Press, Inc., 1941) ; Spann, *op. cit.;* T. B. Maston, *Christianity and World Issues* (New York: The Macmillan Co., 1957) .

146

Rauschenbusch, John A. Ryan, Harry F. Ward, F. J. McConnell, and Kirby Page.

B. Christian Concern for the Welfare State

The foundations of the concerns of the welfare state are deeply laid in the Christian conception of man, respect for personality, and human solidarity. The modern welfare drive or dynamic arises also from the melioristic idea that the conditions of human life can be and ought to be improved. At least a moderate faith in progress in this sense lies at its root. An influential exponent of this position was William Temple. Archbishop Temple stated this principle vigorously in *Mens Creatrix:*

But if progress is either a fact or a real possibility, the dilemma, "good man" or "good citizen" no longer arises in the old acute form. The old alternatives were, "work a rotten system at moral loss to your self," "Leave the world and save your soul." But now there is a third, always recognized in practice but not always in theory, "Go and make the world a better place, even if you have to dirty your hands in the process." And if all moral obligations spring from our membership in society it is clear that this is not only permissible but obligatory, and that a "cloistered virtue" may be exquisite but cannot be moral, except in so far as it is attempted in order that its influence may benefit society as a whole.[3]

Temple's social ethic at this point was an elaboration of his four Christian social principles of freedom, fellowship, service, and sacrifice. These principles motivate and underlie his approach to the welfare responsibility of the state, but they also transcend it.

Temple rightly rejected the view of the state held by Hobbes, Machiavelli, the Fascists, and the Communists that the essence of the state lies in its power of coercion.[4] He maintained that the distinguishing mark of the state is respect for law and that the coercive powers are only an expression of law and never of political authority for its own sake. "The distinguishing mark of the State is not its possession of force, but its self-expression through Law, which employs force as the guarantee of that universality which is its essential nature."[5] Consistent

---

[3] (New York: The Macmillan Co., 1917), p. 193. Used by permission of Macmillan & Company, Ltd., St. Martin's Press, Mrs. William Temple.

[4] This view of the state also dominates such American periodicals as *Christian Economics* and *Faith and Freedom*.

[5] *Christianity and the State* (London: Macmillan & Co., 1928), p. 114.

with this view he insisted that the "nearer we are to a just social order the greater our need of religion." This need resides not only in the moral cohesion of the state and its foundation of law, but also in the danger that the state may become merely a secular institution divorced from its religious roots. Thus Christianity transcends the state:

> The Gospel of the cross, which sends us forth to do all we can for social justice and human fellowship, still stands when our utmost effort is expended, calling to new achievements . . . but we find justice in its perfection . . . only when as penitent sinners we kneel before the Cross; . . . to our need of the Cross the very failure of our merely social enterprise will lead us back.[6]

Temple was one of the immediate predecessors of the democratic socialist welfare state, but he always insisted on the supremacy of the Christian gospel over it.

It is not only in a general relationship to law that the Christian expresses his modern concern through the state, but also through the whole world of work. Such a Christian leader as Dr. J. H. Oldham recognized that much of the social crisis of the modern world was due to the divorce of work and worship. His concern for the sphere of daily work as the testing ground for all conceptions of a just society brought his thinking into direct line with the political and economic thinking behind the idea of the welfare state. The emotional drive behind the welfare state he derives largely from the failure of the economic order to assure men continuous employment or, if it did occasionally seem to do so, employment that carried a living wage or was of inherent value or was clearly contributory to common good. It is at this point that our earlier discussion on work as religious vocation has a direct bearing on the issues of this chapter. The state has been called upon to intervene in the world of work. For the Christian this assumption of governmental responsibility is coupled with the further question of the quality of participation in industry and politics that this intervention by the state makes possible for the worker. No matter what external form modern work takes, whether for public or private enterprise, the Church must protest when work "no longer fosters, as it ought to do, the growth of personal character, by affording opportunities for per-

* *Social Witness and Evangelism* (London: Epworth Press, 1943), pp. 18-19.

sonal decision, exercise of judgment, mastery of intractable material and growth in understanding and skill." [7] The Christian doctrine of vocation leads squarely to protection of the worker by government.

Another leading idea of the democratic welfare state as illustrated by developments in Britain is that of the functional society. This conception was dominant in the views of R. H. Tawney, well known for his *Religion and the Rise of Capitalism*, *The Acquisitive Society*, and *Equality*. He argued that the malaise of English life was due to its deep-rooted class structure and the resultant unjust inequalities.

The inequality which [so many critics] deplore is not inequality of personal gifts, but of the social and economic environment. They are concerned, not with a biological phenomenon, but with a *spiritual* relation and the conduct to be based on it. Their view, in short, is that, because men are men, social institutions—property rights, and the organization of industry, and the system of public health and education—should be planned, as far as is possible, to emphasize and strengthen, not the class differences which divide, but the common humanity which unites, them.[8]

In order to overcome the long entrenched and unjust inequalities of the class structure, Tawney advocated a major extension of the social services. These proposals are much like those which since 1945 have been included in the welfare state. He advocated health services, children's allowances, subsidized housing, rationalization of education, and insurance against unemployment. Against the objections of opponents he defended certain moral claims to equality in fundamental resources. He said:

Burke remarks that all men have equal rights, but not to equal things, and there is a truth in the distinction which is justly applauded. But, unfortunately, Nature, with her lamentable indifference to the maxims of philosophers, has arranged that certain things, such as light, fresh air, warmth, rest, and food, shall be equally necessary to all her children, with the result that, unless they have equal access to them, they can hardly be said to have equal rights, since some of them will die before the rights can be exercised, and others will be too enfeebled to exercise them effectively.[9]

[7] J. H. Oldham, *Work in Modern Society*, (New York: Morehouse-Gorham Co., 1950), p. 14.
[8] *Equality* (New York: Harcourt, Brace & Co., 1931), p. 37. Used by permission of George Allen & Unwin Ltd.
[9] *Ibid.*, p. 176.

Tawney greatly influenced the economic and political thought of William Temple and J. H. Oldham and exerted a major influence on Christian support of the welfare state among English-speaking peoples.

A Christian politician who helped directly to shape the welfare state in Britain was Sir Stafford Cripps. A devout churchman and socialist he found an expression for his sense of religious vocation in left-wing politics. His conception of the role of the Christian Church is constructive action in social ethics.

It is for the church [he argued] to provide the moral force and the driving power for social and economic development. The technical details of government and of legislation are for the politicians. But this is not to imply that politicians should be materialists. We require courageous Christians in our political life more than ever today. For, since this moral driving power is essentially designed to influence political decisions, its creation and its growth must impinge directly upon our political thought and action.[10]

Like Tawney, Cripps advocated industrial democracy. He sought to get this expressed both through government and in the more immediate relationships of workers and management.

The Christian concern for a welfare state arises both in the interest of the conservation of personal freedom and fulfillment and in behalf of justice. Tawney's concern for equality is for a justice which frees. It is a concern for the weaker party. Full freedom is a combination of restraints and liberties which make for the ends which are consonant with the chief end of man. The real issue is, therefore, not the simple individualistic question of whose liberties are being infringed, but the rights of each in the community of inclusive responsibility. It is the classical Christian doctrine of the state which is at stake. This doctrine asserts that the true end of the state is neither the protection of property nor power, but justice itself. There is a common good which is the good of the whole community and its members. The art of true politics is to give proper due to both the whole and the individual members.

C. Problem Areas for Christians

In the previous section were cited Christian leaders who influenced thinking about the welfare state in Britain. They have also influenced

10 *Towards Christian Democracy* (New York: Philosophical Library, 1946), p. 4.

the whole Christian world through the ecumenical movement. The very idea of the responsible society owes much to men like J. H. Oldham. Since World War II many of the earlier goals of social welfare have been in part realized, and a new situation has arisen. Christians have experienced the realities of both collectivist and of democratic regimes. Hence the whole discussion of the welfare state now enters into a new era as churchmen respond to the various forms and degrees of political and economic state action in modern society. The issues are spiritual as well as political and economic. They involve questions of the unity of means and ends.

From one perspective this whole book is a response to the problem of the Christian in the modern world of welfare and power. As Professor Banning [11] has pointed out, there are five groups of problems which must be faced: (1) the challenges of conceptions which tend to shift personal responsibility to the state, (2) problems of state intervention in economic life, (3) problems of governmental intervention into social relationships, (4) problems of the development and maintenance of law, and (5) problems of intervention into cultural affairs.[12]

The Christain faith must seek to conserve the sense of personal responsibility. It is not a priori clear, however, how far it is well for governments to intervene in economic life—for example, on the degree of regulation of production, the question of centralization and decentralization, the guarantee of work and wages, the stimulating of new production, and the redistribution of national income. In the field of social relationships there are problems of Christian concern as to the pattern a nation may set up in the relations of management to labor or the freedom of collective bargaining. Similarly there is the question of the extent to which social work should be public or private, or the extent and patterns of a housing program, the provisions of social insurance and the program of public health. Banning argues, quite properly, that government policy must be concerned with these things, but other questions remain: How is responsibility for social policy to

[11] Professor W. Banning of Utrecht is an influential figure in Christian social thought and action in the Netherlands.

[12] "The Welfare State from the Christian Point of View," Ecumenical Study Documents (July, 1953), Sec. I: "The Changes in Society and State and the Church's Call for a Responsible Society."

be aroused and allocated, and what in the present concrete situation of a particular nation does the claim to social justice amount to?

Social welfare depends in part on the development and maintenance of good law. In some areas the law is behind the times and restrains the best growth of community life. Some thinkers take a fatalistic attitude toward law. But Christians are constrained to ask questions about centralization of authority and administration. What activities may be taken from the state? How can local governments be made to assume more significant responsibilities in the society of today? How can the maximum number of persons and voluntary associations learn to bear responsibility for the formulation of and respect for law? The answers to these questions will vary from country to country and from decade to decade.

Very grave questions arise in the sphere of the state's role in cultural affairs. MacIver has defended the thesis that the state should not command the doing of things the value of which depends on the spirit in which they are performed and not on the mere externals of performance.[13] Whatever may be the merit of this thesis, it is clear from a Christian perspective that the state should be the servant of the enhancement of culture, not its master. Hence the freedom of religion and of voluntary associations must be protected.

D. Christian Responses to Particular Challenges

The bitter encounter with the totalitarian state has crystallized for some minds an identification of the latter with the welfare state. This happened in the case of Bishop Berggrav of Norway. He says: "The specific characteristic of the welfare state is this: on the one hand it is totally secular, and does not in any way whatever acknowledge God as the Lord of life; on the other hand, it acts as though it were Providence itself and assumes the right of entering into all the spheres of human life." [14] Here clearly Berggrav is dealing with the omnicompetent state as a totalitarian political, economic, and social society where all problems of the citizens are cared for down to toothache and bath water. Though he speaks from a Lutheran perspective, all Christians would

[13] *Op. cit.,* chap. xi.

[14] Eivind Berggrav, "State and Church Today," in "The Welfare State from the Christian Point of View." Ecumenical Study Documents on Social Questions: The Responsible Society in a World Perspective (July, 1953, No. 53E/353).

agree to his repudiation of omnicompetence as a conception of government.

The problem arises whether the Lutheran doctrine of the two realms may be maintained under these changed conditions or whether the new state enters so deeply into the spiritual realm that there is no longer any room for the Church. The welfare state does not shrink from violating the secrecy of the individual's conscience; it seeks to exercise total rule. The welfare state aims at being a unified state, a unity state, and because it knows the great importance of personal conviction, it sees to it that all its citizens are provided with the "proper" kind of personal conviction.[15]

Berggrav is concerned to preserve the role of the Church in such realms as the motives of public agencies, the faith of the people, the care of persons in sorrow and need, the diaconate, and social work. He is concerned that the Church protect its social welfare work from being sterilized by the state, that the right of parents to determine the education of their children be preserved, and that the state not try to determine what is good and what is right. On the other hand, he is concerned that the Church stay out of power politics as a means for achieving its ends. He repudiates the political tendencies and strategies of the Roman Catholic Church.

Viewed in the perspective of the Norwegian Church struggle against the Nazi state, Bishop Berggrav's reaction is fully understandable, but it may not, nevertheless, be an adequate response to all forms of the welfare state. The Norwegian pastor Henrik Hauge sees the problems in a more dialectical setting. "It would be a frightful misunderstanding," he says, "if the Church should maintain that there must be a conflict between the Church and a welfare state, and it would be an illusion to think that there is no possibility of conflict between a welfare state and the Church." [16] Specific aspects of this larger question include the following points of conflict: (a) whether the welfare of the citizens is the supreme and only legitimate goal of man's social life, (b) what welfare really means and includes, and (c) who shall be responsible for what aspects of welfare.

The problem of power is a crucial one. There has always been a problem of power in the state. But the roots of the problem of power

[15] *Ibid.*, p. 6.
[16] "The Church and the Welfare State," in Ecumenical Study Documents, No. 53E/353.

are not the same as the roots of the question of welfare. It is in the combination of welfare and power that a special modern dilemma arises. "One dilemma," as Hauge sees it, "is the connection between the new idea of the righteous society in the welfare state and the power." The dilemma is this peculiar combination of power concentration and a welfare state. This leads into the dangers of which Berggrav speaks, should welfare monopoly follow in the wake of the welfare state. The struggle, therefore, between the church and the power state is not against the welfare state but *for* and *with* the welfare state within a responsible society.

Christian leaders, like Heinz-Dietrich Wendland, see three main lines along which power in the modern state must be limited and restricted.[17] First, there is the need to limit power through the faith and conscience of the individual who exercises political power. Second, there is the need of the Church to be active in freedom and love, to instruct the conscience and to counterbalance the state by a political care of souls, and to preach repentance to those in power. Third, power needs limitation by secular justice and democratic controls. These mean that Christian citizens should be devoted to an unswerving search for justice in the state and in the larger community which the state serves.

These observations carry the discussion back to ideas developed in earlier centuries and recall significant observations by men like Edmund Burke, Roger Williams, and de Tocqueville. Burke held that "society cannot exist unless a controlling power upon will or appetite be placed somewhere and the less of it there is within the more of it there must be without. It is ordained in the eternal constitution of things that men of intemperate minds cannot be free. Their passions forge their fetters." Along this same line de Tocqueville remarked that "if faith be wanting in man he must serve and if he be free he must believe." There must, then, always be a quickening of the personal conscience and under God a recognition that the care of men can never be completely turned over to the political order. In his famous pamphlet entitled *The Bloody Tenent of Persecution,* Roger Williams wrote on this theme as follows:

[17] *Ibid.,* "The Control of Power—A Christian Task."

154

For in a free state no man hath power over the bodies, goods, lands, liberties of a free people but by their free consents. And because free men are not free lords of their own estates but only stewards under God therefore they may not give their free consents to any magistrates to dispose of their bodies, goods, lands, liberties at large as themselves please but the Sovereign Lord of all, alone.[18]

Roger Williams' argument has a striking new force and application in relation to welfare and power.

The new situation of the Christian Church in relation to the modern welfare state must be understood also in terms of changes from the side of secular thought as illustrated by certain tendencies in British and Continental democratic socialism. These are of interest especially in view of the new emphasis on personality and revisions of the conception of what constitutes the fundamental human situation. For example, a member of the British Labour Party acknowledges in *The New Fabian Essays: "The evolutionary and revolutionary philosophies of progress have both proved false.* Judging by the facts, there is far more to be said for the Christian doctrine of original sin than for Rousseau's fantasy of the noble savage, or Marx's vision of the classless society." [19] A significant modification in basic orientation is also apparent in the Declaration of the Socialist International meeting in Frankfurt am Main in 1951, dealing with aims and tasks of democratic socialism. It argued that socialists can base their concern for social justice on religious beliefs and need not be Marxists. There is much thinking of this kind now in Holland, Germany, and Sweden. In Asia, too, socialism as an ideology is undergoing a transformation, attempting to hold on to what is true in liberalism, Marxism, and Gandhism, and rejecting what is false.[20]

The new emphases of democratic socialists on personality, on creative

[18] These passages were suggested to me through the essay by Principal T. M. Taylor, "The Scope and Limitations of State Initiative," Ecumenical Study Documents: January, 1952 (51E/331).

[19] Quoted in *Six Ecumenical Surveys* prepared for the Evanston Assembly of the World Council of Churches: "Social Questions—The Responsible Society in a World Perspective," pp. 7-8. The above paragraph owes much to this discussion and the literature cited.

[20] See such literature as *Socialism, a New Statement of Principles* (London: Socialist Union, 1952); Netherlands Socialist Party, *De Weg naar Vrÿheid* (Amsterdam, 1956); Gerhard Weisser, *Sozialismus und Marxismus* (1947); M. M. Thomas, "The Responsible Society in India," *Indian Journal of Theology*, November, 1952.

freedom, on responsible use of power, and on a more adequate doctrine of man and society offer challenges to the churches. On all these matters Christians must provide both adequate doctrinal understanding and insight translated in terms that really meet the concrete issues of political and economic thought and action. Both secular and Christian thinkers everywhere in the world are in a new situation which tests every ism, ideology, and doctrinal system.

An important response to the new situation is that of the Anglican scholar V. A. Demant, whose book *Religion and the Decline of Capitalism* has aroused considerable discussion. Canon Demant, like Berggrav, has seen the state assume some of the functions demanded by earlier proponents of social Christianity and is aware of the decline of the religious component in the ethos of society. He acknowledges some positive values in capitalist society, now that some of its worst abuses have been partly ameliorated. He has also observed some of the dangers of collectivism in Europe and asks such leading questions as the following: "Can economic liberalism go down without losing firstly the advantages of disinterested science and serviceable techniques, and secondly such positive aspects of the liberal tradition as the rule of law and insistence upon the priority of persons over institutions?" [21] There is a danger of making science and law and business, as well as religion, merely lackeys of one overmastering purpose of social solidarity, real or alleged.[22]

On the negative side the collectivist welfare states seem to suffer from obsession with the same values that dominated the earlier bourgeois society. Such values include commodity hedonism, the reckless dissipation of man's estate, the overdevelopment of the technical side of human nature at the expense of the whole person, the arrogance of technically advanced countries toward other nations, economic nationalism, and a false optimism that finds the solution of life's deepest problems in social organization. Demant holds that modern collectivism has erected an elaborate social structure without being aware of the deep decay that has attacked the foundations of social life. Liberalism in the nineteenth century was already living on the borrowed capital of Christianity, and collectivism has done little to replenish it. He finds

[21] *Op. cit.*, p. 26.
[22] *Ibid.*, p. 55.

that collectivism, like capitalism, has no coherent or sufficient doctrine of man. It lacks a profound metaphysics. Since it has no transcendent spiritual element, it deals with social problems in a purely horizontal manner. Having a superficial conception of human nature, it deals even with freedom and justice apart from man's true end. "Collectivism," he notes, "is but atomism packed tight. Men do not find healed the wound left by tearing them away from their spiritual and organic setting, by collaborating with other men maimed like themselves in a state enterprise or planned economy or racial messianism." [23]

At this point Demant's criticism makes contact with that of an English free-churchman, Sir George Schuster, who contends that nationalization has failed to provide the new system and status that the working class has been seeking as an escape from the traditional authoritarianism in business. He contends that legislation does not cut deep enough to deal with the root of the sickness of industrial life. The basic defect lies in human relations that must be improved at the level of the workshop and the individual factory plant and not by the parliament. The focus here is the significance of the local level of reform and social life without denying the place of broad national structures. For Schuster the "greatest need of our modern industrial society is to make industrial employment something which is, and is seen as, an essential part of a satisfactory human life (individual and social) and not as a cause of conflict or an evil burden to be escaped from or reduced as far as possible." [24] An adequate doctrine of Christian vocation must be implemented not only in terms of a broad governmental framework for industrial democracy, but even more in terms of the social process of the individual job situation.

E. Some Emergent Conclusions

The conception of welfare, in relation to which the discussion of the welfare state derives its meaning, is ambiguous in a twofold sense. On the one hand, there is no unanimity among Christians at the present time as to what the specific social good of man is or what the degree of state responsibility in relation to the rights and freedoms of persons is.

[23] *Ibid.*, p. 195.
[24] *Christianity and Human Relations in Industry* (New York: British Book Centre, 1952), p. 29.

On the other hand, experience with the totalitarian state has tended to induce some Christians to reject state welfare action because of the fear of loss of personal freedom and the freedom of the church. Despite lack of unanimity several conclusions may be drawn.

1. Welfare, like responsibility, is an inclusive term with many tensional components within it. Welfare is not the exclusive province of the state but is everybody's business to build up personality and provide the proper conditions for its fulfillment. To welfare belongs the idea of common concern that persons as persons should grow and their true good be actualized. Persons grow both within social groups and in conflict with social institutions. Welfare includes freedom. Therefore, the proper idea of a welfare state is not that of an omnicompetent state, but of establishing the conditions of opportunity for responsible productivity and decision making. These conditions will include a concern for minimal standards in employment, housing, health, education, and the like. Christian concern that such conditions for minimal standards be met is not equated with ultimate sanctions for the programs proposed and applied to establish these conditions.

2. Welfare includes an appreciation for freedom, but it rests primarily on a fundamental respect for persons and on the Christian understanding of the fact that they are members one of another. There are many circumstances in society where some forms of liberty and respect for personality are conflicting values. In a complex economic order a regard for greater personal opportunity of underprivileged people may mean less traditional liberty for the privileged few. A critical appraisal of the total personal good must determine whether, for example, justice or liberty in any situation will be the more dominant. Welfare is not a fixed amount of social or economic goods. With rising abundance, based on high productivity, the relation of freedom to justice takes on different forms from those in a situation of poverty.

3. A responsible welfare state will give due recognition to the role of the natural social units like the family and the voluntary associations. Their role in social welfare will be discussed in a later chapter. There is much truth in the saying that man behaves at his best in small groups. The priority of the family and the numerous subsidiary groups should, therefore, be protected and encouraged by sound social policy. It is even necessary that the state protect them against itself. A high

appreciation for the role of the voluntary associations, especially in the cultural fields, does not preclude the operation of the state in the control of economic activities. State welfare should undertake what private welfare cannot do and must encourage the creative initiative and responsiveness of private agencies and institutions.

4. The problem of power is basic in both the economic and political aspects of a welfare state. Monopoly of power must be repudiated. Democratic limitations of power are essential to effect the optimum of decentralization and devolution of responsibility within the state machine.[25] Where decentralization and devolution of responsibility are effectively worked out, where local government is vigorous, and where government is kept responsive to public opinion, more action by the state may be undertaken without loss of basic liberties than where these conditions do not obtain. As we have seen in previous chapters, the responsibility of government reflects the ethos of the society which sustains it. The family, the school, the church, and the voluntary associations carry a heavy weight of obligation for maintaining the spiritual vitality of the ethos underlying the legal, economic, and political order. Economic power by whomever held must be constantly checked, so that individuals and groups are not exploited, special interests given advantage, access to opportunity restricted, liberty of opinion suppressed, or the creative life of the community throttled.

5. A welfare state is simply not a welfare state from a Christian viewpoint while it leaves unchallenged well-drawn or rigid lines of class division. The mutual separation of one group of the population from another means that both the bourgeoisie and the proletariat are infinitely the poorer because there is no interpenetration or mutual enrichment. The Church may not, therefore, be merely a spectator to a situation which only guarantees civil liberty and safe parliamentary seats for liberals and conservatives. Christian criticism must effect that union of theory and practice which penetrates both the ideology of welfare and the barriers making for class separation. The Church needs to make more experiments which, though unconventional and nonparochial, transcend the walls of separation between the subcultures of the trade union world and the business and professional world of

[25] See Denys Munby, "Moral Problems in the Economic Situation Today." Ecumenical Study Documents on the Responsible Society. May, 1952 (52E/335).

suburbanites. Christian leaders must bring the vocational ethic of the Christian Church jointly to management, shop stewards, foremen and superintendents, apprentices and personnel officers, trade union leaders, and clergy. As they jointly consider the specific issues of economic life and politics they must relate them to worship and ethics.

6. One of the significant ways of influencing the spiritual quality of the welfare state is through better education. Education is a major factor in vertical mobility, that is, in the opportunity of a person to rise in the economic and social scale or to overcome class barriers in society. The Church, therefore, has a stake in keeping the community conscience sensitive to the educational claims of all its young people. This role means that not only at the high school level but also in higher education the churches will pursue policies of encouragement to the less economically privileged. But not only will the churches encourage vertical mobility by assisting able students from the lower economic classes; they will insist on broad integral liberal education that sees community life as a whole, and they will make its offering of philosophy, religion, and theology germane to these objectives. A welfare state not only needs technically well-trained persons; it needs persons of spiritual and moral stature even more.

7. As society takes responsibility for the basic welfare of its members, especially in an age of relative abundance, there is a problem of the effect of this service on the individual, since so much is done for him without commensurate obligations being laid upon him.[26] This situation challenges the integrity and the responsibility of the individual member of society who is tempted to take so much economic and social good for granted. The Church has a special role in reminding its members of their need to become morally and spiritually mature.

8. Welfare is not only a national but an international obligation. National welfare must be analyzed and appraised in the context of world-wide responsibility. Oftentimes actions undertaken by governments in the interest of the welfare of their own citizens are difficult to reconcile with the welfare of other nations and of the community of nations.[27] Welfare thus becomes an inclusive ethical conception. In the light of this perspective nations must consider not only the social good

[26] See essay by J. M. Clark in Ward, *Goals of Economic Life*, pp. 49-51.
[27] See essay by W. A. Brown, Jr., in Bennett, *Christian Values and Economic Life*, pp. 108, 125, 127, 142-46.

of their member citizens but also such world-wide effects as threats of deflation and inflation, credit policies, obligations to consult and co-operate with other nations, exports, sharing surpluses in goods, sharing know-how, and capital for development programs. Out of the sense of responsibility which creates welfare state activities at home arises the further obligation to consider power policies abroad and the rights and duties of technically developed and less developed areas of rapid social change with respect to one another.

CHAPTER IX

Responsible Agricultural Policy

Man's relationship to the land has always had a profound effect upon his way of life and work. Land tenure and agricultural activity have involved him in relationships which include religion, family, and community. So intimately are these relationships observable in many parts of the world that man is often thought of as belonging to the land, even to a particular piece of land. The manner of land ownership, the systems of inheritance, the definition of property rights and use, are interrelated with systems of religion and ultimate ethical sanctions.

A. The Complexity of Agricultural Values

In many parts of the world a vast technical, economic, and social revolution is under way in this tightly cohesive way of life that is man's immemorial involvement in agriculture. Technical changes are directed at (1) the resources available for cultivation, at (2) methods of production, and at (3) the organization of production. These tend to affect the standards of values in family life, in community authority, and in patterns of co-operation. As soon as widespread purposive change, based on Western technical patterns, is undertaken, certain general changes emerge: policies of soil conservation, including reforestation and contour plowing; livestock improvement; seed improvement; pest control; land improvement; mechanization; and the introduction of cash crops. These affect life at every turn.

One of the fundamental issues that has arisen, not only in underdeveloped areas of the world but also in the United States, is found in the transition from agriculture as a way of life to agriculture as a way of earning a living. We shall note this problem more fully when dealing with the family farm in America, but it is important to see it as a world-wide crisis. When agriculture changes from subsistence to farming for cash crops, a number of disruptive factors enter in. The shift from *making* a living to *earning* a living is usually radical in its effects. Oftentimes it means a change from a value crop, around which religious life centers, to a merely utilitarian crop. The land is a unit of belongingness. When this goes, life values may be fundamentally overturned.[1]

The social crisis in American agriculture has given special concern to religious leaders for several decades. During the depression years of the thirties, with their dust storms, farm foreclosures, poverty, and distress, churchmen of various faiths repeatedly gave expression to the need for social policies which would emphasize right land use, conservation, stewardship of natural resources, the family farm and the farm family, human welfare, and the spiritual needs of rural areas.

In 1945 a distinguished group of Protestants, Roman Catholics, and Jewish leaders issued a joint statement of principles which should underlie national, state, and individual land policy. The land, they noted, is God's greatest material gift to mankind. It is a fundamental source of food, fiber, and fuel. Land is a very special kind of property.

Ownership of land does not give an absolute right to use or abuse, nor is it devoid of social responsibilities. It is in fact a stewardship. It implies such land tenure and use as to enable the possessor to develop his personality, maintain a decent standard of living for his family and fulfill social obligations. At the same time, the land-steward has a duty to enrich the soil he tills and to hand it down to future generations as a thank offering to God, the giver, and as a loving inheritance to his children's children.[2]

The values which received special attention are related to different aspects of this affirmation. (1) A unique relationship exists between the family and the vocation of agriculture. The family's welfare must have the first consideration in economic and social planning. (2) The

---

[1] See Mead, *op. cit.*, p. 194.
[2] "Man's Relation to the Land," published August 24, 1945, by the Rt. Rev. Msgr. Ligutti, Benson Y. Landis, and Dr. Gabriel Davidson. It was circulated by the Committee on Town and Country, 297 Fourth Ave., New York City.

land is not to be a source of benefit to a favored few and a means of servile labor to the many. (3) Society has a responsibility to encourage and to educate the land stewards in such use and techniques as will make them masters of their own economic destiny. (4) Rural people have the right to receive directly their just share of the economic, social, and religious benefits in organized society. (5) In addition to appropriate education in land use, production, and community service, a major objective of legislation and planning should be the family-type farm operated by the owner. (6) Large-scale land holdings are to be discouraged as undemocratic and unsocial. Where large-scale production is necessary and advisable, co-operatives are to be encouraged along with local ownership and management. (7) Where and when large-scale industrialized farming exists and requires seasonal or year-round employees, responsible policy demands for such a labor group a living family wage, decent housing conditions, and collective bargaining. (8) Social welfare provisions like those already available to urban workers should be made applicable also to farm populations.

The stewardship of the land involves, in other words, an inclusive stewardship of responsibility to person, family, neighbor, and all those who are affected by the production and distribution of food, fiber, and fuel. To the fact of complexity is added the urgency of the present situation.

The problem of man's stewardship of the land that God has given him is highlighted by the great drought which baked the southern plains of the United States and thrust its tentacles into the bordering northern plains. The most seriously affected section extended from central Texas northward through central New Mexico and Colorado to the southeast corner of Wyoming and thence across Nebraska, western Kansas, and the Oklahoma Panhandle. This area was double the size of the Dust Bowl of the 1930's. Misuse of the land had reverted 2,000,000 acres to dust and put 29,000,000 more in condition to blow. By comparison 9,000,000 acres in Texas, Colorado, New Mexico, Oklahoma, and Kansas actually "blew" in the last great dust bowl year of 1938. The floods which deluged the area in late 1956 and early 1957 added to the havoc already inflicted.

In this situation a number of factors were outside human control. For the most part lack of rain and subsoil moisture are conditions imposed by the vagaries of nature. Some authorities have estimated that the drought is the most severe in seven hundred years. But the human element is also a significant factor. It is essential to adapt the stricken land to its best use and to terminate feast-or-famine economics. Policies are needed to impose restrictions on the use of the land, what land may be plowed and sowed to crops and how long and how often, and what areas may better be put to grass either for a limited time or permanently. Policies are also needed for the use of ground water. Pumping ground water has become a major operation. In some places pumping is going on to such an extent that the water supply is "mined" far beyond the rate of replenishment. Since ground water is becoming almost as important as surface water in daily agricultural and domestic operations, the time has come when it requires regulation and the establishment of ground water rights just as do the surface flows.

In addition to the land and water use there are problems of farming practices and education in conservation. The development of conservation has been slower than the progress of the drought, however. Though thousands of soil conservation districts have been organized, there have been setbacks in the program. During World War II a period of adequate moisture and the lure of high prices and quick profits brought intensive cultivation of easily eroded land. The "plow-up" extended beyond the old Dust Bowl area. Its high point came in 1947. Not until 1951, with the drought already under way, was more land being returned to grass as a protective measure than was being plowed. These problems have been compounded by "suitcase farmers" and townspeople getting into the cattle business. Then, too, farm price supports and the desire of farmers to plant more to offset falling prices are also factors in the situation.

Emergency programs have been quantitatively significant. To date at least $315,000,000 in Federal aid have been pumped into the area. These dollars have been expended for credit loans, cut-rate hay and feed, added technical assistance, and the like.

The extent of the agricultural problem in the United States is symbolized by the fact that in his proposed budget for 1958 Eisenhower asked a record $5,329,880,000 to aid farmers and to carry out other activities of the Agriculture Department. This amount constitutes 7 per cent of the total budget. Of the total $3,826,100,000 would be used directly and indirectly to help support farm prices and to bolster farm incomes. Some issues involved in this program we shall note below. Before discussing them it is important to survey briefly the changing character of rural life.

B. The Changing Character of Rural Life

During George Washington's presidency 95 per cent of the American population was rural; during Lincoln's presidency the proportion was 80 per cent; during Eisenhower's presidency it is only 36 per cent. This census classification is based on size of place; therefore rural means nonurban. To understand the problems of rural life, one must further analyze the population according to rural farm and rural nonfarm. In the nonurban areas of American life there are innumerable varieties of social groupings which range all the way from mining communities in West Virginia and Pennsylvania to factory-farms in California and from unproductive small farms in northern Mississippi to great wheat farms and forestation projects in the Dakotas and Montana.

Building a responsible society in the agricultural sector of the economy requires a sensitivity to these changes, to the variety of American farm problems, to the different types of farming communities, to the dilemmas of the farm family, to the special predicaments of migratory workers, to the relationships of agriculture to industry, to the role of farmers' organizations, to questions of price levels and family income, to the international policies of the United States, and to many other facets of agricultural life. Population changes, differences between agriculture and urban industry, and the technological revolution on the farm lift up concretely the major factors that form the background of farm policy decisions.

The great population trend is from the rural to the urban areas. In the 1920's migration resulted in a net transfer from farms of 6 million persons; in the 1930's there were 3.5 million, and in the 1940's almost 9 million. Since 1950 in spite of a high birth rate migration has reduced the farm population from 25 million to less than 22 million. Only 10 per cent of the civilian labor force is now in agriculture, compared with more than 20 per cent a quarter-century ago. During the present decade at least one fourth of the young men reaching working age on farms will be in excess of replacement of older men who die or retire. In several of the low-income areas a third to a half of these young men will need to take up nonfarm work before 1960 even if no

166

further displacement is forced, for example, by increase in the size of the farms.[3]

This population shift has a relationship to the technological revolution on the farms. During the past quarter century the farmer's annual gains in productivity have exceeded even those in industry, a fact frequently overlooked. From 1947 to 1954 this trend did not abate. The gains in farm productivity averaged better than 4½ per cent a year. Many factors entered into this higher productivity whether measured in relation to man-power or measured in terms of increased yield of farm produce. Such factors include improved skill and research, improvements in management, efficiency and power of farm organizations, the opening of fertile crop land in the Pacific region, government-sponsored irrigation projects, hybrid plants with high yields, and more efficient pesticides and insecticides. Then, too, since 1930 tractors in use have multiplied more than five times, and grain combines and corn pickers have multiplied sixteen times. Though the amount of crop land did not change appreciably between 1930 and 1950, the over-all utilization of implements and machinery about doubled, while the purchases of fertilizers increased threefold. When we relate the greater productivity of farms to population between 1929 and 1954, we note that while farm output increased 46 per cent, the labor force declined in agriculture by almost 38 per cent, or from 10½ million to 6½ million. When both full-time and part-time workers are counted, the labor force on farms is probably now about 8½ million.

General statistics of the kind just cited are significant, but they must be supplemented by data showing the range in productivity, size of farms, and regional disparities. For example, there are nearly a thousand counties in the United States where more than half the farmers are mainly dependent on the income from small, poorly paying farms. What they are up against in innumerable cases is lack of enough good land, lack of equipment, lack of credit facilities, and often lack of management information and skill. The generalized critical farm areas, concentrated largely in the southeastern section of the country and in the deep South, include a million full-time farmers of working age who in 1950 sold less than $2,500 worth of products. The most serious low-

[3] The statistics in this chapter are taken from census reports; from the President's message to Congress, April 27, 1955, entitled "Development of Agriculture's Human Resources —A Report on Problems of Low-Income Farmers"; and the study by the Conference on Economic Progress, "Full Prosperity for Agriculture," November, 1955.

income areas are marked by production, income, and level of living all of which fall below recognized minimum standards. These areas lie entirely within the South and Border South and encompass the old Cotton Belt, with the exception of the fertile Mississippi Delta, most of the Appalachian and Ozark Mountains and plateaus, and northwestern New Mexico. They have a total population of 13½ million but there is not a single city within them of as much as 150,000 people.[4]

When placed in the context of all farms in the nation, small farms bear the following relationships to others in terms of acreage: 37 per cent are 50 acres or less and account for 4 per cent of the acreage; 61 per cent are from 50 to 1,000 acres and account for 54 per cent of the acreage; and 2 per cent are over 1,000 acres and account for 42 per cent of the acreage. From 1930 to 1950 the number of farms decreased from 6,289,000 to 5,382,000 while the average acreage per farm rose from 156.9 to 215.3. Tenancy declined from 42.2 per cent of the total to 26.8 per cent.

Despite the great technological and other changes that have marked the history of agriculture and have brought an air of similarity between town and country living in certain areas, the situation in agriculture continues to exhibit great disparities from the industrialized and urban segments of economic and social life. How different is agriculture? Walter W. Wilcox has lifted up seven significant differences which the maker of responsible social policy must keep in mind. (1) No other major industry except mining and petroleum engineering requires such a high investment in "permanent capital" in relation to the value of its annual production. (2) Agriculture is the only industry in which most of the investment is on an individual or family basis. Farmers are, therefore, very sensitive to deflation not only because of its effect on current income but because of its effect on land ownership and equipment. Farmers tend to be inflationists in hard times. (3) Agriculture is biological by nature and in its production processes. Hence it sustains very special relationship to time and seasons, the cycles and rhythms of animal and plant life, the schedules of crops and the like. (4) Farm families have a tendency to minimize their losses by keeping up or increasing production even when prices fall. Falling prices do not cause production to drop. This fact results in the upward trend in farm out-

---

[4] "Development of Agriculture's Human Resources," Washington: House Document No. 149 of the 84th Congress, 1st Session, April, 1955.

put relatively independent of other factors. (5) Many farms are too small to be commercially capable of effective competition. (6) Farm labor cannot be dismissed in periods of falling prices comparably to urban employment patterns. (7) The tendency has been for technological improvement to exceed the rate of increase in the population as a whole. Consequently prices tend to be relatively poorer rather than better.[5]

These disparities challenge national and local standards of value.

C. Equity and Other Values at Stake

The ethical norm around which much discussion of the farmer's plight in the United States revolves is equity. Walter W. Wilcox takes equity to be one of the basic ethical goals of our society and refers to the "desire that each one deserve what he gets and get what he deserves." [6] It is a question in equity when a farm depression takes place in the midst of general prosperity and when the gains in economic thought and action in other areas of the economy are not being applied with appropriate variations in agriculture.[7] It is a question in equity to confront realistically the plight of farmers because of their chronic relative weakness in the market place, because of their organizational weakness in stimulating consumption or rationalizing production and prices and incomes as others do, because trends in food distribution and prices have reduced their share of the consumers' food basket, and because of inadequate national policies.

The norm of equity must not be confused with the means that may be employed for its realization. For example, parity in farm prices, which I shall presently define and discuss, may be an application of equity, but it must not be identified with it. Equity lifts up the ideal of evenhanded impartiality. This involves other values when viewed in the context of society as a whole. Farm goals must be related to the intent of the whole society. Any merely self-seeking group goals must be rejected. The interests of the various farm groups must be impartially appraised in terms of their relative position of advantage or disadvantage over against one another as well as in relation to the national interest.

[5] *Op. cit.*, ch. 2.
[6] *Ibid.*, p. 4. Used by permission of Harper & Bros.
[7] Conference on Economic Progress, *Full Prosperity for Agriculture* (Washington, D.C., 1955), p. 4.

While equity is a focal norm for agricultural policies, other values seem to be closely related. Equality of opportunity as expressed in desegregation is involved. Along with desegregation must be placed educational opportunity and the rights to enjoy the good things of life which the general prosperity makes possible. This value includes disapproval of great inequalities of income. Farm families have participated in the equalizing tendencies due to the graduated income tax, relief grants, veterans' benefits, social security extension, education, and such social legislation as old age pensions and the like. Equity has a close kinship to equality, though it is not identical with it. For example, adding one thousand dollars to the income of a low-income or middle-income family adds more to consumer spending for most farm products than adding one thousand dollars to the income of a higher-income family. Higher minimums of purchasing power among the poorest quarter of the American people would greatly reduce the "surpluses" of food and fiber because these are the very products which they would most readily consume if they were able to buy them.

W. A. Brown, Jr., points out that the

economists' concept of equality for agriculture and all other industries is a condition in which the real return to labor, management, and capital employed in agriculture (and in each of its parts) is equivalent to what the persons or the units of capital could get in any other vocation or use. The approach to such equality requires the highest possible degree of business flexibility and personal freedom; and the concept itself is very different from that embodied in the parity conception that has actually been employed.[8]

It is, therefore, necessary from a Christian viewpoint to seek to distinguish between those aspects of policy that reflect merely a desire for ever-increasing high levels of agricultural prices and incomes, and those elements that genuinely contribute to a just relation between the economic position of the farming population and other segments of the economy.[9]

Parity has been used in policy making as a measure of equity. We may define parity prices as those "computed for each farm product by

[8] "Some International Implications of Christian Economic Ethics," in Bennett, *Christian Values and Economic Life,* p. 133 n. Used by permission of Harper & Bros.
[9] *Ibid.,* p. 135

a formula designed to indicate what price would be required for it to have a purchasing power equivalent to its purchasing power in the chosen base period." [10] The period generally referred to is 1909 to 1914.

There are a number of equity issues related to parity in addition to those which have already been anticipated above. Parity efforts or farm price stabilization measures are supplements to the so-called free market system designed to make it function more equitably in rewarding those who engage in farm production. These measures are not welfare measures for the redistribution of farm income on the basis of family needs. Indeed, there is grave question whether a policy based on price and commodity adjustments can give adequate income protection for the farmer who needs it most, and whether a different approach is not necessary to meet the personal and family needs of disadvantaged farmers. At the present time the larger farms benefit more than the medium-size farms from the reduction in income uncertainty.[11]

Some of the consequences of price-stabilization measures should now be considered. One is that assurance of relatively stable incomes encourages farmers to invest in labor-saving and output-increasing equipment more rapidly than might be prudent under free market conditions. Such investment may speed up technical progress in agriculture to such an extent that additional "surpluses" of products result from accelerated technical progress. Sufficient farm labor may be freed for nonfarm production to more than offset the increased capital used. "Surpluses" could in this sense be regarded as a bonus to society resulting from increased stability of prices.[12]

Another consequence is that price-supported crops which have the condition of restricted acreage often occur in the same year in which prices in nonsupported crops are sagging. Diversion of acreage to these latter crops may lower the prices of those crops. The farmers affected feel keenly the competition in the very commodities whose price levels are sagging. There is, accordingly, widespread disagreement on the equity of maintaining price supports on specific commodities and not on others and on the regulations which should govern the use of acreages diverted from the price-supported crops by acreage allotments.

A third consequence is that establishment of assured prices at a

[10] Wilcox, *op. cit.,* p. 19.
[11] *Ibid.,* p. 37.
[12] *Ibid.,* pp. 28-29.

higher level than the free market will over the years result in somewhat larger output than otherwise. Hence, if "surpluses" are to be kept small in relation to total farm output, farm price supports must not be too different from the free market prices.

The consequences just mentioned raise the ethical issue of the right balance among equity, stability, and freedom. Freedom is often set over against security. Freedom is also often placed in opposition to governmental action or market interference in the interest of stability. Security and freedom are not always contradictory values. The choice before farmers and the government may not be between stability and security on the one hand and freedom on the other. "Security," writes W. W. Wilcox, ". . . involves freedom from other external forces that may be viewed as more limiting to individual initiative than is the specific governmental intervention. And some farm leaders say they believe farmers prefer freedom from want to freedom from governmental interference." [13] This kind of freedom is really an economic issue: "Is the added stability of prices and income worth the cost in terms of required restrictions on plantings and marketings?" Some insist that the issues of economic freedom and security cannot be separated from the larger questions whether any man can be politically free who depends upon the state for sustenance. It is difficult to find any group in the social economic order which is not thus dependent in some significant respect, either directly or indirectly, on government. Others again focus attention on the goal of government of helping people to help themselves, that is, developing a policy which will strengthen individual integrity, freedom, and moral fiber in each citizen. Freedom, men are coming more and more to realize, can be achieved only in social organization, in social order. Here, again, the word of the Evanston Assembly of the World Council of Churches is applicable: "While the state is sometimes the enemy of freedom, under many circumstances the state is the only instrument which can make freedom possible for large sectors of the population."

D. Farmers' Organizations and Governmental Policy

Agricultural policy which is oriented to commodity control, parity, and price stabilization tends to overlook the income needs of the individual farm family and to favor the owners of the larger commercial

[13] *Ibid.*, p. 34.

farms. These latter types of farms have been better able to take advantage of price-stabilization policies than smaller farms. The technological development on these farms increases at a faster rate than on the smaller ones. Governmental policy has probably been more responsive to the pressure of big farmers and organizations of big commercial farmers than to the needs of family farms of either the commercial or subsistence type. In the establishment and modification of agricultural policy the farmers' organizations play an important role.

Of the farmers' organizations one should take note of the trade association groups, the American Farm Bureau Federation, the National Grange, the National Farmers Union, and the National Council of Farmer Cooperatives.[14]

There is a wide variety of associations serving specific farming interests such as associations for the improvement of livestock breed improvement, field-crop improvement, cattle feeding, lamb feeding, wool growing, dairying, egg production, fruit production, vegetable production, and so on. Beginning and continuing with interests in technical improvements in producing and marketing, these associations have grown in size and specialization and their activities have been enlarged to obtaining governmental regulations in their favor. In this respect they behave just like trade associations in business and industry in urban and mining areas. They are generally more aware of the immediate benefits which can be derived from policies demanded and implemented than of the long-range consequences to themselves, their communities, the nation, or international affairs. Their production and marketing goals often conflict among differing types of commodities and even for the same commodities in different parts of the nation. These specialized associations, some of them very powerful, often create difficulties for the general farm organizations to which their members belong. The general organizations have, accordingly, significant opportunities and responsibilities in relation to the special interest groups.

The largest of the general farmers' organizations is the American Farm Bureau Federation with a total membership in 1954 of 1,609,461 families. Its objectives as stated in the preamble of the organization are "to correlate and strengthen the Farm Bureaus of the several states and to promote, protect, and represent the business, social, economic,

[14] This section is indebted to Wilcox, *op. cit.*, chs. 11, 12, 13, 17, 18.

and educational interests of the farmers of the nation." [15] During the thirties and early war years the American Farm Bureau pressed for higher government price supports, but in the years since 1947 it has advocated moderate reductions in price-support levels in opposition to other political groups and interest organizations. Wilcox points out that in the postwar period it "has maintained a unique position for a special-interest group. In an over-all sense, its program has been one of asking government for less rather than more in the way of special economic assistance." [16] The reason for this program is the belief that farmers' incomes will be improved in the long run and the interests of equity will be better served with lower price-support levels and conservation payments, more emphasis being given on educational procedures to help farmers (1) increase productive skills, (2) develop managerial ability, and (3) increase their efforts in voluntary cooperative action.

The second largest of the general farmers' organizations is the National Grange with a membership of 847,419 in 1955. Grange membership is on an individual rather than on a family basis. In its early years it had a rapid development as a protest movement against monopolistic practices of large corporations and especially against arbitrary and discriminating practices of the railroads. Regulatory legislation is part of its heritage since the 1870's. The Grange supported the Agricultural Adjustment legislation of the 1930's, but it was critical of the original parity formula and played an important role in the modified formula of the Agricultural Act of 1948. A distinctive feature of the Grange program has been its advocacy of self-financing two-price domestic parity measures for commodities having two or more relatively distinct markets. These plans usually require the payment of parity prices for that part of the product which is used domestically while allowing exports to be made at world prices. The National Grange also supports community improvement projects, youth programs, and activities for better farming and better living.

The National Farmers Union was organized primarily to help farmers obtain better prices for their products, to promote co-operation, and to protect their interests. Its strength has been the result in large

[15] Quoted in *Ibid.*, p. 97.
[16] *Ibid.*, pp. 98-99.

part of its efficiently run grain elevators, co-operative services, and co-operative livestock-marketing agencies in the Midwest and Northwest. It has had a closer relation to organized labor than the two other general farmers' organizations. Also, it pays more attention to the small farmer and advocates market reforms which often involve greater governmental participation in production and marketing than the others endorse. It has endorsed farm price supports at 100 per cent of parity on all farm products up to a specified family-farm volume of production per farm. Surplus would be distributed to the needy of this country and to friendly countries through international agreements.

Of these three organizations the Farm Bureau stresses governmental interference least, the Farmers Union most, and the Grange takes an intermediary position. All are concerned primarily with the family-type farm.

The National Council of Farmer Cooperatives is an association of farmers' business organizations. Its members are farmer-owned and controlled co-operatives engaged in the marketing of agricultural commodities or the purchasing of essential supplies for agricultural production. Through its federated co-operatives the Council represents about five thousand co-operatives which serve about three million members. The National Council works with the Congress and administrative agencies of the government in formulating and carrying out agricultural and other economic policies.

One of the crucial problems in the development of a sound agricultural policy is the institutional continuity of the points of view represented by the various farmers' organizations. Wilcox formulates the problem as follows: "How can the organization achieve a sufficiently integrated set of procedures to function effectively on a specific issue and yet maintain sufficient flexibility to bring new insights to bear on new problems?" [17] This is one of the fundamental problems of all great institutions. It is essential that a sound democratic and responsive relation be developed between officers and the rank and file and that a broad educational program and process be achieved if the organizations are to play responsible roles in determining national policy. This need for representative expression by leaders of the attitudes of the rank

[17] *Ibid.*, p. 106.

and file is especially evident in the relation of congressional leaders to farm leaders on the one hand and the voting constituency on the other.

The power of farmers is thus not simply economic but also political. Hardly 10 per cent of the nation's gainfully employed are engaged in agriculture, yet the system of representation in the Senate of the United States is such as to give great power to the predominantly agricultural states. The ethical issue of representation mentioned in an earlier chapter is especially relevant here. Undoubtedly the Farm Bloc is politically powerful out of all proportion to the population involved. Economic action depends on the exercise, finally, of both formal and informal political power. The general appeal of the farmer is that of mobilizing political support for measures purporting to express equity and other ethical considerations. In these efforts the political leadership of the nation is able to appeal to a strong sentimental tradition in favor of those who produce food and fiber.

E. The Farm Family

The farm family has been noteworthy for its emphasis on certain values which have contributed greatly to national life. Such values include honesty, truthfulness, self-reliance, independence, productive work, neighborliness, stewardship of resources, kindness to farm animals, the full utilization of resources, the primary responsibility of the individual and the family for their own welfare with minimal assistance and regulation by government, and the value of the family itself.

Rockwell C. Smith [18] has conveniently contrasted rural and urban society by a schema which highlights some of the values of the farm family and the rural community. The social unit in rural life is the family; in urban life it tends to be the individual. Social contacts in rural society are based on personal sympathy; in the urban life they tend to be categorical. The social bond in the country is custom; in the city it is contract. Social values in the rural setting are dominated by tradition; in the urban environment the accent is on novelty. Social control in the former situation is generally through direct action; in the latter situation it is accomplished through social agencies. The rural environment of life is nature while that of the city is impressively technological. Finally, the social focus of rural society is kinship and locality

[18] *The Church in Our Town* (Nashville: Abingdon Press, 1945), ch. 1.

while in the city it is common or associated interest. Though this schema is obviously oversimplified, it serves to emphasize values which policy for responsible farm family life must take into account.

The family-sized farm is in many relationships at a comparative competitive disadvantage. More and more the welfare of farm families is determined by actions and decisions outside their farms. The farm family is in a critical position because of the disparities between rural and urban life and also because of the increasing number of large-scale farms which depend primarily on hired labor, even on migratory labor. Many economists and sociologists doubt whether these large-scale farms produce and market more efficiently than family farms. Some family farms are, of course, too small to operate efficiently. But even the medium-sized family farm needs a policy which is concerned with the conservation of the values it expresses. The larger farms benefit more from reduction in income uncertainty than do medium-sized farms. This intensifies the disparity of income between the bulk of farm families and the more typical urban families. The most serious discrepancies occur between full-time farm families producing little for commercial markets and the families of the employed skilled and unskilled urban workers.[19]

Though contrasts such as the above tend to place the medium-sized farm on the defensive as an economic institution and tend to suggest that the family farm is on the way out, there is some important evidence that, given the same general cultural framework and family farms of viable size, the latter will produce and conserve a quality of community life much more satisfactory than that produced by the large-scale absentee-owned farm. Farm-family life and community organization must be viewed as an integral whole. Consequently social, economic, and political policies have a decisive bearing on the quality both of family life and of rural community existence. Indeed, they are complementary as shown in the research done on Arvin and Dinuba, California, by Walter Goldschmidt.

The comparative researches of Walter Goldschmidt have achieved an almost classical status in this field as expressed in *As You Sow* and other publications. He has shown the effect which the scale of farm operations has upon the character of the rural community. Rural areas

[19] See *ibid.*, pp. 19, 37.

dominated by large-scale absentee ownership are qualitatively inferior to smaller-sized family-owned and resident farms as judged by such criteria as good and bad living conditions, relative degrees of social equality, relative amounts of social homogeneity and participation, relative amounts of social services and of economic opportunity, and the like.[20] Goldschmidt compared the patterns of life of two neighboring California communities, one of which is characterized by large-scale farming while the other tends to be dominated by small-scale farm organization. His general conclusion is that it is primarily the nature of its agricultural and agrarian organization which has led the community dominated by small farms to have more stability in its population, more sightly homes, better schools, greater community loyalty, and a more democratic structure and government.

The large-scale industrialized farming area produces crops extensively, solely for the cash market, with a high degree of farm specialization. It utilizes great quantities of capital and requires a large input of labor hired on an impersonal basis.[21] As a consequence it accepts the urbanized culture pattern of pecuniary standards of value and a social status system based on money wealth. This set of values leads to a more or less closed class system based on economic status and expressed in terms of occupation. Moreover, this pattern so specializes functions and activities that the individuals tend to be concerned with a single fragmentary role in the total functioning of the economy.

Goldschmidt's recapitulation of the social differences between Arvin, the large-scale factory farm area, and Dinuba, the family-size farm area, shows the following twelve contrasts unfavorable to the former community:

(1) The greater number of persons dependent upon wages rather than upon entrepreneurial profit. (2) The lower general living conditions as measured by a level-of-living scale and the subjective evaluation of households. (3) The lower degree of stability of population. (4) The poorer physical appearances and condition of houses, streets, and public buildings.

[20] *As You Sow* (New York: Harcourt Brace & Co., 1947).

[21] For the United States as a whole it should be noted that most of the million or more migratory farm workers, domestic and foreign, are employed on large-scale industrial farms. In some cases housing and wage scales are adequate, but in every case their employment is intermittent and insecure.

(5) The relative poverty of social services performed by the community. (6) The poorer schools, parks and facilities offered youth. (7) The relative dearth of social organizations serving the individuals in the community and the community as a whole. (8) The fewer religious institutions. (9) The lesser degree of community loyalty expressed. (10) The apparently fewer decisions on community affairs made by the local community and the apparently smaller proportion of the population participating in such decisions. (11) The apparently greater degree of social segregation and greater social distance between the several groups in the community. (This and the preceding items have been labeled apparent because neither is amenable to statistical evaluation, though considerable evidence is at hand to indicate their existence.) (12) The lesser amount of retail trade, the fewer business establishments, and the volume of trade in those classes of merchandise most generally accorded a high place in social values. This constitutes a rather imposing list of social and economic factors reflecting the quality of the society in the two communities, in which the one fulfills rather well our normal expectations of social life and the other consistently fulfills them less satisfactorily.[22]

One of the marks of a responsible society is that power to make effective decisions is widely distributed among the people. For this reason it is important to conserve the family farm. Yet despite its advantages as reflected in the researches of Goldschmidt and others, many farm families are not economically or socially effective. More than one fourth of the families who live on American farms still have cash incomes of less than one thousand dollars a year. They neither share fully in the nation's economic and social progress nor contribute as much as they would like to the nation's production of goods and services. Many of these farm families are caught in a downward spiral of cumulative causation and reaction in the economic and social order. Only a comprehensive program of constructive action will reverse the movement of the spiral. Lacking opportunity and therefore not sharing in the rewards of high productivity, the social roles of these small farmers are seriously affected. Participation diminishes in community, religious, and civic affairs. The spirit of initiative and self-confidence gives way to inertia and apathy. The cumulative reaction affects the

[22] From the report of the Small Business Committee of the United States Senate, *Small Business and the Community* (79th Congress, 2nd Session, December 23, 1946). Goldschmidt was a consultant to this committee. His book *As You Sow* is an expansion of these theses.

characters of the children as well as the parents. Indeed, the whole community suffers.[23]

The essential principle in a program of reconstruction is a co-ordinated assault on all phases of the problem. A co-ordinated many-sided approach will include at least the following elements: (1) new educational techniques; (2) supervised credit; (3) vocational training; (4) retraining for youth and adults who are not needed to replace older personnel; (5) sound employment information; (6) social security;[24] (7) research on agricultural methods; (8) health services; (9) enlargement and improvement of general educational opportunities; and (10) co-ordination of the work of agencies including civic and business leadership, farm organizations, schools, churches, community and service clubs, and governmental agencies at all levels.

The integral approach to the family farm sees the latter in the context of the concrete rural community. In such a setting the church has a special obligation to interpret the meaning of community, to deepen the motivation of the individuals, families, and institutions for improving the community, and to relate the goals of agriculture and rural life to the ultimate meanings of human existence. Since it is the purpose of the Church to increase the love of God and the love of neighbor in the world, the local parish must learn to organize its inner structure, its ecumenical expression, and its community service with these goals in mind.[25] The church represents the power of inclusive concern and unlimited compassion for all persons and groups. Leadership fully as competent and well trained is needed for this situation as for any urban area. This leadership need deserves special attention since great inequity and disparity obtain between the resources assigned by denominations to rural as compared with urban and suburban areas.

F. Relation of Domestic to International Policies

We have seen that mankind is the unit of co-operation. No nation

[23] The government report "Development of Agriculture's Human Resources" (1955), which formed the message of the President of the United States relative to the problems of low-income farmers, details many facets of this situation.

[24] Social Security has been extended to five million farmers and hired workers.

[25] Two usable manuals are Rockwell C. Smith, *Rural Church Administration* (Nashville: Abingdon Press, 1953); and Calvin Schnucker, *How to Plan the Rural Church Program* (Philadelphia: The Westminster Press, 1954).

lives to itself alone. The domestic agricultural policies must, therefore, be coherent with sound concepts of international trade if the idea of responsibility is to be consistently applied. Farm productivity has created a relative surplus at home, and this condition has led to several programs of disposing this surplus abroad. In general the greatest moral weakness of these programs is that they are focused on disposing the "surpluses" in the interest primarily of American farmers. It may appear morally generous to give farm surpluses to the needy and naked abroad, but in an economically interdependent world more than generous intentions are needed. Programs must be formulated that meet long-range human needs. Just as in America the disadvantaged need "not charity but a chance," so in the underdeveloped areas the people need assistance in getting on their feet, not a glut of gifts which undermine their nations' struggling economies. As Wilcox says, "We must continually review the functioning of our international economic system to make sure that it provides equality of opportunity for the diverse groups in the world, especially with respect to their obtaining the essential technical know-how and access to capital with which to improve themselves." [26]

International policy has sometimes been conducted in such a way that consumption has not grown enough at home while consumption through exports has declined severely. This is due to the fact that there is an eye to exports in order to dispose of surpluses, but an unwillingness to import goods so as to provide the purchasing power in dollars abroad to pay for them. Such is the consequence of nationalistic policies which focus on stabilizing the domestic price but ignore the realities of world economic forces. Governmental restrictions on imports and special assistance on exports interfere with the objectives of promoting freer international trade. The difficulties in the way of overcoming this conflict stem in large part from the selfishness of special interest groups and parochialism in defining the true interest of the nation in relation to other peoples.

One of the most imaginative suggestions which I have noted is that by Paul Geren, who suggests that the agricultural "surpluses" might be given to underdeveloped countries so as to turn them into capital assets

---

[26] *Op. cit.,* p. 44. Used by permission of Harper & Bros.

through the medium of workers employed on projects such as building dams, irrigation projects, and the like. The "surpluses" would be given or lent as on-the-spot resources to the workers who are transforming them through labor into capital goods which in turn become resources for raising the productive capacity of the people involved. Such projects serve the purposes of international equity, equality, and self-help and express the concern of one nation for the maximation of the potentialities in others.

Irresponsibility in foreign technical assistance and agricultural policy may have ruinous effects. Such irresponsibility is usually the failure to place proposed changes within the context of a culture or world economy as a whole. Mechanization, for example, can have an overwhelming effect on human welfare by rupturing the nourishing continuity of man with the land, with his own body rhythms, and with his traditional past.[27] Life may become utterly chaotic. Industrialization has often meant that in Africa, for example, men were pulled away from the land at crucial times in the agricultural cycle. Since they were traditionally the key persons at such times, their villages now have to import four fifths of their food.[28] Elsewhere the cutting down of the bush in the hinterland has resulted in the disappearance of game which furnished most of the meat in the diet.[29]

Changes in agricultural policy must embody what Alfred North Whitehead called a "tender concern that nothing be lost." It is especially important that this principle be embodied in the attitudes and policies of the United States, which because of its leadership position and preponderance of power in the world will inevitably affect the personal lives of millions of persons by the program and procedures it employs.

Because of the complexities of international trade and the need to consider the impact of farm "surpluses" on the economies of the receiving countries, careful study should be made of the advantages and disadvantages of international commodity agreements, international food reserves, and expanded foreign aid programs. Such studies should express the moral obligation to examine every aspect of agricultural

[27] Mead, *op cit.*, p. 193.
[28] *Ibid.*, p. 195.
[29] *Loc. cit.*

policy for its influence on mankind as a whole. Responsible international policies must be committed to building up the whole world economy by balancing industry and agriculture in an integrated way. In the short run a special moral obligation rests upon the United States to share its national abundance and to seek the elimination of hunger and distress.

CHAPTER X

Work and Social Responsibility

A. Work and the Doctrine of Vocation

Work and the worker are entangled in the ambiguities and crises of modern man's technological civilization. On the one hand, the person's sense of freedom, self-worth, power, and creative productivity have tremendously increased because of science and technology. On the other hand, certain principles of modern culture and the facts of industrial urban life have threatened his personal freedom with a collective fate, his self-worth with depersonalization, his power with powerlessness, and creativity with mass production and automation.

The principles of modern culture which have increasingly controlled the atmosphere of the worker's world are those of natural law, secularization, and autonomy. In each case the older religious quality of life which pervaded the order of nature, the created world, and human effort has to a large extent evaporated, leaving society more and more impersonal and lacking a sense of ultimate meaning. The effect of man's use of these principles has been to change the biblical and Christian sense of vocation, or calling, into a utilitarian or pragmatic attitude toward work as merely a job. His work has become no longer a "way of life" rooted in an order of creation and a plan of redemption but a contractual relationship for making a living. Technology built on natural science has tended to drive out any personal or subjective considerations and to displace them with purely objective decisions. Secular callings have been radically distinguished from the religious ones, which in turn have been specified and restricted to church-related activities. Man has tended to measure values in terms of success standards which he has imposed upon himself. As a consequence man has become imprisoned in his own finite order of science, technology, and social goals and has lost the sense of depth in his own person, his society, and the universe around him.

This imprisonment in finitude has not, however, entirely obliterated an ethos of work which the Bible and the Reformers bequeathed to the modern world. The ethos which remained suppressed or only latent in certain social movements has begun feebly to reassert itself. Christian vocation as a religious and ethical conception is coming to the fore in the Christian churches, especially through the ecumenical movement.

What are the chief historical elements in this doctrine of vocation? [1] In the Bible man's work is closely related to the work of creation, man's service to God, community responsibility, the redemptive love of Jesus Christ, love of the neighbor, and the mission of the Christian community under the guidance and power of the Holy Spirit. Work is not an independent or separable realm of man's activity but is part of the grand design of God's activity in the creation and redemption of the world. Furthermore, there is in the biblical conception no radical dualism between the necessary work of the common laborer and the spiritual work of priests and clergy, for all are bound together in obedience to God. There is no exaltation of spiritual work, such as prayer, as being on a plane higher than menial activity. All forms of work express diversities of gifts and these, when properly exercised and shared, make for unity and harmony in the service of the Lord.

Work in the biblical perspective is no autonomous individualistic effort but an expression of membership in the community of Israel, as in the Old Testament, or of the congregation, as in the New Testament. God sets the goals for his people. Man receives from God his assignment and purpose. This conception must not, of course, be understood in a static sense. Man is to serve God; work serves man; and man serves God with and through his work.[2] Man does not exist for work, but work exists for man, and man exists for God. Man is God's steward as the earth is subdued and cared for. Man's work is thus included within the purpose of God. As he provides for his own necessities of life and fulfills himself in creative activity, man finds the limits

---

[1] See Muelder, *op. cit.,* chs. 11 and 111.
[2] Walther Bienert, *Die Arbeit Nach der Lehre der Bibel* (Stuttgart: Evangelisches Verlagswerk GMBH, 1954) , pp. 390-91.

of work in God's order of creation and the meaning of redemption. Thus man is not to make of work an end in itself or to fix his desires on bigger and bigger material treasure. The true ends of life always set the goal and the limit on his investment of himself. For work to fulfill its proper end, it must have God's blessing. It is, indeed, a kind of continual thank offering to the giver of every good and perfect gift.

To serve God in obedience and thankfulness is to work without anxiety or self-sufficient pretension. In the New Testament the admonition is to be not anxious for the morrow but to seek first the kingdom of God, trusting that God will add material blessing. Here the great example is Jesus Christ himself, who in his whole person is a servant. He does not present himself to man as one who seeks to be served but who serves. Through Jesus Christ work is shown to be an activity of love. The twofold commandment of love to God and neighbor has in this way a direct relationship to man's daily work. Love binds man to God and to his fellow men. Responsibility is both vertical and horizontal. These two dimensions are not isolated from each other; for as one does service to the least of Christ's brethren, one does it unto Christ.

The New Testament spirit of love, the work of creation redeemed in the work of Christ, manifests itself in the work of the cross and in the apostolate of the early church under the power and guidance of the Holy Spirit. To work for the glory of God in the service of Christ and for the love of the neighbor is not, as many suppose, a realm of labor apart from daily responsibilities but part and parcel of one great vocation. In the present day the renewed interest in the ministry of the laity arises out of this recognition of the continuity of the realm of love in man's whole life and destiny. To regain this sense of depth is to recognize that wherever men and women are bearing the burdens of work with a sense of divine responsibility, there is the frontier of the kingdom of God.

B. Separation of Work and Vocation

During the past two hundred years social and historical forces have conspired to separate the economic sphere from the controls of the rest of culture and to encourage its relative autonomy. Through the cumulative reinforcement of science, technology, and the factory system an attitude emerged that held economic activity to be as impersonal as natural law. The leaders of the economic realm developed both theories and institutions for the greater expression of this autonomy over against the church, the state, and the mores of the community. This attitude has been challenged in both theory and practice. We are now observing the slow reintegration of economic life into the whole of culture. Despite great resistance the domination of capitalist enterprise over society is being overcome by a reassertion of the political, religious, and social claims of culture as a whole over economic life.

Impersonal attitudes tended especially to victimize the worker. The realm of labor, being increasingly tied to the powers of the factory system, was separated from the vocational perspectives of the Christian Church. Workers were separated from their hand and cottage tools and massed in great industrial centers. Efforts to organize unions for their protection and welfare were ruthlessly suppressed. Only in the present century, more particularly since 1935, have American workers secured political guarantees to organize unions of their own choosing. By the time that trade unions had gained any measure of power the whole ethos of work had become thoroughly secularized. Only latent spiritual perspectives remained. Collective bargaining necessarily focused on issues like the right to organize, the wage contract, conditions of work, and worker welfare. Meanwhile job descriptions and employment practices lost all connections with issues of the sacredness of the person, the claims of community, and ultimate meaning. Such values were seldom considered in a hiring hall, a placement or personnel office, or a governmental employment agency. Industrial labor relations became a matter of the private wage contract. Not even the solidarity of the family was taken into account. Consequently, training for jobs and vocational guidance accommodated themselves to the individualism of the wage contract.

This secularist point of view is still dominant today. The focus is on the efficient productivity of the worker as a functional unit in large specialized enterprise. Work is still viewed largely as an end in itself or as a means to a successful change in the world of work. The full-orbed ministry of work has not penetrated industrial relations very far.

To this despiritualized result the churches have also contributed their share. They have separated the sacred from the secular, the clergy

187

from the laity, and have increasingly identified Christian callings with church work. Only in recent years have they recovered any sense of the inclusive character of religious vocation. At the same time by institutional identification with the dominant classes in society they alienated the masses of the workers. This alienation went the furthest in Roman Catholic countries and in Protestant nations with close ties between throne and altar. In Europe and Britain the churches have not recovered from the alienation, though there are significant signs of renewal.

The plea for the recovery of work as a spiritual vocation must not be confused with a quest to subject work or the worker to the domination of the church.

Despite the depersonalization of work and the worker the latent values of human dignity have begun to assert themselves in terms of new understanding. The whole person goes to work. He brings to his work situation his motivations and goals, his desires for satisfactory family life and for personal fulfillment. Psychological, sociological, and spiritual factors enter into the worker's struggle for recognition. It is these factors that must always be noted when considering the organized labor movement and collective bargaining. Union security and collective bargaining define today for millions of workers a significant aspect of the responsible society. To these we must next turn.

C. Collective Bargaining and Union Security

Collective bargaining, according to the Taft-Hartley Act of 1947, is the

performance of the mutual obligation of the employer and the representatives of the employees to meet at reasonable times and confer in good faith with respect to wages, hours, and other terms and conditions of employment, or the negotiation of an agreement . . . and the execution of a written contract incorporating any agreement reached if requested by either party.[3]

Collective bargaining is by no means a simple affair. Differences of opinion of law develop on the subject matter of bargaining, on the meaning of good faith, on the scope of bargaining, on the process of

[3] Sec. 8-d. See Jack Barbash, *The Practice of Unionism* (New York: Harper & Bros., 1956), ch. viii.

bargaining, and on the administration of a labor contract. There are also likely to be differences of assumption regarding the prerogatives of the labor union and of management.

On labor's side three preconditions to collective bargaining must obtain. (1) The practice of collective bargaining takes place only after an organization of employees exist. (2) Management must recognize that the employees or a considerable number of them are members of the organization. (3) Then, too, management must be willing to negotiate with unions, through representatives chosen by them to bargain in their behalf. Much of the history of trade unionism in the United States has gone into the struggle to bring into being these three steps precedent to collective bargaining. The struggle for recognition and the problems of bargaining have brought into existence a group of experts or specialists in the larger unions, flanked by permanently employed staff and researchers.

From the employer's side the aspect of collective bargaining that concerns him most is the loss of "management prerogatives." Trade unions set limits to unilateral power of the employer which existed before they were organized. A. J. Hayes of the Machinists Union says bluntly: "Unions came into being specifically for the purpose of interfering with management's right to make unilateral decisions affecting the welfare of its employees." [4] Management has repeatedly sought to induce labor to agree on an area within which management decisions could not be questioned.[5] Although labor recognizes that there is such an area, it is unwilling to set limits to it. The agenda for managing a business and the subject matter involved in the process of collective bargaining are not mutually exclusive problems. The same considerations may affect both managing and bargaining. Ultimately, there is the problem of balancing the interests of the parties involved and of providing enough information for intelligent negotiation.

From the standpoint of Christian vocation both management and labor are jointly viewed within a common integral responsibility. Their counterpositions and roles are historically determined and largely prag-

[4] *Machinists' Monthly Journal* (February, 1955), quoted in Fitch, *op. cit.*, p. 46.
[5] Walter Reuther's proposal in August, 1957, for a reduction in the wholesale price of automobiles was rejected by the manufacturers on the ground that it was not a matter of collective bargaining.

matic arrangements which carry no inherent ultimate claim of right and authority.

Collective bargaining depends for its development on union security. Because of the fear of management organized labor has sought agreements to secure the status of unions. Bitter opposition by management in times past has encouraged the belief that most employers would destroy the unions if they could. The current resistance to the organizational campaign of the AFL-CIO in the South and the spread of "Right-to-Work" laws sponsored by employers' associations stimulate such fears afresh. When the causes of these fears have been thoroughly allayed and responsible bargaining in good faith has become a fully national practice, the demand for protecting the union through various types of security clauses—closed shop, union shop, and maintenance-of-membership shop—will probably decline.

In the tension between the values of freedom and security unions seek justice through the freedom which security provides.

Is there any foundation for the current fear that "Right-to-Work" laws are intended to damage unions? The Virginia law is described by the Supreme Court of that state as follows:

> It provides in substance that neither membership nor nonmembership in a labor union shall be made a condition of employment; that a contract limiting employment to union members is against public policy; and that a person denied employment because he is either a member of a union or not a member of a union shall have a right of action for damages.

A national Right-to-Work Committee is promoting the passage of such laws. These laws are actively promoted also by the National Association of Manufacturers, the Chamber of Commerce, and other organizations of employers of a regional and statewide character. Both these associations support "Right-to-Work" laws as a protection of the freedom of the individual. Some students of labor union history view this championing of the individual worker against coercion as a bit ironical. It is of interest that the states which have passed such laws are largely in the sections of the nation with least industrial development or where great resistance to organized labor has been fomented. Unions may be pardoned for relating these movements and activities to one another and to earlier management hostility to the trade union movement.[6]

The ethical issues in "Right-to-Work" laws are of two kinds, those dealing with the merits of union security clauses in contracts and those dealing with the intervention of the state in such matters. The position taken by the Department of the Church and Economic Life of the National Council of Churches reflects considered judgment on these questions as follows:

> With specific reference to the issues currently raised by state "right-to-work" laws, it is recognized that either requiring by law or forbidding by law union membership as a basis of continuing employment involves grave moral problems. Under the varied circumstances prevailing at different times and places throughout this large country the National Council of Churches discerns no simple judgment on these moral problems upon which highly diverse opinions are held by dedicated Christians. However, it is the opinion of the General Board that union membership as a basis of continued employment should be neither required nor forbidden by law: the decision should be left to agreement by management and labor through the process of collective bargaining.[7]

Justice must be found in the freedom of equals to negotiate, not in the freezing of individual freedom by laws which inhibit collective bargaining.

Industrial experience in America has shown that the union shop is a prerequisite of much successful union-employer relations. An assured status for the union does not guarantee good collective bargaining, but it is a prerequisite of it. The union shop assures this status. The employer is likely to enjoy more freedom in a shop where the status of the union is established than in one where it is precarious. Union insecurity—a likely consequence of "Right-to-Work" laws—forces it to attempt to restrict the employer's discretion at every point where he may discriminate against union members in favor of nonmembers. Hence it is an irresponsible social policy to seek to destroy the integrity of labor unions under the guise of the so-called "right to work." The individual

[6] See John G. Shott, "How 'Right-to-Work' Laws Are Passed: Florida Sets the Pattern" (Washington, D.C.: The Public Affairs Institute, 1956). " 'Right-to-Work' Laws: Three Moral Studies" (Washington, D.C.: International Association of Machinists, 1954, 1955).

[7] Voted by the Executive Board of the Division of Christian Life and Work, June 5, 1956, as modified by the General Board on June 6. The General Board authorized the circulation of the statement but neither approved nor disapproved it.

worker has no effective legal right to work under conditions worthy of human dignity where strong unions have been eliminated. Since collective bargaining is under present circumstances a proved condition of stable industrial relations, a worker has a moral obligation to accept his share of responsibility through membership in organized labor. "Right-to-Work" laws do not create jobs; they only victimize the worker, make his organization ineffective, and deluge the community with industrial irresponsibility.

If collective bargaining is to fulfill its function in promoting industrial peace and responsibility, a corresponding legal, moral, and spiritual climate—an ethos of mutual respect—must prevail. On the whole, where unions are accepted and strong, the process of collective bargaining is mature and constructive.[8]

Government coercion to limit the free exercise of judgment by the negotiating parties violates the democratic spirit of America. What is supposedly gained by protecting the freedom of the individual employee is more than offset by the disproportionate advantage given to the employers in dealing with unions and the loss of freedom in the bargaining situation. In a significant percentage of excellent industrial situations of peace achieved through collective bargaining, as studied by the National Planning Association, signed or *de facto* union shop agreements were in effect. [9]

D. Problems of Responsibility in Organized Labor

Labor organization has made some outstanding contributions to economic life. It has given the worker a sense of personal and group dignity. It has shortened the hours of labor and helped raise the rate of wages. Conditions of work have improved. Education has been encouraged and health improved. There has been a fuller participation by union members in the life of the community and the nation. In many places the barriers among the races have been broken down. Unions have aided in the safety legislation of the nation as well as in various forms of insurance and pension protection. Increasingly labor leaders as well as rank and file members take an integral part in

[8] See Muelder, *op. cit.*, ch. iv.
[9] See *Causes of Industrial Peace Under Collective Bargaining*, ed. Clinton S. Golden and Virginia D. Parker by National Planning Association (Washington, D.C.: National Planning Association, 1955). Fourteen case studies were made.

church life, community chest campaigns, parent-teacher associations, youth club programs, and the like. Within twenty years labor has grown economically powerful and politically effective. As a consequence of this power corresponding criteria of the responsible society must be applied to it as well as to management and government. Seven of these criteria have special relevance.

1. A union owes its members a democratic and responsible organization. By its very nature, composition, and life a trade union is as much a political as it is an economic organization. [10] A union must, therefore ever be accountable in its exercise of power to those whose welfare is affected by this power. There is a tendency in the direction of centralization of authority. Representative democracy inevitably makes for a separation of the officers from the membership, unless corrective measures are consistently employed. Like management, government, and the church, the trade union is not immune from the diseases of bureaucratic administration. Constitutions and bylaws must therefore provide not only for efficient action on behalf of the members by the staff and officers, but also for vigorous democratic self-determination by the members. The spirit of democracy is needed not only on the legislative side of union business but also in the handling of penalties. A "bill of rights" for union members has been urged to implement these goals. Moral dilemmas of the union in this connection often arise because on the one hand, it is a parliamentary type of organization and, on the other hand, it is a limited purpose organization which must safeguard union integrity and strength in the economic struggle. These two types of organization and goals may be in conflict with each other.

Because of the size of many unions and the manner in which established unions grow, the problem of responsible member participation is acute. New recruits come in as a response to skilled organizers whose impetus and direction come from the top. Recent high school graduates, recruits from rural areas, and housewives—who have not experienced the early days of labor struggle—comprise many of the new members. Finding the union already functioning, they tend to take it for granted. Often they join because it is the thing to do or,

[10] John M. Clark distinguishes the political character of a trade union from that in towns and states by the dominance of external relations in its scheme of activities and interests. "America's Changing Capitalism: The Interplay of Politics and Economics," in Berger, *op. cit.*, p. 202.

in case of a union shop, because they have to join to hold their jobs. John Fitch says: "These workers are not acquainted with labor history and have a middle-class outlook. They are neither pioneers nor agitators—they pay their dues and hope not to be disturbed." [11] The presence of this group creates many serious problems such as bureaucratic management with its temptations to go its own way. A solution to the problem of bureaucratic isolation is suggested by the practice of the International Typographical Union. It fosters two recognized political parties which regularly nominate candidates for offices and campaign vigorously for them. This union also has an effective constitutional procedure for handling trials and appeals. "Nothing is more important from an ethical point of view," writes Fitch, "than recognition that human beings of whatever class or station are susceptible of corruption by the lure of power, prestige, and financial advantage and must be held strictly accountable to those from whom their authority derives." [12]

2. In freedom and with justice the trade union movement must resolve the conflicts of extreme autonomy and exclusive jurisdiction. The problems of autonomy and jurisdiction affect the handling of racketeers, Communists and Fascists, rival organizations, membership drives, ethical practices, and the like. A new framework for handling these problems came into existence in December, 1955, with the new federation known as the American Federation of Labor and Congress of Industrial Organizations. Within this federation procedures are established for handling all serious jurisdictional issues. One of its basic principles is expresssed in the determination to "be and remain free from any and all corrupt influences and from the undermining efforts of communist, fascist or other totalitarian agencies who are opposed to the basic principles of our democracy and of free and democratic trade unionism." [13] The AFL-CIO has a degree of authority and scope of power not previously possessed by either parent body.[14] It has established a Committee on Ethical Practices with suitable initiative power and has set about to develop principles and guides for imple-

[11] *Op. cit.,* p. 97.
[12] *Ibid.,* p. 101
[13] *Ibid.,* p. 113.
[14] See Arthur J. Goldberg, *AFL-CIO: Labor United* (New York: McGraw-Hill Book Co., 1956), pp. 145-49, 192-94.

menting its determination to "be and remain free from all corrupt influences."

3. There must be serious determination to eliminate malpractice in unions. Of course most unions are not honeycombed with racketeering and corruption as some enemies of labor allege. Nevertheless, the scope of the problem is sometimes of major public concern. Malpractice has included the use of physical violence or its threat to accomplish robbery or extortion, bribery of public officials and others, participation in organized vice and gambling, employment of thugs and gangsters, mishandling of union funds, abuses in the management of "welfare funds," and others. An investigation conducted by the Superintendent of Insurance of New York in 1954 found "serious abuse" in the handling of 34 out of 162 welfare plans studied.[15] These abuses included welfare funds, loans or gifts to unions and union officers in order to finance projects having no connection with the purpose of the welfare fund, lack of proper administrative procedures, discrimination in benefit payments, "kickbacks" to union and fund officials, and nepotism. Widespread public and union investigations of fund handling probably result not only in stricter legislation but in reorganizing the administration of the funds and establishing appropriate codes. Leaders of American labor are concerned to drive out the criminal element which fastens itself to the unions.[16]

4. The process of collective bargaining must be made and kept responsible. In the earlier days of bargaining, negotiations were often carried out in an atmosphere of conflict and even of open hostility. Today most bargaining conferences are carried on in good faith and in a spirit of reasonable contracting. Both management and labor have yet, however, to take the voice of the community fully into account. The voice of the community should be felt in some representative capacity other than that of the government, if that is possible.

Collective bargaining not only should be carried on in an atmosphere of rational problem solving and with the interests of the community in mind, but it should also be done without prior public commitments and fanfare which prejudge the negotiating process and introduce rigid and defensive elements into the situation.

[15] *Ibid.*, pp. 172-74.
[16] Barbash, *op. cit.*, ch. xiii.

5. Management expects and the public endorses the principle of a "fair day's work." The issue is comprised of various make-work practices which exist largely because of the uncertainties of employment. These problems obtain not only among organized workers but among nonunion employees as well. Though organized labor generally approves of technological advance, some unions enforce rules involving the unnecessary employment of individuals. Obsolete arrangements often obtain in the building trades. On the railroads the definition of a day's work which was realistic a generation ago keeps in railroad service thousands of men not needed there. The demands of the Musicians Union are often properly designated as "featherbedding," that is, devices to force an employer to pay for "services which are not performed or not to be performed." [17] It is difficult to determine objectively what a fair day's work is, but the effort to do so remains an inescapable obligation.

6. Trade unions have responsibilities to nonmembers and to the unorganized. These responsibilities are largely in the area of more inclusive membership policies. Unions have rights in protecting their own integrity, but grave moral questions arise when persons are excluded because of national origin, religion, sex, or race or are confronted with admission fees that frustrate all expression of creative talent because of monopolistic control. The AFL-CIO constitution is positive in its declaration of equality of rights as here indicated. The new federation has taken an unequivocal position in advocating civil-rights legislation and has gone far in the removal of racial barriers in its own ranks.[18] In some states organized labor takes an ambiguous position because of historic prejudices associated with segregation and desegregation issues. National leadership is often far ahead of local performance in unions as it is also, it must be added, in churches and schools.

7. Organized labor has responsibilities for the common good. This point of view is urged and represented by such a leader as Walter Reuther. In addressing the CIO convention in 1952 he said that the CIO was an organization that united its work with the efforts of the whole people in seeking a "democratic solution to the complex problems that beset us." Not only good housing but better social security

---

[17] As defined in the Taft-Hartley Act.
[18] Goldberg, *op. cit.*, pp. 195-202.

benefits and educational programs need labor's support. Reuther represents a philosophy in labor that accepts the world context of cooperation. He says:

We have a job . . . of doing much more than just bargaining for our membership. We have to assume ever increasing social responsibilities. . . . We must find a way to realize the tremendous spiritual reservoir that resides within a free people, and translates that power into constructive approaches to the world's problems—if we do that, we can win the battle for peace and freedom.[19]

In considering the responsibility of labor to promote the public good, it is important to remember that labor is a large part of the public. Its educational success is an important contribution to the adult education of the people as a whole. For this reason it represents a political force of great dimensions. Its power is thus an issue not only in the sphere of economic responsibility but in political responsibility as well.

E. Social Responsibility Toward Classes of Workers

We have thus far considered work from the standpoints of religious vocation, depersonalization in the factory system, collective bargaining, and union security and have noted briefly seven types of social responsibility connected especially with organized labor. Much of this analysis has been focused on trade unions and some of their problems. This analysis must now be supplemented by considering certain other issues. We shall consider in turn the young worker, women workers, the middle-aged employee and the older employees. These classes of workers present challenges to the community as a whole and not simply to labor organizations and employers.

1. Social Policy and the Young Worker

The problems involved in sound policy for young workers are quite complex in contemporary United States. Today many of the issues focus on the relation of sound basic education and employment. Child labor laws, for example, attempt to keep school-age youth in school. It is estimated that the average American production worker uses

[19] Quoted in Fitch, *op. cit.,* p. 208.

$12,500 worth of equipment. Employers naturally want workers with a proportionate sense of responsibility, and it is understandable that they regard quitting school before high school graduation as prima-facie evidence of irresponsibility. In the midst of technological changes involving increasing automation it is understandable that employers stress better education and training, not lowering of child-labor standards.[20]

Part-time work for school-age boys and girls is on the increase. In 1940 only 310,000 or 4 per cent of all school-enrolled youth aged fourteen to seventeen worked outside school. In 1955 the number stood at 1,722,000 or 22 per cent of those in school. At the same time the number of out-of-school youth working full time had decreased. Just after the war about a million or two thirds of the one and a half million dropouts aged sixteen and seventeen had jobs. Ten years later when the number of dropouts in the same age bracket dropped to one million, only about 55 per cent were employed.

So far as job opportunities go, youth today share in the benefits of the general prosperity. This situation is in sharp contrast to the conditions prevailing during the depression of the 1930's. In that decade youth between the ages of fifteen and twenty-four bore a disproportionate share of unemployment. Indeed, the difficulty of youth in finding jobs emerged as one of the most serious problems of the depression. About a third were unable to find jobs.

There is a vicious circle in the relations of unemployment and inadequate education for work and life. Persons without good basic education find it increasingly difficult to get and to hold jobs. The failure to find work and hence to earn adequately handicaps educational advancement. Youth need both sufficient opportunities for work and work which fulfills appropriate standards.

2. Women and Work

The participation of women in the labor force has been a significant fact for several generations. However, the rate of present participation constitutes what the National Manpower Council has described as a veritable "revolution" in employment and a "new dimension" to the nation's available labor resources. This research group anticipates that

[20] Clara M. Beyer, "Youth Employment—Opportunity and Protection," in *Social Action*, February, 1957, pp. 7-15.

nine out of every ten American women are likely to work outside the home in the course of their lives. The effect of this widespread employment on their participation in major social institutions—family school, church, and government—will be great and far-reaching.

One third of all women aged fourteen and over are now in the labor force at any one time. Some twenty-eight million, or over two fifths, work in the course of a year. Schoolgirls today may expect to work as much as twenty-five years or more outside the home. They will constitute an increase of ten million in the labor force in the next ten years. Working women receive one fifth of the nation's income in wages and salaries, some forty-two billion dollars, and are responsible for more than one fourth of the total man-hours worked.

Family and school are directly affected by this new situation. Six out of every ten working women are married, and half are over age forty. Three out of every ten married women are working. Even more striking is the fact that two out of every five mothers with school-age children are in the labor force.

There is great need for sound principles of guidance for women entering the labor force. These will include attention to the following: (1) expansion and improvement of educational and vocational guidance on the part of school and college officials, boards of education, federal, state and local governments; (2) sound programs of self-development and training employment opportunities; (3) education for the complex and successive phases of a woman's life including preparation for her varying roles at each stage; (4) encouragement of more young women of high ability to continue their formal education in college, professional, or graduate schools; (5) adherence by employers and unions to the principle that all individuals, regardless of sex, should be hired, assigned, trained and promoted on the basis of their personal qualifications; (6) rigorous application of the rule of "equal pay for equal work"; (7) more flexible work arrangements so as to adapt to the part-time availability of women workers; and (8) constant review of the hiring, assignment, training, and promotion practices of employers in the light of the changing situation.[21]

At the present time it is hard to foresee the tremendous conse-

[21] See Henry David and Eli Ginsberg, *Womanpower* (New York: Columbia University Press, 1957). The National Manpower Council was established at Columbia University in 1951 under a Ford Foundation Grant.

quences of the unprecedented participation of women in the labor force. Two types of study are needed in connection with this phenomenon: descriptive research dealing with the impact of the increased employment of women on family life, the rearing of children, the self-development of women, and the prosperity of the economy, on the one hand, and normative research on the goals and values at stake. The latter will include an evaluative analysis of motivations for entering the work force, the rate and quality of consumption, and the institutions affected judged in the light of the norm of the responsible society.

3. Middle-aged Workers

Increasing attention is being given to youth, women, and older workers in the labor force. Belatedly the middle-aged worker is also receiving consideration because of the special problems which attend his situation. For many people the full brunt of life's responsibilities are upon them in the years from forty-five to fifty-five. Their children have not yet finished their education; the challenges of their work, trade, business, or profession are at a peak point; they feel the pressures of expectations by their associates as well as their competitors; they are carrying many social responsibilities in the community and these are on the increase; and they are confronted by their own goals of personal achievement.

In the midst of these problems there is often a severe shock when employment ceases and new adjustments must be made. The worker's status and self-esteem may be rudely shaken. New inventions may callously overrule old relations of production. Where employment, social status, and personal worth are closely related, unemployment for a middle-aged person may mean treatment as a "has-been." When seeking new work, workers find that experience does not seem to be a sufficient recommendation. Studies in unemployment clearly show that the relationship of employment and education is closer than the relation of employment and age. Education helps to get and to hold a job. It also affects the level of income while employed and hence the security of the worker when unemployment strikes. The number of years of school completed in youth is a general indication of earning ability and the capacity to get and hold jobs in middle age.

Today many American industrial workers in the range of years from

200

fifty-five to sixty-four have had the educational handicap of being born on a farm or near it, or of coming from foreign countries where educational opportunity was minimal. There has been a major shift of population from rural to urban industrial areas without a corresponding adaptation in educational resources for the middle-aged workers. These workers are confronted with difficulties which deserve the special attention given to them here. Samuel H. Thompson of the U.S. Department of Labor after a thorough statistical analysis of older middle-aged workers points out three significant factors:

(1) Deficiencies in basic education indicate a lack of basic skills among millions of workers and especially older workers that make difficult their adjustments to technological change, and that sharply limit their opportunities to contribute to national economic progress and to share in the fruits of that progress, without some degree of educational rehabilitation. (2) To remedy these deficiencies would constitute a major problem in adult guidance and educational services. Yet these people will have to compete in a labor market where high school or better will soon be the rule rather than the exception. (3) The analysis casts a glaring light on the economic as well as the social urgency of basic educational opportunity beyond elementary school for all the people." [22]

Such problems are a challenge to schools, employers, trade unions, and government as well as to the worker involved. They continue acutely in the age group to be considered next.

4. The Older Worker

By the older worker is meant those aged sixty-five and over. Since 1900 the number of persons over sixty-five has grown fourfold, from 3.1 million to 12.3 million in 1950. The percentage has doubled, from 4 to 8. It is estimated that in 1954 there were 13.7 million people in this age group; by 1960 it will number 15.7 million; and by 1975, 20.7 million. As the number of older persons has increased, a gradual decline in the proportion of them gainfully employed has taken place. Between 1940 and 1955 men sixty-five and over in the labor force decreased from 41.5 to 39.1 per cent of the age group.[23] This decrease obtained

[22] "Unemployment, Income, and Age," *The Personnel and Guidance Journal*, XXXV (February, 1957), p. 383. Used by permission of the American Personnel and Guidance Association.

[23] John J. Corson and others, *Economic Needs of Older People* (New York: Twentieth Century Fund, 1956), p. 468.

despite the large use of older people in the labor force during the war and the growing labor force since the end of the war. Nevertheless, about a third of all men and women in this age bracket receive income from current earnings as workers or as spouses of workers. In the present situation a person aged sixty can look forward to fifteen years of life but only to nine years of work.[24] This group is thus growing older, is predominantly women, and frequently no longer part of a family unit.[25]

Earnings in old age are significant because of the work-centered philosophy of our culture. Both men and women continue to judge their individual usefulness largely in terms of their capacity to hold a wage-paying job. Lack of job opportunities often undermines a person's self-respect as well as his social status and his economic security. A supplementary consideration is the nation's need of his productive contribution. With younger marriages and larger numbers of children per family the rate and amount of consumption of those too young to earn must be considered, along with the claims of those too old to earn, in formulating policies. Both the very young and the very old are increasing in the size of their respective groups and hence also increase their consuming demands on the productive output of the economy.

Old age may constitute a real crisis for the worker's morale. There is eventually a decline in physical strength and alertness or the onset of disabilities which require retirement. Often persons in good health are forced by employers to retire because of declining efficiency. Others are forced out by retirement policies of one kind or another regardless of suitability to continue at work. Those who are thus unemployed confront considerable reluctance by employers to hire them.

The Twentieth Century Fund Committee on Economic Needs of Older Persons [26] includes among its recommendations a number of ethical norms and social policies which are specifically relevant to the older worker. These norms and policies may be approvingly noted here as objectives for social action: " (1) Each person has the responsibility —as a right and a duty—of making whatever contribution he can toward his own support and that of his family during the later years of life." To preserve such an objective requires not only the effort of the individuals involved but also the co-operation of employers,

[24] *Ibid.*, p. 469.
[25] *Ibid.*, p. 17.
[26] *Ibid.*, p. 473.

voluntary associations, mutual aid in the family, and local, state, and federal governments. This co-operative planning must be guided by a second principle. " (2) The individual should not be denied adequate opportunity to earn and incentive to save." Most Americans prefer responsible activity to idleness, and this preference must be constantly remotivated; but if older persons are to continue reasonable careers of productivity, society must alter attitudes and circumstances that now impede employment of those able and willing to work. In this change of attitudes employers, trade unions, and the community generally must all play constructive parts. " (3) Employers and unions should endeavor to provide greater opportunities for the productive employment of older people who can and want to work." In order to accomplish this goal, it is necessary to study ways of reassigning older workers to tasks within their capacities and of providing appropriate facilities for their retraining and placement. It will also be necessary to be more flexible in policies involving age limits so that persons with the proper skills may continue in their employment. Similarly, it will be necessary to modify employment policies which now preclude consideration of mature workers regardless of skills.

Any responsible social policy for older workers will be based on a total concern for their welfare and hence will seek the optimum combination of employment and retirement schemes with sound pension, insurance, and old age assistance programs. These latter programs will involve both private and public factors. Both private and public plans are in effect today. Experience seems to indicate that government must play a guiding role in providing for the well-being of older people.[27] We shall return to this theme in a later chapter.

F. Responsible Relations of Religion and Labor

On the basis of the foregoing survey of religious vocation and the problems of contemporary labor, we may return to the question of the relation of organized religion to the labor movement under the general perspective of responsible common aims and criticisms.

In some respects the aims of religion and organized labor are identical; in some respects religion supports the aims of labor conditionally; in some respects the aims of labor fall short of religion inherently; in some respects religious aims are critical of labor's aims; and

[27] *Ibid.,* p. 480.

in some respects labor and religion confront common challenges in the contemporary world.

1. Religion and labor as defined above both stress the dignity of man and hence the dignity of the worker. He is not a commodity; his labor is not a mere commodity. Labor and religion recognize that the whole person goes to work. The world of work is a personal world in which the drama of meaningful existence is being enacted. Religion is interested in meaningful jobs for whole people. Religion and labor both believe in the right of voluntary association, the right to organize, and the freedoms that make these possible. Religion and labor are both concerned with the struggle for justice, the protection of the weak and the young, and with adequate support for decent family life.

2. Religion supports organized labor in its effort to raise the standards of living of its members, but it calls attention to the fact that only a fourth of the labor force is yet organized. It supports labor in its struggle against arbitrary power in industry, but calls attention to its arbitrary power struggles. It supports the civil liberties of workers and unions, but asks for a greater expression of democracy in the unions. It supports the right of workers to look after their interests, but calls upon the whole community to integrate labor more fully into itself by wider participation of labor in all general boards and agencies of community life. It supports adequate wages for labor, but recognizes that the economic order is complex and that all essential factors in production and distribution be given due consideration. Religion supports the historic democratic role of labor in America, but raises the question whether it has as yet developed an adequate economic and political philosophy. Is business unionism good enough? Does labor accept too naïvely the American economic order? Is labor playing a fully responsible role in relation to basic economic decisions and as a power in the field of politics?

3. Labor organization cannot fulfill many of religion's aims. It is wrong to assume that the union can be a worker's church. The scope of religion should not be trimmed down to trade union goals. Of itself labor cannot make of work a real Christian vocation, yet a new sense of man's ultimate vocation is absolutely essential in today's world.

4. Religion must be critical of labor today whenever it fails in the following issues: full interracial participation; respect for individual and group criticism within unions; workers' education; appreciating the

204

community's stake in industry; correcting corruption; efforts at trade union harmony, and misuse of power.

5. Religion and labor confront common challenges in today's world and should co-operate closely in the following areas: They have a common concern to protect civil liberties and promote civil rights. They have a common stake in constructive proposals for the aid of the retired worker, not only through pensions but in productive and creative expression. They have a common cause in slum clearance and adequate housing. They have a common responsibility in the conservation and democratic integrity of public education. They have a common obligation in the struggle against militarism and war. They have a common goal in integrating the human resources and leadership in community life. They have a common challenge to help raise the standards of living all over the world.

CHAPTER XI

Responsible Management

A. Issues of Managerial Responsibility

No one believes any longer that an "invisible hand" transmutes self-interest into the welfare of mankind.

In one way or another all markets are today managed markets. Competition is, therefore, not perfect, but neither is it blind. More and more men recognize that economic life is a network of choices and decisions. Economic life has goals not only in the experience of individuals but also for organized groups of businessmen and governments. Where decisions and choices are presented to men, there is a moral situation. Purposive action enters into vast orders of economic activity. This involves planning. The planning may be private or public. In some giant American corporations today the internal network of decision making is as complex, bureaucratically speaking, as that found in the whole governmental structure of certain small nations.

What is responsibility in economic leadership? [1] From an individual perspective it involves an attitude toward the decisions one makes for oneself and with regard to their consequences to others. In Chapter II we noted that moral responsibility involves a margin of discretion and a voluntary choice. Closely related to responsibility is the idea of accountability. Accountability refers not only to the requirements of the law but also to the ethos of the community, the reasonable expectations of the community. H. R. Bowen suggests two closely related definitions of the meaning of responsibility for businessmen. Responsibility

refers to the obligations of businessmen to pursue those policies, to make those decisions, or to follow those lines of action which are desirable in

[1] See Clark, *Ethical Basis of Economic Freedom*, p. 37.

206

terms of the objectives and values of our society. . . . [The term] refers to the idea . . . that voluntary assumption of social responsibility by businessmen is, or might be, a practical means toward ameliorating economic problems and attaining more fully the economic goals we seek.[2]

It is evident that Bowen's definition refers to responsibility within American "capitalism" or "free enterprise." It does not of itself question the goals of economic activity or place them within the critical context of world economic life. Moreover, this definition does not meet the full test of the idea of a responsible society as defined in Chapter I.

Nevertheless the conception presented by Bowen does open a number of significant avenues of approach. Some of these may be specifically indicated in terms Harry A. Bullis of General Mills has raised concerning the challenges confronting modern management. Bullis' fivefold group of questions suggests answers which show how far economic thought has moved beyond the era of the "invisible hand." He asks:

[1] Is industry planning well ahead to be able to absorb future job hunters in our rapidly increasing population? [2] Is it giving equal opportunity to everyone who is willing to pay the price in intelligent hard work, regardless of race, color, or creed? [3] Is it providing opportunities for our handicapped citizens who are capable of limited employment? [4] Is it cooperating with Government in areas where the combined efforts of Government and industry are needed to stablize our economy? . . . [5] Is industry contributing unfettered money in the forms of grants-in-aid, scholarships, and endowments to underwrite American education? [3]

It is Bullis' contention that a properly prepared business manager today will be able to give constructive answers to each of these questions. These issues lead to yet other questions as we consider the complexity and organization of economic life, its power struggles, its relation to the Protestant ethic, and its growth through professional leadership.

B. The Organizational Revolution

One of the major features of contemporary social life is its involvement in what Kenneth E. Boulding has called the "organizational revo-

[2] *Op. cit.,* p. 6. Used by permission of Harper & Bros.
[3] "The Future Belongs to the Educated Man," *Saturday Review,* January 21, 1956, pp. 12-13.

lution." [4] This revolution manifests itself not only in labor, farm, and professional groups but also in government and business. Up to 1900 there was a marked rise in the size of business enterprise and a growth in trusts and combines. To some extent this movement has been checked in the United States because of unfavorable political attitudes. There has been a great rise in the number and power of trade associations, which now number about one thousand five hundred. Boulding argues that the tremendous rise in organization is due not only to the sense of need for it, such as desire for status and power, but also because of the development in the skill of organization itself. To this must be added the growing recognition that persons by themselves are not very productive, while organization of men and materials may be highly productive.

Most organizations are not the result of a spontaneous coming together of their members; they are organized by organizers, and the rise of organizations often goes hand in hand with the rise of a special class of full-time paid organizers—whether the minister of the church, the business agent or "walking delegate" of the trade union, the county agent of the Farm Bureau, the managing director of the corporation, or the secretary of the trade association.[5]

The dynamic and expanding character of the American economy may be graphically portrayed by a few charts showing the gross national product or expenditure, the national income by distributive shares, the business population, and the billion-dollar companies. (See *Information Please Almanac,* 1956.) Agricultural statistics have been indicated in another chapter.

GROSS NATIONAL PRODUCT OR EXPENDITURE

(in millions of dollars)

Item	1945	1955*
Gross national product	213,558	375,300
Personal consumption expenditures	121,699	245,800
Durable goods	8,105	34,400
Nondurable goods	73,222	122,400
Services	40,372	89,000

[4] *The Organizational Revolution* (New York: Harper & Bros., 1953).
[5] *Ibid.,* p. 207. Used by permission of Harper & Bros.

Gross private domestic investment	10,430	54,100
New construction	3,833	31,200
Producer's durable equipment	7,654	21,500
Change in business inventories	-1,057	1,500
Net foreign investment	-1,438	-400
Government purchases	82,867	75,800
Federal	75,923	46,400
National security }	......	41,200†
Other }		......
Less: Government sales	2,158	......
State and local	8,071	29,400

* First quarter at annual rate, seasonally adjusted; detail will not necessarily add to totals because of rounding.
† Less government sales.
SOURCE: U.S. Department of Commerce.

NATIONAL INCOME BY DISTRIBUTIVE SHARES
(in millions of dollars)

Type of Share	1945	1954	% of total
National income	181,248	299,673	100.0
Compensation of employees	123,181	207,901	69.4
Wages and salaries	117,577	196,244	65.5
Supplements to wages & salaries	5,604	11,657	3.9
Income of unincorporated enterprises and inventory valuation adjustment ..	30,835	37,876	12.6
Business and professional	19,011	25,876	8.6
Farm	11,824	12,000	4.0
Rental income of persons	5,634	10,539	3.5
Corporate profits and inventory valuation adjustment	18,413	33,815	11.3
Net interest	3,185	9,542	3.2

SOURCE: U.S. Department of Commerce

BUSINESS POPULATION
(in thousands of concerns)

Item	1946	1954
Total operating businesses[1]	3,487.2	4,196.7
Manufacturing	285.9	317.6
Wholesale trade	229.2	287.1

Retail trade	1,555.4	1,850.7
Transportation, communications,		
public utilities	162.2	178.8
Finance, insurance & real estate	320.3	340.2
Service industries	656.5	742.3
Mining and quarrying	33.8	38.8
Contract construction	243.8	441.3
New entrants [2]	617.4	330.7[4]
Discontinued businesses [2]	208.7	334.3[4]
Commercial and industrial failures [3]	1.1	11.1

[1] 1929-51, annual average; 1953-54, as of June 30. [2] Annual totals. [3] Closures resulting in a known loss to creditors. [4] Based on incomplete data.

SOURCE: U.S. Department of Commerce, Dun & Bradstreet.

BILLION-DOLLAR COMPANIES

(Assets in millions of dollars as of December 31, 1954)

Company	Assets	Company	Assets
Bell Telephone System	$12,850	Consolidated Edison	
Standard Oil Co. (N.J.)	6,615	Co. (N.Y.)	1,542
General Motors Corp. ...	6,021	Atchison, Topeka &	
U. S. Steel Corp.	3,539	Santa Fe Ry.	1,485
Pennsylvania R. R.	2,456	Sears, Roebuck & Co.	1,470
Socony-Vacuum Oil Co. .	2,257	Union Pacific R. R.	1,386
Standard Oil Co. (Ind.) .	2,199	Westinghouse Electric	
Ford Motor Co.	2,000*	Corp.	1,329
Texas Co.	1,996	Baltimore & Ohio R. R. .	1,274
Southern Pacific System .	1,986	Union Carbide & Carbon .	1,252
New York Central R. R. .	1,974	Humble Oil Co.	1,245
Gulf Oil Co.	1,969	Commonwealth Edison	
E. I. du Pont de		Co.	1,188
Nemours & Co.	1,946	Sinclair Oil Co.	1,187
Pacific Gas & Electric Co.	1,786	Shell Oil Co.	1,102
General Electric Co.	1,692	Phillips Petroleum Co. ..	1,093
Standard Oil Co. (Cal.) .	1,678	Cities Service Co.	1,067
Bethlehem Steel Corp. ...$	1,613	Chrysler Corp.	1,035
		American Gas & Electric	
		System	1,035

* Estimate

SOURCE: *Business Week*

The "organizational revolution" has transformed the whole scope of capital accumulation, production, consumption, and power of the American economy. The transition from a small business economy to a big corporation economy has been rapid. Within the lifetime of America's older citizens this transformation has gone forward so gradually that many have hardly known that they were living in the midst of a major revolution in ownership, in concentration of power, and in corporate management. The revolution was not planned or intended by the nation. It occurred pragmatically, and despite a great depression it evoked only political reform but no major radical response. In the spring of 1957 the Supreme Court handed down a decision which may check, if it will not reverse, the fifty-year trend toward concentration and bigness, when it charged General Motors and Du Pont with violation of the antitrust acts. Joseph C. Harsch, correspondent of the *Christian Science Monitor,* in observing the prominence of this trend toward bigness, noted that if unchecked the time would come inevitably when to all practical purposes the United States would be a corporate state in which most individuals would be employed directly or indirectly by some one of the giant corporations. At such a time the highest available goal for a young man would be to become an officer in some "corporate hierarchy." [6] It is significant to note that recent checks to concentration have come not through special legislative or executive action by the federal government but from the judicial branch.

Organized economic power, in either corporations, associations, cartels, or labor unions, tends to have effects on economic life that challenge the responsible manager. In the first place, there is a tendency to replace direct person-to-person transactions and price setting by indirect and impersonal patterns of relationship. Transactions by large organizations often have a quasi-monopolistic character. In the second place, the process of price setting is increasingly "public" rather than strictly "private." Regulations by commissions and collective bargaining in basic industries illustrate this tendency. In the third place, organizations tend to make parts of the market more rigid than they would otherwise be. This results in a sharp division of the price system

[6] "The Supreme Court and Leadership," *The Christian Science Monitor,* June 12, 1957.

between flexible and inflexible spheres of decision. In the fourth place, where prices tend to be inflexible, there is a threat of deflation. Since this would be disastrous, there is a marked effort to keep national money income from declining. Indeed the national income must be kept rising. In the fifth place, powerful economic organizations demand vigilant budgetary and monetary policies on the part of government. Intervention is inevitable. Finally, since deflation must be avoided, inflation threatens to get out of hand. Inflation is a result of the other factors operating as indicated above. They are not, of course, the sole causes of the inflationary spiral.

Boulding points out that with the chronic presence of actual and threatened war the risks of inflation are considerable. A highly organized society is easier to run in an inflationary period. Both labor and management are tempted, for example, to pass on the results of their bargaining and marketing schemes in terms of higher prices to the consumer. Chronic inflation poses many problems:

A great many of our economic institutions are based on the assumption that the price level may be expected to be reasonably constant in the long run—an assumption which over the past 150 years has been justified. The accounting system, the financial system, including the whole structure of borrowing and lending, provision for old age in the form of pensions, insurance, and money or bond savings, are all based on the assumption of a constant value of money. If the value of money is constantly going to decline, most of our pension and insurance plans will be worthless, and unless nominal rates of interest rise markedly the real rate of interest will become permanently negative, with consequent disorganization of the whole system of finance.[7]

The inflationary threat is not the only major problem of organizational rigidities and power. Another is the increase in conflict. As the internal problems are solved in growing organizations, the external conflicts become more important. For example, as business firms run into imperfect markets, sales expansion requires either price cuts or greater selling costs. When there are many small organizations seeking to expand, they may do so without affecting any single rival so as to provoke notice or retaliation, but one large organization among a few can expand only at the obvious expense of its rivals. Such expansion prompts

[7] *Op. cit.,* p. 212. Used by permission of Harper & Bros.

counter measures. "The very success of an organization may spell its doom. It grows to the point where it cannot live with its neighbors, and yet it cannot grow to the point where it absorbs its neighbors."[8] Boulding holds this principle of conflict to be so universal that he calls it the "Principle of Increasingly Unfavorable External Environment."

The problem of conflict raises the issue of respect for moral order. Powerful organizations in competition or rivalry with one another tend to undermine the traditional "rules of the game" and to choose any means which may bring about their desired ends. The goal of "success" tempts group power so far as to induce a state of *anomie,* or normlessness. Moreover, giant corporations experiment with and institutionalize certain forms of coercion in order to assure "success." This action may go so far as to attempt, directly or indirectly, to capture the powers of the state for the interests of business. Other coercive efforts involve direct action against businesses.

Agricultural policy also illustrates the effect of conflict among organizations. Farmers' associations have used both economic and political means to improve their positions. It is often necessary for the government to increase its intervention in order to keep organized business and organized labor and organized farmers from nationally destructive measures. Irresponsibility by any group invites state intervention. Coercion checked by counter-coercion does not necessarily make for the common good. "Two opposite coercions do not necessarily cancel out, and, indeed, frequently result in extremely destructive forms of competition, both economic and political."[9]

If conflict is to be transcended, some form of integration of interests and some workable organ of control are required. This latter principle means that the "interaction of organizations must itself be organized." Since this involves an over-all organ of control, it is necessary that government play a major role, directly or indirectly, in the interests of responsibility.

As an illustration of the problem of responsible economic life I shall emphasize once more the question of inflation. In Chapter I we noted the special memorandum on inflation by the National Council of Churches which criticized the tendencies of powerful groups to accept sacrifices only on condition that other groups make equal or greater sac-

[8] *Ibid.,* p. 213.
[9] *Ibid.,* p. 218.

213

rifices.[10] The injustice and futility of this type of action are evident. Such practices place the burden on those parts of the community least able to defend themselves. The warning sounded in the National Council memorandum in 1952 must be even more sternly uttered today when inflationary prices persist despite recession and unemployment.

One effort to combat the tendency of organizations to get more and more monolithic is decentralization. I may fruitfully illustrate the nature of decentralization by referring to what has taken place in General Electric. Managerial control is divided among a large number of individual units. Decentralization does not necessarily imply the breaking up of a company into smaller units except for purposes of managerial effectiveness. R. J. Cordiner of General Electric regards decentralization as a philosophy which applies with equal force to any large organization of free human beings such as a government, a university, a union, or a business. He regards it as a way of making a creative response to certain challenges of bigness and a way of preserving and enhancing the competitive enterprise system, what he calls the "people's capitalism."

This type of decentralization does not reverse the organizational revolution but is a way of acting more flexibly within it. Large enterprise has ardent proponents. The president of General Electric sees positive values in large business enterprise. Cordiner says:

The economy of the United States, and its position as a world power, make large enterprises both an irreversible fact and an actual necessity for economic and national security reasons. Any attendant perils lie not in bigness itself, but in the way energies of large organizations are organized and managed. Centralized administration of large institutions of any kind can lead to irresponsibility, shortsightedness, inefficiency, and the abuse of power—but this need not happen under wise and self-disciplined guidance. Responsible decentralization—as a philosophy—makes it possible to provide at once the big results that come from big enterprises, with the human freedom that comes from respecting the competence and dignity of every individual in the enterprise.[11]

The interest by corporations in a degree of decentralization is emphasized also by Charles E. Wilson of General Motors. Overcentraliza-

[10] See above page.
[11] *Op cit.*, p. 79. By permission from *New Frontiers for Professional Managers* by Ralph J. Cordiner. Copyright, 1956. McGraw-Hill Book Company, Inc.

tion makes sense neither in business nor in government, he contended as Secretary of Defense.

About every three years some one would raise the question wouldn't we save money in General Motors if we centralized the thing and did all the buying in one big place, pointing out that the Buick company paid a few cents more a thousand for some nuts or bolts or screws or something. We would look it over again and decide no, that it wasn't the right way to do it. Our big problem was to decentralize the thing and clarify the policy, simplify the administration and promote efficiency and avoid the concentration of stupidity.[12]

C. The Ethical Situation of the Businessman

From the rapid review of certain illustrative problems rising from the "organizational revolution," it is apparent that considerations of responsibility relate both to matters of the economic order as a whole and to matters of individual ethics. They are inextricably interwoven.

The modern businessman is in a strategic position in the economy. Although his strategic position does not place on him alone the obligation of responsibility toward economic life, yet it does place a greater onus of responsibility upon him than upon other functionaries in the system.[13] This strategic position is his by virtue of the historical development of business society, the businessman's demands for freedom of enterprise, and the favorable position which law has given to private property as it functions in production, distribution, and consumption. With the evolution of the economy from the period of *laissez faire* to that of the "mixed economy" or "people's capitalism" or "welfare capitalism" —however it is designated—there has been a shift in the focus and emphasis of moral responsibility. This shift is of special interest.

H. R. Bowen summarizes the earlier tacit moral obligations of businessmen as follows:

(1) to observe the rules of property; (2) to honor contracts; (3) to refrain from deception and fraud; (4) to be efficient and to promote economic progress; (5) to protect life, limb, and health of workers and of the general public; (6) to compete vigorously, and in case of failure of competition to act with restraint; (7) to accept and respect the economic

[12] *Time*, June 3, 1957, p. 13.
[13] Bowen, *op. cit.*, p. 29.

215

freedoms of consumers, workers, and owners; and (8) to have regard for the human rights of workers.[14]

Since this earlier period it has been necessary to expand the businessman's scope of responsibilities in two directions. One of these involves complex social effects; the other involves government.

Making private business decisions is often a complex organizational network of operations. In making these decisions managers must consider broad economic and social effects. Large enterprise planning must envisage decades of economic life and the interaction of national and international processes. The decision maker must more and more be able to identify his personal interest with the social welfare. When it becomes fully evident that mankind is the unit of co-operation, the world economy will be recognized as the field of force which conditions the decisions.

The second direction in which the modern businessman must learn greater responsibility is as a partner with other major decision-making groups, especially with government. Since government is the guarantor of both justice and freedom in a democratic society, the businessman is increasingly expected to co-operate with government in the formulation and execution of policies affecting the public welfare.[15] Not least among the values to be conserved by this partnership is economic stability. Stability contributes both to domestic tranquillity and to international order and peace. Since America constitutes a large part of world business, stability at home is decisive for the policies of many foreign governments.

Unfortunately the attitude of much business is still one of negative criticism and even hostility toward government. Government may contribute to a degree of freedom in economic life. This contribution arises from the inability of "free enterprise" to assure freedom. John M. Clark observes "that if American business were left to its own devices, it would probably seek to mitigate competition by informal understandings, then discover that these were not binding, and then would substitute various methods of enforcement." The result would be "that business in America would become cartellized, to an extent not too different from

[14] *Ibid.,* p. 19. See Alvin S. Johnson, "The Soul of Capitalism," *Unpopular Review,* April, 1914, pp. 227-44.
[15] *Ibid.,* p. 28.

216

what prevails in Europe." [16] Freedom requires at least a minimum of order which only government can provide.

D. Protestant Perspectives of Business Responsibility

We are now ready to place the problem of responsibility in the context of Protestant ethical analysis.

Over a period of about eighty years a number of American Protestant perspectives on business responsibility have emerged. There is, of course, no unanimity of conviction on economic life among Protestants and Protestant sects. General convergence of ethical doctrine would seem to focus on the following themes: the economic system itself, private property, power, motives and values, vocation, distribution of income, social consequences of business policy, and questions of participation.[17] On these themes a number of characteristic propositions may be formulated: (1) No particular form of social or economic organization is ordained by God's will or has any special claim to support on religious grounds. (2) Social institutions are relative to time and space. A form of social organization which is desirable in one environment at one stage of human development may be unsuited for the proper service of mankind at another. (3) Economic life is not dominated by quasi-natural "laws" such as are not subject to human choices or regulation. (4) Leaders of social institutions have an obligation to adapt them to the demands of the kingdom of God. (5) An owner is a trustee accountable to God and society. There is no necessary presumption that all types of property must be held on identical terms of ownership. Experimentation in varying systems of ownership is not only allowable but required. (6) Different forms of property and their relation to power, freedom, and justice must be constantly scrutinized in the light of the ideals of personality and community. (7) Power in property and organization entails the responsibility to use it in the public interest. (8) Large power groups are probably here to stay and hence must be realistically treated in the light of a just ordering of power responsive to basic human need and personal fulfillment. (9) Motivations and values in economic life must be constantly scruti-

[16] *The Ethical Basis of Economic Freedom*, p. 38.
[17] The chapter "Protestant Views of the Social Responsibilities of Businessmen" in Bowen, *op. cit.*, is one of the best brief summaries available and written specifically with the businessman as reader in mind. This chapter draws heavily on this book.

nized, criticized, and directed to proper ends. Under capitalism men tend to be dominated by the desire for material acquisition, luxury, power, and self-aggrandizement. For many millions of persons money and material prosperity are the accepted symbols of success and hence are made the central aims of human striving. Profit must especially be criticized.[18] In this connection it is instructive to note that a company like General Electric has begun a thorough study of motivation and economic incentives. R. J. Cordiner says: "This area of human motivations is an exciting frontier for modern industry, and is perhaps the ultimate challenge of the industrial society." [19]

The above perspectives have a direct bearing on the Christian doctrine of vocation, which is assuming increasingly greater attention in the Protestant churches and is of special concern to the ecumenical movement. (10) Management must get its orientation, its motivation, and its goal from religious vocation.[20] At the point of vocation all work, including that of decision making in large and small business, finds its point of reference in the life and work of Jesus Christ. (11) The doctrine of vocation places both the worker and the owner in a community of power, respect, and service to society.

(12) Distribution should be determined primarily on the basis of justice. Many Protestant pronouncements while not devoted to simple equality of income are concerned for the level of purchasing power consistent with not only satisfying minimal needs but maximizing personal fulfillment.

These Protestant criticisms and pronouncements involve principles and suggest policies which some leading businessmen have themselves recommended. They inform the decision-making process of advanced professional managers. In their depth of understanding of personal motivation and their social scope they stand in significant contrast to the limited ethical orientation of the earlier period noted above. Business codes need to take into account the actor, whether in his individual capacity or as member of a corporate body, the goals of economic activity, the social context of the business, and the adjustment of means to ends. These aspects of moral and business action comprise an inclusive social obligation. In so far as a manager has power and

[18] See Muelder, *op. cit.,* pp. 78-82.
[19] *Op. cit.,* p. 25.
[20] See Muelder, *op. cit.,* ch. iii, "Religious Vocation: Management."

218

authority, he ought to hold himself accountable to the best interests of the community; to devote himself to conserving natural resources; to advancing the productivity and efficiency of economic life; to enhancing respect for human beings in the persons of associates, suppliers, competitors, employees, and consumers; to developing freedom of opportunity and growth for persons of all races, religious backgrounds, and national origins; to protecting the dignity of the family through sound business and social policies; to enlarging the scope of distributive justice in relation to the co-operation of men and women in status and job classifications; to promoting the diffusion of property and power in the interests of decentralized responsibility; to cultivating ever better relations with unions in collective bargaining, in co-operating in political policies for the national good, and in assisting the nation to understand and meet its obligations in world economic relations.

In addition to these moral goals we must consider the important idea of participation. Some Protestant social ethics have stressed the participation of workers, consumers, and possibly other groups in business decisions. Management has shown little interest in adopting this idea, but it may be involved in that aspect of social obligation which affirms that those who hold economic power "are responsible for its exercise to God and the people whose welfare is affected by it." This duty cannot be discharged by a paternalistic interpretation of decision making. As F. E. Johnson says, "it is a truism in a democratic society that no person or group of persons is either wise enough or good enough to control others, except as specifically delegated to do so." [21] As management becomes more and more professional and hence more and more a private government, accommodating the interests of equity, stockholders, customers, workers, and the community, it is essential that these interests have effective participation in policy making. Extensive experimentation in this field would seem to be indicated.

E. Responsible Management as a Profession

In the age of Adam Smith the managerial art was quite undeveloped. It was his opinion that in a manufacturing industry a corporation could not be well managed, and therefore the savings of the investors would

[21] Bowen, *op. cit.*, pp. 248-49.

be squandered.[22] Today management has become a profession in which ofttimes high standards of conduct, both personal and administrative, are realized. With capital stock widely owned, investors in many corporations have developed faith in the competency and integrity of the directors and executives to whose stewardship the funds are trusted. In some cases the board of directors is composed entirely of professionals, no one of which holds his position by virtue of the amount of money he has invested in the company. For example, in 1956 General Electric had 358,000 owners, of which 13,000 were institutions, but no one individual owned as much as one tenth of one per cent of the shares outstanding.[23] General Electric is managed by professional managers. Cordiner says, "These managers, including myself, are not the owners of the business, but employees hired by the share owners through their elected directors to manage their business in the balanced best interests of all concerned." [24] An analogous pattern obtains in Standard Oil of New Jersey and other companies.

What does the professional approach involve? This question invites an answer suggested earlier in this chapter, that management means leadership of a social system. It requires a

dedication of the man's self and service not only to the owners of the business through his Board of Directors, but also as a steward to the Company's customers, its industry, its employees, and to the community at large. The professional manager must consciously place the balanced best interests of these ahead of his own personal interests. The corporate manager today thus has an opportunity and an obligation for service comparable to the highest traditions of any professions in the past.[25]

The manager of even a moderately sized business is the guide and administrator of a social system. For this reason it is not enough that he be technically competent in fields such as engineering, marketing, or accounting. Modern business administration is not substantially different in principle from administration in other major institutions like government or universities and colleges. In all cases, as Melvin T. Copeland remarks, "business enterprise is rife with vibrancies and

[22] Melvin T. Copeland, *The Executive at Work* (Cambridge, Mass.: Harvard University Press, 1951), pp. 3-4.
[23] Cordiner, *op. cit.,* p. 12.
[24] *Ibid.,* p. 16.
[25] *Ibid.,* pp. 16-17.

vibrant personalities." [26] To manage such a social system, it does not suffice to have a title or legal responsibility alone. The authority of the executive must be won by effective leadership expressed through intellectual competence, interpersonal respect, and moral control. Copeland says, "His appointment to office merely gives him an opportunity to demonstrate his qualities of leadership, to win the esteem, respect and support of the members of the organization with whom he is to work." [27] Title and, sometimes, economic power come from above, but effective social authority must come from below—from the persons who are expected to follow his leadership.

Two types of problems which may arise from leadership have to do with (1) avoidance of conflicts of interest and (2) compliance with the law. The first group of moral issues relates to such acts as commercial bribery, where an executive accepts a personal gratuity as an inducement for making a decision; or granting loans to officers of a company; or an executive selling property in which he is personally interested to the corporation of which he is an influential officer; and many others. Much has been made of conflicts of interest in cases where business executives have become governmental officials. Conflict of interest is sometimes involved in nepotism. Again, the question arises in connection with bonus payments paid to executives when they are themselves the initiators of the plan.

The problems of compliance with the law are many because of the multiplicity of laws at all levels of local, state, and federal governments. There is the problem of the attitude toward law itself, as well as the complexity of compliance. In the field of anti-trust laws the attitude of a corporation as well as the need for clarifying the law are involved. Copeland suggests that one good moral test for executives is the "light of day" test. "In situations involving potential conflicts of interests for directors or executives of a company . . . ability to stand the light of day is a useful test for application. Arrangements or dealings with directors or executives which cannot readily stand up under full exposure are not wisely undertaken." [28]

Administration is a network of decisions.[29] In a responsible managerial system consistent with democratic ideals, the decision-making

[26] *Op. cit.*, pp. 3-4.
[27] *Ibid.*, p. 5.
[28] *Ibid.*, p. 213.
[29] *Ibid.*, p. 15.

process is a chain of actions induced by leadership. Consultation is of the essence of this chain of actions. Contrariwise, unilateral decision in a democratic society is unethical. As F. E. Johnson says, "a democratic philosophy of management calls for sharing in proportion to proved capacity to take responsibility, and to stand the gaff. This is something that only experience can determine." [30]

The education of a professional manager today requires not only practical knowledge of modern technology but also thorough grounding in humanistic values. Even on the engineering side of his training he needs broad economic, sociological, and psychological understanding of the technical processes. Moreover, since he is a significant actor in the co-operating unity of mankind, he needs a world perspective. This space span must be matched by a time span. Especially in larger businesses survival value requires relevant planning which considers not only immediate profit possibilities but developments throughout decades and generations. Political trends and the determination of peoples to have personally and socially significant lives must be considered. Business practice must accommodate to social welfare or it will in the long run be repudiated by consumers, workers, and citizens alike.

F. Responsible Economic Power

Professional managers may contribute to the increase of accountability in economic life, but they cannot resolve the ultimate questions of economic power in a democracy. As employed personnel, managers are not free to take a radical position on corporate power. To be sure, the quality of management makes a contribution to the ethos of responsibilty, but managers have limited authority to deal with the final problems of power. The centers of economic power are also found in ownership, trade unions, and government. Because government defines property, the basic formulation of responsible economic policy is political. Political decision is finally responsive to the goals which pervade culture as a whole.

Political, economic, and military power are naturally very closely related. In the United States the intimate relation of these three forms of power is becoming increasingly explicit. The violent and nationalistic character of the twentieth century are partial causes of this phenome-

[30] In Bowen, op. cit., p. 249.

non. Equally important is the fact that corporate economic powe. seeks close relationships to government, because government has the power to control and to define all property relations. Men of property and managers of property have an interest in influencing and controlling those positions in the state where decisions are made which have consequences for business activity.

It is not surprising that private business leaders are close to the current government in Washington. Today the political activities of corporations are almost as significant as their economic ones. C. Wright Mills is probably correct in saying of many corporations that

as political institutions they are of course totalitarian and dictatorial, although externally they display much public relations and liberal rhetoric. . . . Not the politicians of the visible government, but the chief executives who sit in the political directorate, by fact and by proxy, hold the power and the means of defending the privileges of their corporate world. If they do not reign, they do govern at many of the vital points of everyday life in America, and no powers effectively countervail against them, nor have they as corporate-made men developed any effectively restraining conscience.[31]

Whatever the desires of individual men of property or managers of others' property to be responsible, the fact remains that corporate power acting collectively has not shown more than a token of interest in such common needs as better schools, well-paid public-school teachers, adequate university support, and socially approvable housing for the common people but has consistently resisted legislation and other programs to make these values actual. On the contrary, many business leaders do all things possible to mold the minds of the masses with the complacent slogan of "peace and prosperity."

Within their great bureaucratical organizations many corporations have not made much improvement on behalf of that freedom for the individual which is consistent with autonomy and self-respecting dignity. Despite the trend toward high professional standards in industry, there is the widespread fact of the "organization man." William H. Whyte voices a realistic concern because of the regnant spirit of "contemporaryism." [32] As men in organizations are increasingly dependent

[31] *The Power Elite* (New York: Oxford University Press 1956), p. 125. See the significant review by Robert S. Lynd in *The Nation,* May 12, 1956.
[32] See his *The Organization Man* (New York: Simon & Shuster, 1956).

on an environmental business order over which they have decreasing control, they may be robbed of real spiritual independence. Though some large organizations give a certain leeway for decision making, theirs is a kind of feudal domination over all essential decisions. Bureaucratic heads are skeptical of the original thinker and often go to great lengths to stifle, confuse, and block individual thought. They "double-guess" men in the lower feudal hierarchy of a corporation. The result is the triumph of mediocrity in reducing "organization men" to a common denominator of thought. When men surrender to organizational thinking, their individuality is destroyed. Mass society, mass production, mass media of communication, and mass distribution prove to be enemies of the person.

Man under God must ever be on his guard against the encroachments of standardized, mediocre, uninspired, and uncreative organizational conformity.

CHAPTER XII

Responsible Consumption

A. Responsible Consumption: An Undeveloped Art

There is a common assumption that if a person has the economic means and the facts about available goods, he will make rational choices as a consumer. Because of this assumption the problems of consumption are often reduced to those of income and distribution. Give people enough income and distribute it equitably and the ethical issues of consumption are resolved. But the art of consumption is actually quite complex and difficult. Moreover it is undeveloped in comparison with the art of production. The ideal of responsible consumption raises many questions which this chapter can consider in only a preliminary way.

One initial question is: Who is the consumer? Persons, of course. But there are more than individual persons to consider. Institutions consume. Producers consume; so do middlemen. The army is a consumer, and so is the government. From one perspective all buyers are consumers. From another perspective consumers are those who finally consume the goods and services produced in the economy. They are the ultimate consumers. It is with these that we are primarily concerned in this discussion. They are the individuals and family units for whose sake the economic order finally exists.

There are other preliminary factors in the consumer's situation to be recognized. The grossest problems of consumption are reflected in the inequalities of living standards both within a nation and among nations. Consumption as a problem of equity is, therefore, closely related to the problem of distribution of income. President Roosevelt challenged the social conscience of the U.S.A. in the 1930's with the fact that one third of the people were ill-fed, ill-housed, and ill-clothed.

There has been a general improvement in domestic standards of living since then, though, as the discussion on agricultural policy showed above, there are still many farm families living in substandard conditions. They are matched by millions of poverty-stricken urban dwellers. However, when we compare the average American income to that of most nations in the world today, we note that the capacity to consume is many times greater in the United States than anywhere else.

Consumers' problems are made additionally complex by the dynamic factor in satisfying needs and wants. Consumption is relative because of this dynamic factor. There are, accordingly, levels of consumption. Luxuries in one period become necessities in another. Luxuries suggest the presence of abundance, though the goods and services in the period when they are considered luxuries are relatively scarce. When the luxuries become necessities, a new level of scarcity as well as of abundance appears. Automobiles, once a luxury, are today necessities for millions of people and call for production on a scale undreamed of in the period when they first appeared. Therefore, in the art of consumption it is perplexing to distinguish between real needs and wants. Nevertheless, the distinction is ethically significant.

In America the art of consumption is confused because the nation, in entering an age of comparative abundance, still uses ethical standards which were fashioned in an age of poverty. Relative abundance is a challenger to older consumer ethics both in the traditions of Christianity and in the theory of the classical economists. The great moral and spiritual teachers of the past never faced the issue of widespread material prosperity, for it was not there for them to face. Men as a whole were too poor. Today mankind seems to be determined to get rid of poverty everywhere in the world. Yet when abundance becomes generally prevalent, the spiritual problem still remains as to how the consumption of goods and services can be transformed into an abundant spiritual life.

The question is not simply one of the amount of goods to be equitably distributed and consumed. It is a question of fundamental education in values and standards. Patterns of culture are involved. Every culture has its designs of consumption. They are deeply rooted in the customs, mores, and folkways. They change slowly, because to change them means to upset the stable relations of people to one another in families, neighborhoods, classes, and status systems. Nevertheless, in the United States they have been significantly modified in a few decades. Individuals and families who acquire great wealth may not know how to spend it wisely. Furthermore, the technological revolution in production keeps on modifying the whole design of modern life. Almost overnight dominant rural habits of living are transformed into urban patterns for satisfying wants. Appetites are whetted for new products. Hungers unknown or only dimly felt in an age of scarcity become insatiable. In such an age the need for an ethic of responsible consumption is imperative. Such an ethic must express the relevance of the moral law of the ideal of personality and the moral law of the ideal community. What kind of person and what kind of community will the decisions of consumption develop?

The major educational effort of mankind today is devoted to the sphere of production rather than to the art of consumption. It is generally recognized that if mankind is to get above the poverty level, it must produce a larger pile of goods and services to divide. It is less generally recognized that sound principles of equity must attend the distribution of the goods and services which have been produced. It is even less understood that men and women need to learn responsible consumption as well as the arts of production and distribution. Most secondary and collegiate institutions of education emphasize production in their curriculums. Even in liberal arts colleges, where the official ethos has been to make not just a living but a life, the major motivation has been to enhance the earning power of the student. The various fields of specialization reflect the accent on developing efficient producers in the form of teachers, engineers, lawyers, doctors, scientists, economists, agronomists, ministers, home economics experts, and so on through the whole range of specialists. The creation of goods and services dominates over the art of consuming them. Even just distribution does not guarantee responsible consumption.

An ethic of responsible consumption involves at least four types of issues: (1) Consumption is a broader and deeper concept than mere widespread distribution of consumer's income. Distribution and consumption, though inseparable, must be clearly distinguished. We shall note this situation in the next section. (2) Consumer's education is a much broader field than teaching persons to buy advantageously in the market place of available goods. It includes the ethics of acquiring goods and services, especially the critical analysis of the standards of acquisition and possession. (3) Responsible consumption has a close relationship to the ethical evaluation of culture in relation to needs, wants, and their satisfactions. When Jesus said, "Man shall not live by bread alone," he was speaking negatively about the priorities of life. When he added "but by every word that proceeds from the mouth of God," he laid down an ultimate evaluation of all consumption systems. (4) Consumption raises a complex of basic problems concerning abundance, sharing abundance in a world of poverty, the determination of the patterns of consumption, the ethics of advertising, the freedom of the consumer to spend his own, and the responsibility of the state to protect, regulate, and assist consumption.

B. The Ethics of Consumption in Relation to Distribution

The distribution and consumption of goods and services are closely related, but they must be distinguished as processes and experiences. Distribution refers to the structure and forms in which goods and services are made available, primarily through income, to the various individuals, groups, and institutions in the community. Consumption refers to the degree and manner in which the goods and services are appropriated.

Distribution and consumption interact upon each other. On the one hand, consumption patterns tend to fall in line with class incomes. There is a discernible profile in the consumption habits of various income groups. On the other hand, consumption habits also influence the patterns of distribution. An increase in income does not proportionally affect the whole population in the same way. A thousand dollars added to the income of the lowest 20 per cent of families in the United States will affect the distribution of food and clothing in a marked degree. A thousand dollars added to the income of the upper 20 per cent of families will affect the food and clothing market in only a minor degree. In many other ways also distribution and consumption are closely related but distinctive problems.

Since the ability effectively to procure consumer's goods is dependent on distribution of income, responsible consumption has a close relation to distributive justice. The discussion of agricultural policy above may be regarded as a particularly striking example of equity as a problem in national income. The emphasis on equity tends toward a policy making for the leveling of gross inequalities, eliminating the extremes of income and increasing the number of persons in the middle or median range.

The Christian ethic of responsibility and love for the neighbor tends to place a strong accent on the value of equality. The possibility of economic "plenty," or abundance, underscores the moral obligation to do what can be done for the alleviation of poverty. Where all are poor, poverty is obviously not the moral scandal that it is when the privileged few dominate a large share of goods in an age of potential abundance. In the light of the moral ideal the Christian effort in the economic order must shift from charitable paternalism to the realization of more equal justice in the distribution of wealth. Christians who live in the more privileged geographical areas must recognize that securing economic plenty and greater justice in its distribution within their national groups is not the whole of their duty in this connection. Mankind is the unit of co-operation, and international disparities in incomes are hence an acute challenge to the Christian conscience.

In 1949 per capita real income, translated into U.S. dollars, showed more than a thirtyfold differential between the United States and some countries in Asia and Africa. Selected nations may be indicated as follows: United States, $1,450; Canada, $870; Bolivia, $60; Switzerland, $850; Italy, $230; Israel, $390; Syria, $100; Communist China, $30; Egypt, $100; Northern Rhodesia, $40. The death rate is in inverse proportion to national incomes. This international disparity is also true of educational standards.

The lowest level of consumption needs is that of strictly vital necessities. Every person has a moral claim to vital minimums, for such rights are rooted in basic needs. The claims are made against society and are balanced by the duty of each person to recognize the claims of all others on him. Not every nation is able to fulfill these elementary moral claims, but the claims are inherent in personality and are directed to mankind as a whole. The cry of the hungry, the naked, and the sick transcends the legal boundaries of nations. A correlative duty is for persons and communities to be productive so as to satisfy as much as possible the moral claims to vital minimums. In societies that have the natural and technological means, the moral claims can be more readily translated into legal terms and provisions than in underdeveloped areas. Each community has an obligation to recognize basic needs and to seek to provide for conditions that make possible their satisfaction.

Within the United States there has since 1939 been a trend toward greater equality. The indicators of this trend may be listed as follows: (1) The per capita income of the low-income regions has increased by a greater percentage than that of the high-income regions. Between 1929 and 1954 significant percentage increases of per capita income for selected states may be illustrative: Maine, 149; Massachusetts, 111; New York, 87; Indiana, 200; Illinois, 125; South Carolina, 294; Alabama, 237; Mississippi, 206; Arkansas, 221; California, 117; Connecticut, 129. (2) There are increasingly more people living in the regions of highest per capita income. (3) The net migration from 1940 to 1950 is clearly away from low-income to high-income regions. (4) In the same period wage-or-salary income for low-paid occupations increased by a greater percentage than for high-paid occupations. (5) The number of workers in high-paid occupations increased by a greater percentage than in low-income occupations. (6) The average income of nonwhites increased at a somewhat greater rate than for whites.[1] There is, however, still a marked inequality in American incomes.

Consumer expenditures for food and housing vary percentagewise according to levels of income. For example, in 1941 a national sample of urban families yielded the following schedule.[2]

Per Cent of Total Consumer Expenditures

Annual Income Class	Food	Housing	All other consumer goods
Below $1,000	37	37	26
1,000-1,500	36	32	32
1,500-2,000	33	31	36
2,000-3,000	29	33	38
3,000-5,000	27	33	40
5,000 and over	22	31	47

In studying such a table it is important to remember that low-income families have poorer diets than better-income families despite the fact that they devote a higher percentage of the budget to it. Similarly more substandard housing and dilapidated dwellings are found among

[1] Elizabeth E. Hoyt and others, *American Income and Its Use* (New York: Harper & Bros., 1954), pp. 133-34.
[2] *Ibid.*, p. 160. The ultimate source is the U. S. Bureau of Labor Statistics, *Bulletin* 822, 1954.

the low-income groups. The higher the income, the greater the amount of medical and related services used per person. Yet because of diets, housing, and related factors, low-income families suffer from more illness and the like. When we expand our perspective to include India and China, we must note that the proportion of national income spent for food is estimated at 75 to 80 per cent.[3]

Who are the poorest? To understand the extent and nature of the problem of poverty, it is important to analyze the composition of the low-income groups in the United States. As of 1949 it was estimated that two thousand dollars annual money income was a proper dividing line between poverty and a minimum adequate income. Of these 39 per cent were unrelated individuals, and they constituted 72 per cent of all unrelated individuals. Of these many were beginners in gainful work and many were 65 years of age and over. Nine per cent were families with no earners, and these constituted 87 per cent of such families, made up mostly of the aged, the disabled, and the widowed with young children to care for. Ten per cent were composed of families whose only earner was in the armed forces, and 38 per cent of such families were in the group. These three groups thus accounted for 58 per cent. Twelve per cent more were made up of farmers or farm managers, and 62 per cent of such families were in this income class.

We have noted a moderate trend toward equality of income in the U.S.A. The trend toward equality is a response not only to income changes but also to the tax program of the state and Federal governments and the direct services provided to the whole people through government. Schools, roads, libraries, parks, hospitals, museums, welfare services, low-income housing, food stamp programs, hot lunch programs, and the like not only equalize distribution, but they do it in a way which directly affects consumption. These types of distribution should be distinguished from distribution of income such as social security programs, old age and survivors insurance, and aid to dependent children, which leave the consumer free to choose the goods to be consumed.

C. Government and the Welfare of Consumers

The issues of widespread poverty and of trends toward equality involve, as we have just observed, the participation of government on be-

[3] *Ibid.*, p. xvi.

half of consumers. Responsible and adequate participation on the part of government is hindered by widespread misunderstanding and attacks on what is called the "welfare state." [4] In contemporary societies, like Britain and America, welfare has come to include a wide range of activities which have a bearing on the problems of consumers. Welfare includes state action to ensure good working conditions in factories, to prevent exploitations of the weak, to ensure that houses are safely built, and to control the sale of dangerous drugs. Sometimes welfare means state action to affect prices, as for example in agriculture, public utilities, and rent control. Welfare may be expressed through insurance to provide income for those unable to work through ill health, unemployment, and old age. In these relationships men and women receive benefits because they are persons and not because they add to the national product. Then, too, welfare may take the form of providing consumer's goods free or at less than cost, such as milk to expectant mothers and to children, subsidized dwellings, and general education.

State welfare action may involve expenditures on goods and services which cannot as well be provided through the market such as defense, law courts, and other services already noted in the discussion on equality. The concept of welfare even includes the question of general planning as to the proportion of the national income that should go into the consumption of civilian goods and into military goods. Diversion into military expenditures of goods needed to raise the general standards of living is one of the greatest social evils of the age.

There are probably four types of governmental action which are clearly conducive to improving consumer participation in the economy.[5] (1) There is action to give the consumer more effective freedom in his choices. "Consumer sovereignty" is an essential application of the freedom of persons. (2) It is appropriate that government protect consumers from their own inevitable ignorance by legislation covering such items as accurate labeling, pure food, construction codes. This list is bound to be very long in a complex and interdependent urban society. (3) It is necessary for government to interfere in protecting the public from consumption practices involving moral degeneracy, drug addiction, organized gambling, prostitution, and the like. (4) It is the

[4] See above chs. vii and viii.
[5] See my chapter, "Ethical Aspects of Income Distribution and Consumption," in Hoyt, *op. cit.*, p. 334.

232

responsibility of government positively to raise the level of consumption in ways that are generally beneficial. These include public provision for education, road building, general sanitation, recreation centers, housing programs, libraries, museums, and other cultural benefits. The "best things of life" can be directly brought within reach of all the people by appropriate governmental action. In the interest of freedom it is wise to keep a healthy tension between private initiative in the field of culture and education and public initiative. Sound social policy will encourage the optimum of creative participation on the part of all people.

Beyond these four types of governmental action lies the realm of income distribution. The government should constantly review the various levels, aspects, segments, of the economy in special need of improved income. Policies should be devised so that the individuals and families involved not only may have the means to meet the vital minimums of existence but also may have a dignified level of consumption.

Anthropological studies have shown that in many cultures the improvement of income may not be an improvement of life because traditional values and ways of living have not been properly modified. Increased income is sometimes squandered while old patterns continue to dominate. Societies may reflect greater license and vice because labor-saving devices and cash incomes are not interpreted and the new ways of life have not been internalized. It is not enough to introduce more efficient and more productive ways of making a living; education is necessary so that added income and productivity may have a beneficent effect. On the other hand, cultures may have levels of aspiration which most persons have never been able to reach. The improvement of productivity and income must be intelligently related to these aspirations. As in many other cultures, American consumption reflects both kinds of problems, the sheer waste or license attending increased income where there has been no improvement in goals or value-habits and the need to teach the people how their hidden aspirations can be meaningfully realized by the proper stewardship of their resources.

D. A Profile of Consumers' Goals

When we turn our attention from questions of income distribution, from general considerations of equality and inequality, and from the role of government in protecting the consumer and providing certain goods and services, to the consumer himself, we are faced by many difficult ethical problems. Such basic ethical problems of the consumer are coextensive with those of general value theory.[6] When man has the appropriate means to express himself, his consumption habits will reflect his effective criteria of the good life. Pleasure, utility, aesthetic interest, religious devotion, duty, self-realization, and the like will be largely determinative according to their place in his scheme of values. In fact, however, we cannot assume that most men have the means to an effective expression of their values. Culture in its many dimensions tends to determine the range of available values among consumers' goods and the criteria by which they are organized and chosen. The problem of consumption comes finally very close to the practical problem of the ideal of personality and community which one embraces.

An adequate ethics of consumption must rest squarely on the foundations of Christian self-realization theory if it is to have consistency and coherence. As a matter of fact, however, the profile of American consumer interests has been determined by the composite of many antithetical tendencies. American social life is eclectic and pragmatic. Social psychiatrists like Karen Horney [7] have noted its neurotic conflicts between a naturalism of competition and individualistic self-interest, on the one hand, and certain Christian virtues like mutuality, co-operation, and responsibility on the other. The distinguished panel of social analysts who produced *The Goals of Economic Life* under the auspices of the Federal Council of Churches and the National Council of Churches noted a mixture of utilitarian, social self-realization, personalistic, and activistic Christian norms at work. Some sought to find a possible coincidence of self-interest and altruism in economic life. There is no present coherence among actual consumers' goals and distinctively Christian norms. This lack of coherence is clearly evident from profiles drawn, on the one hand, by anthropologists and, on the other, by statisticians of income expenditures. Both these profiles, as we shall note, stand in sharp contrast to a religiously responsible outlook on life.

The consumer interests of Americans reflect the fact that despite many paradoxes they regard themselves as middle-class people. Some

[6] See E. S. Brightman, *Moral Laws* (New York: Abingdon Press, 1933).
[7] In *The Neurotic Personality of Our Time* (New York: W. W. Norton & Co., 1937).

234

studies show that 70 per cent of those who recognize that they have low incomes still claim middle-class social position. There are some "culture-wide goals" which tend to tear down class divisions. Clyde Kluckhohn and Florence R. Kluckhohn have schematized with a word or phrase the generalized value orientations of Americans into three groups: the View of Life, the Individual in Life, and the Individual and Social Values. The View of Life, the portion of the schema most relevant here, is characterized by "Effort and Optimism" with attendant traits of "moral purpose" and "rationalism." Americans are eager to get things done. For them this is a world in which effort triumphs. Their efforts are usually clothed with moral justifications, even when these are only rationalizations. The Kluckhohns make the incisive comment:

> The actual pursuit of power, prestige and pleasure for their own sakes must be disguised (if public approval is to be obtained) as action for a moral purpose or as later justified by "good works." Conversely, a contemplative life tends to be considered "idleness." "Externalism" combined with "moral purpose" gives "virtuous materialism." [8]

There is a tendency in all this to assume that reasonable behavior and morality coincide and that morality and expediency are quite compatible.

American culture is still strongly characterized by romantic individualism in which both liberty and equality are affirmed. Social mobility and fluidity and the history of opportunity have tended to encourage both the idea of the "second chance" for the individual and his desire to prove that he is "as good as the next one." The cult of the individual who wants to get ahead plays into the cult of work and worldly success. Striving for money reflects a deeper competition for power and prestige. "The only way to be safe in American life is to be a success. Failure to 'measure up' is felt as deep personal inadequacy. In a phrase, the American creed is equality of opportunity, not equality of man." [9]

The American social situation with its many tensions and social

---

[8] Clyde and Florence R. Kluckhohn, "American Culture: Generalized Orientations and Class Patterns," in Lyman Bryson, and others, eds., *Conflicts of Power in Modern Culture* (New York: Harper & Bros., 1947), p. 110. Used by permission of the publisher.

[9] *Ibid.,* p. 113.

stresses makes for a neurotic uneasiness which in turn affects the value patterns of consumption. We have earlier noted the mass economic upheavals of urban and rural life, the historic lack of attention to the human problems of industrial civilization, the impersonality of the social organization of cities, the still bubbling melting pot, the transitory geographic residence of millions of people, the social mobility from class to class, and the weakening of supernatural sanctions. All of these tend to make individuals feel adrift and lacking in significant meaning. They may encourage even more the drive for status and prestige and for the immediacy of pleasure, delusive though these may all be in relation to man's fundamental needs.

A characteristic American trait has been the "cult of the average man." On the one hand, this has meant the conception of a society where the lot of the common man would be made easier, where the same opportunities would be available to all, and where the lives of all would be ennobled and enriched. On the other hand, the "cult of the average man" tends to mean conformity to the standards of the current majority.[10] This tendency has been brilliantly described in Riesman's *The Lonely Crowd* as the social character called "other directedness." In a sense everybody wants to be himself and everybody wants to be like everybody else. Advertising has played on this paradoxical theme with great success. Wanting to be with people like oneself has also made of America a nation of joiners.

Change is an important value to Americans. Carl Becker has shown how deeply the idea of progress has taken root in the culture. He says, "The doctrine of progress makes a virtue of novelty and disposes men to welcome change as in itself a sufficient validation of their activities."[11] Consumption habits make conformity to current changes almost imperative.

Pleasure is also an important principle. Increasingly people want to have a good time. This principle is in conflict with some of the traditional Puritan virtues which tended to stress "work for work's sake." There is a resultant bipolarity of recreation and guilt feeling for it.

Another trait which influences the consumption profile of Americans is externalism—the love of bigness. This trait tends toward the worship

[10] *Ibid.*, p. 115.
[11] Quoted from *The Heavenly City of the 18th Century Philosophers* in the article by the Kluckhohns.

of size and evaluation in terms of numbers. Along this same line the criticism is made that Americans are "contemptuous of ideas but amorous of devices." Money tends to be the symbol of "success." "Status in the United States is determined more by the number and price of automobiles, air-conditioning units, and the like owned by a family than by the number of their servants or the learning and esthetic skills of family members." [12]

Consumer profiles are related also to the goals of the middle class. They lay great stress on the acquisition of property and on piling up capital goods. Property and ownership are both important. Good standing in the community is also emphasized, involving strict sex taboos (now breaking down), cleanliness, emotional control, good manners, belonging to respectable companies and businesses, respect for law, good works of charity, and good education. Parents are willing to go to great lengths to help the children get ahead. Education is one of the major means of improving one's class and social status. Indeed education is often evaluated in terms of the earning power of persons of different levels of formal education.

The profile of American consumption can be fruitfully analyzed by noting how consumers spend their dollars and by relating this division of the dollar to the value profiles of Americans. In 1954 the U.S. Department of Commerce reported that American consumers had a total outlay of $236,532,000,000, divided as follows:

Group	(Millions) Dollars	Per cent of total
Food, alcohol, and tobacco	78,586	33.1
Clothing, accessories, jewelry	24,545	10.4
Personal care	2,759	1.2
Housing	27,758	12.6
Household operation	30,776	13.0
Medical care and death expenses	11,756	5.0
Personal business	11,379	4.8
Transportation	26,928	11.4
Recreation	12,220	5.2
Private education and research	2,605	1.1
Religious and welfare activities	3,202	1.4
Foreign travel and remittances—net	2,018	.8

[12] *Ibid.*, p. 118.

This table is very revealing in confirming the anthropological profile presented by the Kluckhohns. It makes quite vivid also the difficult problem of bringing consumption more into line with Christian ideas of sharing and responsibility. The educational task of changing the materialism of American life involves coming to grips with the forces in society that din the values now prevalent into the minds and desires of the people. One of these forces, itself characteristic of the culture, is advertising. Through the study of advertising, the larger forces which determine values become evident. Advertising is the showcase of desire.

E. Ethical Problems in Advertising

In the field of consumption advertising plays an important and powerful role. Advertising is an aggressive force in a market situation where production takes the initiative, not waiting for consumer demand to determine the kind or quality of goods to be produced and distributed. For example, the increased demand for cigarettes is not a wholly spontaneous one. Cigarette companies have devoted millions of dollars and great skill to inducing consumer desire and manipulating choices. Many other great corporations have similarly striven to convert "supply" into "demand" and have been effective in changing consumer habits.

Advertising is an offensive weapon to increase the business of one company at the expense of another and which tries to penetrate the consumer field even to the extent of "high-pressure" invasion of personality, tastes, and time of individuals. In the war of competition advertising is also defensive, of course. Counteroffensive action is generally the best defense. But between offensive and defensive advertising, and other sales methods, the consumer is generally the victim, for the cost of the battle is passed on to him in terms of waste and higher prices.

Advertising as such is not necessarily a social evil. It may be argued with plausibility that much advertising performs a public service in that it promotes mass distribution and makes mass production more effective. Advertising frequently provides useful and reliable information about products, business, and technological advances. Because of advertising newspapers, periodicals, radio and television stations, are developed and supported. Widespread advertising through the media of mass communication helps to keep the market national and even

238

international in scope to the advantage of the consumer who otherwise might have his choices limited to more parochial dimensions.

Three points of view [13] are often presented on the relation of production to consumer demand: (1) that the businessman should produce only in response to a given consumer demand and that, accordingly, he should not attempt to influence that demand except by offering information to the consumers as to the availability of the goods; (2) that the businessman can legitimately attempt to influence consumer demand, but because his power over standards, values, and wants is so great, this power must be exercised with great restraint; and (3) that businessmen are not and should not be the guardians of morality and hence should be entirely free to employ sales techniques and advertising methods as they choose. One's response to these points of view depends in part on the question of fact as to how influential advertising is in shaping cultural patterns. Advertising, one may assume, continues to be employed because it is effective in the market place.

When we recall the basic function of the economic order, that production does not exist for its own sake but for the service of the consumer, it becomes clear that the burden of proof is on the producer. Consumers have some freedom, but they are unorganized and weak in comparison with producers. Advertising plays a conspicuous part in the wholesale commercialization of culture and is in this regard an agent of the materialistic miseducation of the people. Some of the worst middle-class tendencies which threaten Christian standards are especially encouraged by the appeals used in advertising. Sexual display, class status, outdoing the neighbors, appearing wealthy, and self-display are all incessantly encouraged. To predetermine the choices of buyers, appeals are made to family love, emulation, pugnacity, imitation of social leaders, sex attraction, and the fear of failure in some part of life's natural expectations. Advertisers also often make a perverse use of religion, patriotism, state and local pride, and group loyalty. The advertising itself involves in many cases not only the questionable device of the indefinite comparative, but downright duplicity, the raising of false hopes, a superficial view of life, and the debauchery of national standards.

[13] Bowen, *op. cit.*, p. 215.

These ethical problems of advertising are closely related to all the other devices used today to influence buying. What justification is there for the invasion of the privacy of persons by door-to-door selling by salesmen who come unannounced? What defense can morally be made for systematically seeking to make people dissatisfied with what they have? What can be said for the ballyhoo methods, the chances, the prizes, the hawking, and the contests which in addition are frequently in poor taste? In an appeal for freedom of the consumer Moneta Soper writes:

> I would like:—freedom from coupons . . . —freedom from stamps that can be collected for prizes . . . —freedom from liquor ads in my mailbox addressed to Occupant . . . —freedom from fancy, expensive packaging; and from buying six big refrigerator covers I don't want to get the three little ones I need . . . —freedom from contests and prizes . . . —freedom from opulent chrome and nauseous color combinations . . . —freedom from advertising pressures based on stimulated wants, not needs; and appeal to motives that are false.[14]

The chief moral issues that arise from advertising and closely related salesmanship today may be summarized as follows: the distortion of economic goals through the domination of production over consumption, the problem of truth, the freedom of the consumer, the manipulation of the person, and the perversion or debauching of cultural standards. These problems are so acute that they require action not only on the part of responsible businessmen but on the part of government to protect the welfare of the people. As in all forms of effective cultural change the approach has to be many-sided.

In seeking to bring advertising under rational and moral control, it is well to be reminded, as J. K. Galbraith seeks to do,[15] that a mere diminution in the waste of advertising will not inevitably result in a qualitative improvement in consumption. He points out that the waste of advertising is only a part of the larger waste which results from the fact that we have production facilities in excess of our ability to use them intelligently at present. It is part of the problem of learning to live in an age of increasing abundance.

[14] *Christian Advocate*, 138 (September 1, 1955), No. 33.
[15] *American Capitalism* (Boston: Houghton Mifflin Co., 1956), pp. 102, 108-9.

F. The Educational Challenge

Changing advertising methods and techniques is not the royal road to responsible consumption. Advertising exhibits the need for an all-out educational effort to define and refine the economic goals of society. If it is true as C. Wright Mills argues in *The Power Elite* that our national purpose is business prosperity measured in dollars and volume of production of those things it is profitable to private business to produce, then education is challenged to examine whether the nation should continue to make "democratic welfare" an adjunct to "business welfare." If it is true that private business is not really interested in such social needs as better schools, well-paid public-school teachers, socially adequate housing for the mass of the population, qualitative human adequacy and balance in the development of persons and families, then education is challenged to make these consumers' needs more dominant than it has in the past. If it is true that the people are pressure-sold, or "presold," so as to lose sight of those unseen group and personal values which are indispensable to a responsible democratic society in favor of values which are transiently popular and visible, then education is challenged to come to grips with the whole profile of consumers' values.

The critical power of the educational apparatus of American life is enormous. The quality of consumers' decisions is amenable to the educational process. Through widespread efforts extending from elementary public schools to the universities in co-operation with P.T.A.'s, boys' clubs, girls' clubs, churches, and the like significant transformations in the critical capacity and refinement of tastes can be achieved. As a result the consumer can achieve a greater initiative with respect to the goals of economic life. If tender love, imitation, emulation, pugnacity, sex attraction—everything human—can be used to predetermine the choices of consumers, the educational process can be employed to bring these under more rational control. Religion, patriotism, state and local pride, and group loyalty need not be placed on just one side of the scale of preference.

Consumer education must take into consideration the total cultural context as it affects values. Better consumer education is a function of the whole community. It must become a matter of university research, of ethical investigation, of professional training, of church discussion,

241

and of community planning. The goal of such education is the free and responsible consumer. Let us note briefly a few of the elements in such a community-wide approach:

1. Relating the present behavior of the system of production and distribution to the acknowledged spiritual and moral goals of the culture. There is need to face frankly the contradictions among the values now being sought. Those values coherent with personal and community ideals of responsible living must be emphasized.

2. Measuring the economy and economic life by qualitative rather than predominantly quantitative standards and teaching the habit of doing so. Education and action should not be authoritarian. Consumers need the tools for improving the quality of their choices.

3. Improving the educational opportunity of all young persons so that they may develop their own potentialities to the full.

4. Helping persons to gain insight as to why values like prestige, power, material success, conspicuous display, and the like are so prominent.

5. Developing community codes regarding the activities of youth, so that parents are not victimized by competitive family pressures.

6. Developing programs of family-life education, including training in budgeting, so that good taste and community concern are the common possession of future family units.

7. Teaching the soundest principles of private and public assistance to persons and families whose incomes fall below an acceptable minimum.

8. Developing an intelligent concern for those portions of the world where the people are newly awakening to the possibilities of a better life and a sense of solidarity with them in the struggle against poverty, ignorance, and disease.

Social Welfare and Church-State Relations

In an earlier chapter we surveyed some contemporary Christian attitudes toward the welfare state and drew certain conclusions about the role and limitations of governmental action. Much welfare is fostered privately by individuals and by voluntary associations. As we shall see, the voluntary association is a significant force in social life far beyond the field of social welfare. After acknowledging this fact we shall turn to such issues as the church's response to the new situation created by the vast development of public welfare, the relation of church welfare agencies to other private agencies, the modification of roles which is now taking place, and the distinctive emphases of the church. Then I shall present some of the problems in the relation of church and state which social welfare and public education today involve.

Between the institution of the state and the individual exists a wide range of subsidiary organizations based on the principle of voluntary association. These associations serve a great variety of ends such as professional standards, taxpayers' interests, family services, consumers' needs, health and social welfare, and so on. Every American community is honeycombed by multifarious societies such as these. They serve to keep society pluralistic and responsive to the felt needs of its members. Here untold millions of persons in tens of thousands of small groups participate in creating the ethos of national and international community. Through these agencies much of the power and concern of the people is expressed on specific issues. Here the ethos of the community is renewed or adapted to the changing social scene. Here, in part, the policies of the state and the efforts of national power groups are subjected to the critical responses of the people. Through these voluntary associations minority groups of all types get a name and a voice and seek to express their point of view with effectiveness.

Of the voluntary associations those related to social welfare and social work have played a significant role. Historically, the churches were dominant societies in caring for the sick, the destitute, the orphaned, and the bereft, but later private nonsectarian and public agencies have assumed larger roles. The expansion of participation in and responsibility for social welfare on the part of private nonsectarian and governmental agencies has raised important issues of the relation of church and state, the relation of churches to specialization and professional competence, and the co-ordination of all services in the community. Since social work and social service embody the values of improving the social environment and experiences of persons, they have a close relation to social welfare as it affects social action and reform.

A. Churches and the New Situation in Welfare

Greater resources, greater sensitivity to the range of human need, and greater acceptance of the goal of human fulfillment have nurtured the rapid development of the concept of social welfare.[1] Under Protestant, Anglican, and Eastern Orthodox church auspices more than 3,000 health and welfare agencies and institutions are operated with the help of some 25,000 "church social workers." These centers include homes for the aged, children's institutions, placement services, community centers and neighborhood houses, day nurseries, sheltered workshops for the handicapped, counseling clinics or centers, residences for young men and women, hospitals, clinics, homes for unmarried mothers, and the like. In the order of importance the bulk of the churches' welfare agencies are homes for the aged, hospitals, neighborhood houses and settlements, and institutions for the care of children.

Social welfare has expanded in a way that parallels society as a whole: the complexity of social life, the rapid shift of much of the population from a rural to a more urban society, tendencies toward specialization in industry and the professions, and the growth of specialized scientific knowledge. Private welfare programs have, however, expanded less than public programs. John W. McConnell points out that

---

[1] Horace Cayton and Setsuko Nishi, *Churches and Social Welfare*, Vol. II. *The Changing Scene: Current Trends and Issues,* "Churches and Social Welfare," Vol. II (New York: National Council of Churches, 1955).

total private welfare expenditures were probably $1,278,000,000 in 1930, $1,419,000,000 in 1940, and $4,526,000,000 in 1950. Public welfare programs expanded from $1,288,000,000 in 1930 to $5,428,000,000 in 1940 and to $12,348,500,000 in 1950. Percentagewise private welfare constituted 49.8 of the 1930 total and 26.8 of the 1950 total expenditures. The total welfare expenditures in 1930 comprised 4.1 per cent of the national income, 9.5 per cent in 1940, and 8.3 per cent in 1950. Church welfare expenditures were approximately 3.4 per cent of the total welfare expenditures of the United States in 1949 and 1950. They were about 13.5 per cent of all private welfare expenditures.[2]

Along with the expansion of social welfare has gone a development in the pattern of the financial context. McConnell's summary is instructive, covering a thirty-year period:

1. The shifting of the financial burden of individual dependency (direct relief) from private agencies, local government, and religious groups to state and federal government;

2. The devotion of professional skill and resources of the private agencies to personal and family adjustment, group recreation and education, experimental programs and research;

3. The co-ordination and improved administrative efficiency of private and voluntary welfare agencies;

4. The growth of the concept of systematic provision in advance for presumptive need through social insurance, planned public works and government fiscal policy;

5. The assumption by industry of a major share of the financial responsibility for welfare and the increasing initiative exerted by both industry and unions in the development of private welfare.[3]

The participation of the state in welfare expresses the growth of a sense of inclusive community responsibility for well-being of persons, but it has precipitated a reaction in the churches with respect to many issues, the most basic of which is a concern for deepening the theological and philosophical foundations of welfare. Although the churches were among the earliest groups to minister to the inadequate or the unfortunate, there was a tendency to hold that charity was intended

[2] John W. McConnell, "Welfare," in J. Frederic Dewhurst and others, *America's Needs and Resources: A New Survey* (New York: Twentieth Century Fund, 1955), p. 430. Used by permission of the publisher.
[3] *Ibid.*, p. 430.

for the deserving, that is, for those of the right religious faith. It was necessary to expand responsibility and to co-ordinate charitable efforts. Protestant leaders often took the initiative in these programs especially in the family welfare field, but the task was complicated by the multiplicity of agencies representing nonsectarian groups, not to mention the Jewish, Catholic, Lutheran, and other societies. Complete and well-organized coverage of welfare needs required not only co-operation, consolidation, and co-ordination but also the direct involvement of public institutions. With the entry of the public agencies the questions of the right division of labor and the rationale of church-sponsored welfare naturally arose.

F. Emerson Andrews has shown how private voluntary work today is supplementary to sound public welfare provisions. He says:

In broad generalization, public agencies undertake to meet, more or less adequately, basic economic, health, and education needs; in some cases for the whole population, in others for only certain specific classes of the disadvantaged. To voluntary agencies remain the important tasks of filling in gaps and inadequacies in these fields, of establishing standards and checking the work of public agencies, of covering many additional needs not now met by government, and of doing most of the exploratory, experimental, and research work.[4]

Some feel that the supplementary role of private agencies is in fact that of caring for residual needs.

B. Responses of the Churches

The response of the churches to the new situation referred to above has been more than trying to find residual functions in the interstices of public welfare. There has been a renewed concern for the foundations, motivations, and responsibilities of persons and programs. Theological and philosophical perspectives have been enriched and deepened. These include a renewal of the Christian conception of God and man and their implications for service and social transformation. Christian faith sees man as a total person, rooted in a living relationship with God, a relationship which involves decision, commitment, and harmonious life in community with one's fellow men. Christian

[4] *Philanthropic Giving* (New York: Russell Sage Foundation, 1950), p. 112; quoted in Cayton and Nishi, *op. cit.*, p. 27.

faith emphasizes the initiative of God in love for man and the world, a reconciliation of the world to God through the life, death, and resurrection of Jesus Christ. Christian faith expresses itself in the new community of the people of God, the church, in which the Holy Spirit enlivens the forgiven and forgiving sinners. This fellowship has as its vocation under God not its own ends but a ministry for the sake of the whole world. From the Christian perspective social service has a twofold task, one remedial and philanthropic, and one preventive and positively humanitarian. This means that Christian social welfare embraces both social work and social action. The Christian Church is committed by its very nature to personal redemption and social salvation, that is, to acts of redemptive love in the lives of persons and to programs seeking the transformation of society as a whole.

Though institutional church welfare represents only 13 per cent of private welfare and only 3.4 per cent of all welfare as measured in dollars, the churches have an inclusive concern for the motivations of all welfare, the quality of its personnel, and the aims and objectives of its programs.

There emerge from the interaction of nonsectarian, public, and church-related types of social welfare certain areas of agreement and disagreement between the churches and secular social welfare. The points of agreement are numerous as the preparatory studies for the National Conference on the Churches and Social Welfare in 1955 indicated.[5] Both are concerned with the search for and the realization of the highest conceivable personal and social values. Both believe in the dignity of man, his intrinsic worth, his right to achieve an abundant life, to exercise freedom within the law, and to enjoy as much happiness as is possible in an imperfect world. Family discord and disorganization are sources of deep concern to the churches as well as to other social welfare agencies. Such problems are often so involved and complex that unilateral diagnoses and treatments are both inadequate and unrealistic. The churches and other welfare agencies often work in partnership in the amelioration of many such community problems.

The points of tension and disagreement also tend to cover a wide range of topics. Churches in their concern for the spiritual needs of persons often feel that social welfare generally and on occasion only

[5] See Charles G. Chakerian, *The Churches and Social Welfare,* The Hartford Seminary Foundation, Bulletin No. 20, Fall, 1955, pp. 14-15.

superficially honors spiritual welfare while serving temporal or physical requirements. Welfare agencies tend to see spiritual welfare as only one among man's many needs, whereas the churches regard this standpoint as a violation of the basic situation of man. Social work tends to look askance at the professional "do-gooder," the reformer, the zealously and protestingly generous person who is poorly grounded in the theory and practice of social work and yet enters the field professionally. Then, too, there lingers the idea of the "worthy poor" which causes misunderstanding. Social workers sometimes feel that the churches exploit the poor or the disadvantaged through their "charitable" activities because the church leaders use biblical passages to show how virtuous it is to minister to the needs of the poor.

From the side of the churches the complaint is frequently made that professional social workers are not generally concerned with the religious welfare of their clients and that they ignore or sometimes even offer advice or help which is contrary to the religious beliefs or convictions of their clients. Many social workers apparently lack a deep religious experience. Religious insight is needed to keep a wholesome attitude toward those for whom one has responsibilities and to preserve perspective and wholeness in one's outlook toward life and one's vocation within it. Religion gives significance to welfare work and the causes which it serves by relating them to one's ultimate concern and the purposes of the divine love.

In addition to this general difficulty many church people find that some social workers are religiously illiterate, lacking knowledge of the teachings, history, and philosophy of Christianity and an ignorance of church polity and policy. These weaknesses are sometimes at the root of the breakdown of communications between the churches and social agencies. On the one hand, social welfare finds the division of Christianity into hundreds of competing church bodies a source of bewilderment, confusion, and practical chaos. On the other hand, churches find that welfare agencies often do not know the churches' place in community organization as well as they know that of secular institutions. The church is by its nature a community welfare resource.

A special challenge confronts the professional education of both the Christian minister and the social worker. Churches have a responsibility to help recruit personnel for the whole welfare field, for there is a great dearth of qualified workers. Instruction in theological seminaries should be in close co-operation with the resources of graduate schools of social work. All ministers need to be able (1) to recognize the symptoms of individual and social problems; (2) to know the techniques of making proper referrals; (3) to understand effective participation in community welfare work; and (4) to appreciate and co-operate with the professional social worker's role in the community. Where fully trained staff are not available, church-sponsored services should take maximum advantage of professional consultation and, where relevant, supervision by their own national consultants. Similarly there should be constant communication with national social work organizations and state and community-wide standards-setting bodies in the social work field.

Since clergymen and social workers have so much in common in direct service to persons and groups, they also have common interests in the field of social action. Many problems can be successfully attacked only by community-wide approaches which involve new state and Federal legislation or local political action. Christian leaders in social action need a good grounding not only in theology and social ethics but also in economics, sociology, anthropology, political science, and history. To accomplish the above goals calls for a widespread and persistent educational program in the churches so that enough workers properly motivated, well-educated, and grounded in the historic religious origins of our civilization may be available. Graduate schools of social work need also to become more inclusive in their understanding of and co-operation with religious leadership and institutions. Both clergymen and social workers need to understand one another's language, aims, goals, and methods more fully. This understanding involves an appreciation of one another's limitations. Such interprofessional knowledge will not of itself resolve differences in approach, philosophy, and social objectives, but it will tend to clarify the areas of responsibility, agreements, and differences.

C. Church-State Issues

Contemporary concern that no person should fall below a certain standard of well-being economically or go without certain essential services raises consequently a number of questions in the field of church-state relations. We have already noted that the sheer bulk of public welfare evokes the question of the role of private agencies, especially those which are church-sponsored. Some leaders maintain that the major role of private agencies is (1) to pioneer new areas, (2) to introduce new methods and (3) to stand as watchdog over the social and spiritual life of the individual. The creative role of private agencies in general and of the church within the field of private agencies needs constantly to be redefined.[6]

The church has clearly a responsibility for keeping the whole community sensitively motivated to all welfare needs. It can render assistance in interpreting previously unrecognized need. It can help interpret the role of the so-called "welfare state" in its community outreach. The church can be more selective in the area of welfare responsibility than the government. But the question arises of what conferring, if any, a church-related agency should do with public agencies before initiating a new service or expanding an existing one.

Church-state relations are involved in the question of professional standards. Comparisons are sometimes made to the detriment of church social agencies. On the other hand, private agencies sometimes view public welfare efforts with condescension. It is often assumed that because the state can command through taxation and legislative grants large sums of money, it is the pace setter in social work standards, in facilities, and in educational requirements for social workers. On the other hand, it is sometimes assumed that private agencies are in a position to set the standard for the profession. In any case church social welfare is challenged to come to terms with the question of standards. Social work associations in setting standards should constantly review them in the light of changing conditions and scientific knowledge and should give impartial guidance to all types of agencies and their personnel.

Some look upon standards setting by government as an attempt to impose the authority of the state on church-related agencies. Yet it is clear that adequate standards of welfare work must be met no matter who renders the service. This is reflected in the license procedure of some states. There is evidence that sometimes church social agencies mask low standards by an appeal to the spiritual dimension of church social welfare as contrasted with that of a "secular" agency. Perhaps the churches along with all private agencies should seek to be pace

---

[6] See Chakerian, *op. cit.*, "Church-State Issues."

setters in the matter of standards and then help the public agencies by arousing community support and motivation for excellent standards in these agencies. If the sectarian agency is to serve as a yardstick for public enterprise, it must be free of public restriction and caprice to do the experimental projects which blaze new trails.

In addition to standards there is the question of the ministry of religion within public welfare agencies. In spiritual service the church is unique. It is recognized as occupying that field, and its resources should be utilized. Within public welfare agencies the churches feel a stake in an adequate religious ministry to persons who are served by these agencies. What over-all policy should govern the relationships here involved? What is the limit of the responsibility of public agencies for providing for a religious ministry? I have already indicated that church leaders may help to sensitize the community to its welfare needs. This may be done through direct participation as board members, as local, state, or national study committee members, as responsible citizens, as educators of the people, who in turn make decisions affecting policy and financing of public welfare. Ministers also serve as counselors in working co-operatively with social workers in public programs. But further questions of the direct relations of clients to religious ministration remain. How will a public institution deal with multifarious denominations, especially when they press their individual claims and interests strongly? In some places the public agencies will deal only with ecumenical agencies such as councils of churches. Is this the proper solution? Beyond ecumenical co-operation among Protestants, what is the proper relation to interfaith problems?

With their belief in the separation of church and state and their more pluralistic approach to the community, Protestants tend to be more hospitable than Roman Catholics to the assumption of welfare responsibility by secular institutions. At the same time the right of sectarian agencies to protect their own vested interests and therefore to oppose certain public assumption of welfare responsibility must be affirmed. The role of the state as against sectarian effort should be clearly marked and rigorously separated. Much research is needed to help redefine the separation of church and state as public welfare expands.

Closely related is the question of proper referrals. There is considerable concern that the process of referrals be improved so that the person in need can be most adequately served. The special claims of religious

251

groups sometimes make this difficult. Perhaps the principle of sound reciprocity in referrals is the key concept. Sound referrals are based on knowledge of the resources, on good working relationships, on professional confidence among the workers, and on efficient working procedures.

Another issue in church-state relations has to do with the role of the church in welfare legislation and administration. The situation in the field of religion and public education tends to color or even determine the pattern outside education. We may therefore pause to consider education briefly. Protestants and Roman Catholics differ strongly on this matter. The Roman Catholic Church places the educational responsibility under the family and the family under the church. Therefore it takes a strictly authoritarian position both on all matters relating to the family and on the education of its members.

In 1947 the Everson case arose in Ewing, New Jersey, when an effort was made by Roman Catholics to obtain tax aid in the payment of bus fares for their children who attended parochial schools. The United States Supreme Court ruled five to four that bus fares were paid not to schools but only to individual pupils. In this case the Supreme Court interpreted the First Amendment of the Constitution as follows:

No tax in any amount, large or small, can be levied to support any religious activities or institutions, whatever they may be called, or whatever form they may adopt to teach or practice religion. . . . Neither a state nor the Federal Government can, openly or secretly, participate in the affairs of any religious organizations or groups or vice versa. In the words of Jefferson, the clause against establishment of religion by law was intended to erect "a wall of separation between Church and State." [7]

In 1948 in the McCollum case from Champaign, Illinois, the court ruled that religious instruction conducted in public-school buildings in collaboration with school authorities was plainly a violation of the First Amendment.

Churches are bound to be concerned about political action and legislation on such themes as social security, family assistance, adoptions, planned parenthood, hospital facilities and services, housing projects, and the like. They are therefore bound to educate their constit-

[7] Quoted in J. M. Dawson, *America's Way in Church, State, and Society* (New York: The Macmillan Co., 1953), p. 37.

uencies, the public, and legislative committees about their convictions in this matter. On some of these issues, primarily education and family matters, Protestants are to be expected to take a different stand from Roman Catholics. In so doing they will be concerned not only about the legislation involved but also about the administration of the law. Much legislation is necessarily written in broad terms and leaves large discretion to administrators and administrative commissions. The stake of the church in public administration is, consequently, quite as significant as in legislation itself. Private agencies should be watchdogs not only of the standards of public welfare but also of the administration of the law in which the program of welfare is cast.

Another significant area of church-state relations has to do with policies determining the expenditure of public funds. Here again the tensions created in the field of education carry over into welfare. In many church-related agencies, such as hospitals and nursing homes, the question of use of public funds arises. Protestants have shown greater reluctance to take advantage of the provisions of the Hill-Burton Act (1946) than Roman Catholics. Up to June 1952 of a total of $87,476,600 the Roman Catholics had received $68,143,000, or 78 per cent, for church hospitals. A Roman Catholic hospital is not a nonsectarian institution. Protestants in general, but especially Baptists, have opposed such federal grants in principle. There is not only the question of facilities but also that of grants for service. Should the principle of "fee for service" be the policy? How can the freedom of a church-related institution be maintained if it receives public funds? Then there are issues such as the legitimate expectations of the community from a hospital which receives public funds but which is a sectarian institution, no other hospital service being available in the community. What modification in sectarian policies may be expected especially in the service rendered to patients of other faiths under these circumstances? What standards may the government impose as a condition of expenditure of public funds? May the government request a modification of sectarian practices if it gives fee-for-service support? Some would argue that when a church-related agency offers service not provided by a public agency, the entire community should support this program and public funds should be expended for such service, especially when it has been evaluated by competent personnel and by scientific research methods. Others would propose that the church in

253

the above situation should regard its role as that of guiding a pilot project, relinquishing its sectarian character when the community has become aware of its general responsibility to meet the particular need. In this field of co-operation much research on sound policy remains to be done.

Tension in church-state relations frequently arises in the area of family service and adoption procedures. The family has been accorded through religious tradition the basic role of determining the character development of children, along with many other values. Historically, the church has maintained a close tie to the family and a sense of obligation for protecting it as the basic unit of society. Sectarian and nonsectarian social work has been extensive in the family field. But here, too, public agencies have increasingly developed family case work and other services and concerns.

Some of the conflict areas arise out of various church attitudes toward legislation and procedures in the setting up of mothers' clinics, in developing planned parenthood centers, in adoption policies, and the like. Questions of significance in adoptions include the following: How are the wishes of the natural mother, her baptismal status, her religious perferences, the claims of her church, the suitability of the foster family, and the individual needs of the child to be balanced against one another? How can welfare service and the necessary work of the courts be brought into the most fruitful relation to each other? How can the administrative process be made to serve the best human values in this field and be faithful to the legal intention of the community? The churches must always press the question: What guidance does love give to justice in personal and interpersonal relationships?

D. *Religion in the Public School*

The problem of religion in education is a crucial one for the schools play a decisive part in inculcating and developing the ethos of contemporary society. The public school is a community creating agency of vast and pervasive power. Its ability to create democratic unity amidst the diversity and plurality of various national and ethnic strains in American life can hardly be overestimated. Religion is related to basic education in three ways: through what religious institutions do in parochial schools and in part-time instruction in their own facilities,

254

through what churches and synagogues are permitted to do in public school buildings and curriculums, and through what public schools themselves provide. The decisions of the Supreme Court define what churches and synagogues are permitted to do in the public school. They do not define what the public school of itself is able to do and responsible for. It is the meaning of this responsibility with which we are here concerned.

The separation of church and state ought never to be confused with the idea of the separation of religion and public order. The Northwest Ordinance of 1787, re-enacted in 1791, provided that every sixteenth section of public land should be sold or held for school buildings and maintenance. In Article 3 of this ordinance it says: "Religion, morality, and knowledge, being necessary to good government and the happiness of mankind, schools and the means of education shall forever be encouraged."

Some denominational groups have condemned the public school as "godless" or atheistic. We may dispose of this sophism at once. To conduct education for the community within the framework of secular control is not equivalent to secularist education. Indeed, some spiritual values may be possible of realization within the democratic freedom of the public school that are not possible under authoritarian ecclesiastical control. In the next place, the democratic values of public education rest on conceptions of personality which in American culture feed on its religious heritage. Churches and synagogues have a stake in the preservation of the democratic valuation of man. This value is not only personal but interpersonal and intergroup, as is evident in the support which the churches have given to the decision on desegregation by the Supreme Court. To affirm that democratic public education is in principle "godless" means to deny the sacred character of moral law and the natural law in all its forms.

The public school sustains a complex relation to the whole community. Since it represents all the people, it stands, in a sense, above all social, economic, and political issues which confront the nation. At the same time it provides one of the great avenues of meeting, where all creeds, beliefs, and values are treated in an atmosphere of mutual respect and fair play. Moreover, the school of the whole community recognizes the place of minority or deviant groups. Finally, it has the additional responsibility in a democracy as a training ground for citi-

255

zenship where persons learn to take a stand on the issues of the day.

The public schools cannot do everything which religious groups hope for in the education of their young, but they can do much as is evident when once one distinguishes between the religious quality of experience and its structured doctrinaire sectarian expression.[8] For one thing, the schools can foster appreciation for the religious attitude toward life. This attitude includes a cosmic perspective in which daily problems and individual needs are evaluated. It includes an awareness that the good things of life are not only of man's own making but the result of all things working together for good. It includes a sense of man's continuity with the rest of humanity, with nature, and the vast resources which are at his disposal. It includes an attitude toward reality of which he is a part and which sustains him. It includes, as Tillich says, an "ultimate concern about the ultimate," an attitude toward those values which are supremely worthful. Thus we may conclude that the public school may properly nurture the religious attitude by involving young people in experiences which give rise to it. They may be led to have insight as to how religion includes dedication of the whole self to seek ideal values and to serve others in the community.

The public school not only may develop appreciation for the religious attitudes, but it may teach appreciation for the place of religion in the community. There are many opportunities in historical and social studies to acquaint young people with the constructive functions of churches and synagogues in society. Religious institutions are an integral part of social life and should be discussed along with other community-wide institutions. The atmosphere of the school is the product of many factors and affects the quality of the appreciation I have been stressing. Thus the curriculum, the attitude of the administration, the philosophy of the faculty, the counseling program, and the extracurricular activities play their respective parts in a sound approach to the issues under discussion.

In addition there is much that may be learned about religion as it comes in naturally in history, literature, art, government, and social studies. This phase of the problem is so rich that it can only be mentioned here. No one can be a responsible member of Western society,

[8] See Ward Madden, *Religious Values in Education* (New York: Harper & Bros., 1951), p. 11.

nor adequately prepared to act responsibly with respect to the non-Western world today, if he is not reasonably well informed about the religious factor in culture. Many educators are convinced that world religions and the facts about American denominations can be successfully presented at both the elementary and secondary school level.

There are many practical problems that attend the realization of adequate religious instruction in the public school, but the value of it is too indispensable to be evaded or superficially approached. Spinoza's maxim may be appropriate that all things excellent are as difficult as they are rare. Nevertheless the community must continue to experiment in educational methods to fulfill the twofold aim of achieving wholeness of culture for every child and a democratic cohesive commmunity enriched by its diverse heritages.[9] The basic responsibilities of the home and the church are not impaired by such aims in the public school. Their duties of nurturing and instructing children in specific religious commitment, faith, and discipleship remain, for no agency of the state may take upon itself the task of ultimate dedication.

[9] See Claud D. Nelson, "Church and State" (New York: National Council of Churches, 1953), p. 33.

CHAPTER XIV

Responsible World Community

The idea of the responsible society is an inclusive world concept. Mankind not only is a natural unit of interaction and co-operation at the material level; it is also a moral society subject to moral law. More than this it is a community of the spirit whose Lord is Jesus Christ and who calls nations and the churches to responsible social action. The responsible society, as we have seen, is not a monolithic or authoritarian structure, neither is it a new *corpus Christianum,* an effort to revive medieval Christendom on a world basis. Responsibility is a quality of personal and social existence which must be developed at all levels of group life and in all its manifestations. In freedom and in justice men in political and economic authority are responsible to God and the people, whose welfare is affected by their power. In this concluding chapter I must now speak as concretely as possible on certain themes which follow in order: the Christian and war, international law and ethos, the Universal Bill of Rights and Freedoms, the penetration of the scientific attitude, the drives in the new nationalisms of the non-Western world, economic well-being, responses to the appeals of Communism, and the levels of responsibility which emerge in the present world situation.

A. *The Christian and War* [1]

The threat of war hangs over the head of all decision makers today. Three general positions on the question of war as an act of justice

[1] For a good outline of the background material in this vast field see Maston, *op. cit.,* ch. v, "War and Peace," and ch. x, "War and the Christian Conscience." A representative bibliography is cited in each of the chapters.

were recognized by the Amsterdam Assembly of the World Council of Churches:

(1) There are those who hold that, even though entering a war may be a Christian's duty in particular circumstances, modern warfare, with its mass destruction, can never be an act of justice.

(2) In the absence of impartial supra-national institutions, there are those who hold that military action is the ultimate sanction of the rule of law, and that citizens must be distinctly taught that it is their duty to defend the law by force if necessary.

(3) Others, again, refuse military service of all kinds, convinced that an absolute witness against war and for peace is for them the will of God and they desire that the Church should speak to the same effect.[2]

These three positions have not been further resolved since Amsterdam. Yet there is a persistent desire for a clearer and more common witness among Christians across the world. The Evanston Assembly made this quite definite and called for fresh efforts to bring the pacifist and nonpacifist perspectives into active communication with each other.[3] In response to the Evanston Assembly report Christian groups from many parts of the world have particularly endorsed the efforts to hold pacifist and nonpacifist attitudes together in a common Christian witness. A statement from India expresses the opinion that this portion of the report should lead to a deeper comparative study of violence and nonviolence as methods of political action.[4]

Despite marked differences among earnest Christians there are a number of convergent agreements[5] which should be noted: (1) that violence in war has become indiscriminate; (2) that it is highly doubtful that the injustice war seeks to overcome is actually greater than the injustice embodied in war itself and its aftermath, wherefore the "tradition of a just war is now challenged"; (3) that war may be suicidal and hence bereft of sanity. They further agree (4) that war virtual-

[2] W. A. Visser 't Hooft, ed., *The First Assembly of the World Council of Churches* (New York: Harper & Bros., 1948), pp. 89-90.

[3] Visser 't Hooft, *Evanston Report*, "Christians in the Struggle for World Community," par. 12. The three positions noted above are substantially those recognized in the Oxford Conference in 1937. See *Official Report*, pp. 162-65.

[4] R. S. Bilheimer, ed., *Response to Evanston* (Geneva: World Council of Churches, 1957), p. 36.

[5] See "The Christian Conscience and War," a Statement of a Commission of Theologians and Religious Leaders appointed by the Church Peace Mission, 1951.

ly knows no moral bounds. According to the report of the Dun Commission of the Federal Council of Churches, issued in 1950, we are now witnessing "an overwhelming break-through in the weak moral defenses to keep war in some bounds." (5) There is agreement that "preventive" war must be ruled out as well as (6) the doctrine that "war is inevitable" or ever anything but a last resort. (7) There is a common recognition that the struggle against totalitarianism is not exclusively or even primarily a military one. This struggle must be fought on political, economic, and spiritual grounds. There is real danger that military measures may actually interfere with the more basic economic, political, and spiritual strategy by which alone a democratic and humane regime or culture can ultimately be preserved. (8) Finally, there is a theological consensus that "war is always a demonstration of the power of sin in the world and a defiance of the righteousness of God as revealed in Jesus Christ and Him crucified." [6]

Pacifists and nonpacifists alike are becoming increasingly aware that all are involved in a perplexing and complex situation full of ambiguous moral decisions. Pacifism is not immune from ambiguous compromise. It is worth noting, however, that the Dun Commission, speaking in the main as a nonpacifist group, said:

> The clearest and least ambiguous alternative is that urged upon us by our most uncompromising pacifist fellow-Christians. . . . We believe that God calls some men to take the way of non-violence as a special high vocation in order to give a clearer witness to the way of love than those can give who accept responsibility for the coercion in civil society. We rejoice that God has called some of our brethren in universal Christian fellowship to bear this witness and are humbled by their faithfulness in bearing it.[7]

Not all Christians actively engaged in the ecumenical conversation are willing to take this view. Paul Tillich holds that theologically we should not require that war be renounced except in the ultimate sense in which we say that all crime and the like must and will end in the kingdom of God. Indeed, all social life exists in the context of power.

[6] Oxford Conference, *Official Report*, p. 162.

[7] Quoted from *The Christian Conscience and Weapons of Mass Destruction.* Copyright 1950 by The Federal Council of Churches (now the National Council of Churches). Used with permission.

Professor N. H. Søe of Copenhagen definitely disagrees with the concession made by the Dun Commission to pacifists: "If the pacifist position were a clearer witness to the way of love, I do not see how we could possibly consider it permissible not to take that position." Christians are certainly all called to a "special high vocation." There is no higher vocation than that of being in the fellowship of Christ. Søe is not certain that this special high vocation rules out war absolutely.[8]

The nature of the Christian peace testimony may be clarified to some extent by a frank recognition of some sources of confusion. Five of these may be briefly listed: (1) the accommodation of the church as a social institution to its cultural environment, especially to the nation-state and to countries involved in imperialism and counter-colonialism; (2) the anxiety of the church for its own institutional preservation; (3) the doctrine of the "lesser of two evils"; (4) the conflict with Communism; and (5) the spurious character of certain "peace movements."

This latter point we must dispose of first. The peace witness of the church must have integrity. It must front for no one. The church must unmask all peace fronts which are deceptive devices for aggression. In our time the most scandalous evils are perpetrated in the name of peace, democracy, justice, equality. So too in our time the worst public injustices are perpetrated in the name of anti-Communism and rooting out subversives. At the moment in America many people are afraid to be openly and honestly engaged in constructive peacemaking which is critical of the nation's foreign policies. The church should give morale to all conscientious peace action.

The greatest source of confusion in the peace witness of the church is its involvement in national feelings. This is so universal a phenomenon that it is largely overlooked. Nationalism is still man's other religion. The price of spiritual independence is as high as its virtue is rare.

Because the church is so important a factor in national unity and morale, it is in constant danger of being exploited for political and propagandist purposes by the nation. This problem confronts the in-

[8] "War and the Commandment of Love," *The Ecumenical Review*, April, 1954, p. 256. He adds: "An appeal to the idea of 'justice' or to the concept of a 'just war' as being something more fundamental and indisputable than what the New Testament calls love is of no Christian validity whatsoever."

tegrity of the Christian community in every part of the globe.[9] It takes subtle or gross forms, sometimes through efforts to identify the freedom of the Christian man and the claims of religious liberty with democracy and free enterprise, sometimes in the proposals of preventive war, and sometimes in the form of peace propaganda itself. The art of psychological manipulation today has gone to such lengths that aggression and tyranny often wear the masks of the people's peace and democracy, and reaction and colonialism wear the masks of self-righteous defense against totalitarianism.

The churches have yet to make clear to themselves and to their respective national cultures that the Christian cause may not be equated with any political or social ideologies or systems. Its capacity for discriminate judgment and its ability to transcend cultural ties must be greatly increased if it is to bear a united witness to a divided world. One of the church's greatest contributions is, therefore, to foster the sense of responsibility to God among people who are deluged by forces making for conformity to either East or West. Because Communism claims to provide a complete answer to all questions of life, the first answer of the church must be the renewal of the church itself. This answer is not military but spiritual. Christians in Communist-dominated countries and in portions of Asia where such domination is imminent must distinguish, as they give evidence of demonstrating, between the "social revolution which seeks justice and the totalitarian ideology which interprets and perverts it." On the other hand, this same insight must assist Christians in the West from a simple negative judgment about the East. As Professor Søe points out, "we must not forget that there is sufficient kinship between Christianity and the social ideals proclaimed by the East, to make considerable collaboration possible." [10] We are not permitted to bear false witness about either East or West.

There is a different problem in accepting the reality of the unity of

[9] Søe observes rightly: "We certainly ought to rejoice when a recent Vatican proclamation (*Institutiones Juris Publici Ecclesiastici*) declares that a war of aggression undertaken for the purpose of enforcing the rights of the aggressor state can no longer be regarded as a just war. But our rejoicing is somewhat tempered when we consider 'that it has always been possible for each government to satisfy its own citizens that a given war was essentially defensive on its part, or on some other ground just and unavoidable,' as the Statement rightly observes." *Ibid.*, p. 256.

[10] *Ibid*, p. 261.

means and ends. The Christian Church has a duty to civilization in holding this plumbline against the wall of argument regarding the use of violence and the institution of war. The doctrine of the lesser evil is often carelessly separated from the doctrine of the unity of means and ends. One line of argument is sometimes used to condemn totalitarianism; another line of argument is then used to permit the use of arms of mass destructiveness. Thus the Central Committee of the World Council of Churches argued in July, 1949: "Justice in human society is not to be won by totalitarian methods. The totalitarian doctrine is a false doctrine. It teaches that in order to gain a social or political end, everything is permitted. . . . It sanctions the use of all manner of means to overthrow all other views and ways of life." [11] On the other hand, the committee of the National Council of Churches dealing with weapons of mass destruction put themselves in a position where they are not willing to put a limit on the degree of destructiveness that may be permitted with Christian sanctions. The line of argument is familiar:

There can be no justice for man and no responsible freedom without law and order. . . . The law which gives any just order must be sustained by power, and, when necessary, by coercive power. . . . Can we extend the beginnings of this order in the United Nations, if we do not undergird it with effective power? In the last resort, we are in conscience bound to turn to force in defense of justice even though we know that the destruction of human life is evil. There are times when this can be the lesser of two evils, forced upon us by our common failure to achieve a better relationship.[12]

From this point it is not difficult to refuse to say in advance how vast the evil may be which in the name of justice and in the name of Christ one is permitted to inflict. In view of the total character of modern warfare and its incalculable consequences the difference between this ethic and the Communist position may not ultimately be as great as is frequently supposed. Can it be that for an alleged good end anything is allowed? The problematic character of all moral choices does not absolve the Christian from discovering the "lesser evil" and acting in love. But recourse to modern warfare is an appeal to incalculable evil.

[11] Central Committee of the World Council of Churches, "Statement on Totalitarianism," Chichester, July 9-15, 1949. *Statements of the World Council of Churches on Social Questions* (Geneva, 1956), p. 39.
[12] Dun Commission, *op. cit.*

Military budgets have a tendency to become insatiable. Hence war is the most serious danger to the life of abundance in the modern world. Economists like Kenneth Boulding and Roy Blough have repeatedly emphasized the gravity of this threat. A major war would destroy not only hope for increased abundance but the economic system, the political order on which it rests in large part, and perhaps even a major segment of the human race. Short of war, the armament race itself is a form of economic suicide. "Armament races have a tendency to expand as far as the economies of the countries will permit," according to Blough.[13] This may be an understatement. In the eighteenth century perhaps no country turned more than 5 per cent of its resources into a war effort. The Napoleonic wars, according to Boulding, could not have absorbed more than 10 per cent. But the Second World War absorbed about 50 per cent of the national income of the participating countries and penetrated deeply into the individual lives of all.[14] The arms race makes all systems of defense so unstable that it may absorb so ever-increasing a proportion of life and activity as to become intolerable. There are, therefore, other costs to the good life than the economic. "As long as the military establishment is inefficient it can be tolerated; when it becomes efficient it becomes intolerable because of its insatiable character." [15]

The unity of means and ends requires a radically fresh and creative approach in the Christian witness for a responsible society. The church cannot bear a clear testimony against war today without repudiating the H-bomb. It cannot today reject the bomb without repudiating war itself. But it must do more than repudiate war. It must seek the structures of peace.

B. International Law and Ethos

A growing ecumenical consensus favors the development of the UN for the defense of peace and justice, for the progressive development of international law, and for the building of a genuine world community. To accomplish an effective legal order above the states and achieve an international law with binding force for peace are both complex and difficult. Naturally the churches seek recognition of the

[13] "Christian Perspectives for an Age of Abundance" (New York: National Council of Churches, 1956) , p. 11.
[14] Boulding, op. cit., p. 61.
[15] Loc. cit.

sovereignty of God in the ordering of international affairs. They have long recognized that one of the root problems of international conflict is the power politics of sovereign national states.

International law in its present stage of development reflects the weakness of world society. Classical international law is by definition a complexus of contracts among sovereign national states. Baron von Asbuck, professor of international law at the University of Leyden, pointed out to the delegates of the Amsterdam Assembly that contemporary international law is hardly the "expression by a superior authority of the common conscience of a community, as is national law in homogeneous states." It is, rather, he said, in its "insincerities, inconsistencies and uncertainties . . . a compromise between group-interests determined by their relative power." [16] The importance of good law is not diminished by the obstacles to achieving it, however.

Much of this law came into existence at the time when several European imperialist powers were the rival leaders of vast colonial systems. In the revolutionary upheavals of today there is no common international ethos which can provide the substratum of law. It must be grown and forged amidst the emergent rivalries of powerful movements and ideologies.

We should not say that the world community has disintegrated. In a very real sense it has never existed. There never has been a genuine world community, bound together by a prelegal decision of a common conception of justice, common convictions on the purpose of man and human society. Scholars speak of a *corpus Christianum* in Europe which broke up at the end of the Middle Ages, but in the context of world society that body of Christendom was hardly more than a regional community. Today various religions, social conceptions, legal orders, and ideologies exist side by side, insulated or interrelated. Some of them are fundamentally disunited, connected by no common norms.[17] They are bound up with rival economic systems, procedures, and standards of living which add to the strain of foreign relations. The difficulties which this situation presents challenge the churches to take seriously every opportunity to contribute to the development of a

[16] World Council of Churches, *The Church and International Disorder* (New York: Harper & Bros., 1948), p. 57.
[17] *Ibid.*, p. 64.

true ecumenical ethos.[18] International law is more the fruit than the source of community.[19]

An international ethos must emerge from all the groups which participate significantly in world society. No one nation, group of nations, economic society, or religious body can provide such an ethos for others. But all countries must enter into an encounter with all others and trust that in the free market of ideas the common values will in due course elicit a common consent. The debates in the General Assembly of the UN and the many-sided discussions in the agencies of the UN play a great part in nourishing great universal ideas. Since ideals play a definitive role in channeling the energies of persons and groups, the education of mankind in terms of the universal rights and freedoms of man has a significant appeal. In the decades immediately ahead we may anticipate the most vigorous interaction of religions, philosophies, and rival ideologies. Unfortunately the market place of ideas will not be free. Ideas are weapons for power groups to use, and these groups will control the minds of men as they can. Nevertheless, the call to open and universal communication is the only call which fulfills the claims of responsibility.

Even where external power groups do not control them, diverse cultures are in conflict. The various cultures and nationalities represent not only twentieth-century conflicts but many different eras, epochs, and centuries of social, economic, and political development. Functioning at different stages in their technical development and bound together by the most varied internal ideals, they do not measure each other by the same yardsticks of value. Yet there are indications of general approval on many basic human values.

C. Declaration of Human Rights

The greatest significance of the Universal Bill of Rights and Freedoms is that it shows general unanimity among the personal and social goals of many nations. Such goals tend to canalize the imagination and the energies of various peoples. To fulfill these goals will mean a period of intense unrest and even of revolutionary activity. A platform

[18] The Evanston Assembly cited a list of points which should be included in such an international ethos.
[19] See "Christians in the Struggle for World Community." Report of Section IV, International Affairs, Second Assembly, World Council of Churches.

266

of such goals provides a basis for understanding much of the conflict and the direction of its resolution.

Though the nations, including the U.S.A., have been slow to adopt the Declaration of Human Rights as a legal convention, it has a role in the moral education of mankind. It sets the direction for social habits, for settled values, and for generally accepted norms. In the last analysis such norms give moral and spiritual force to law. There is evidence that the values embodied in the charter of the United Nations and in the work of the Commission on Human Rights have already affected the nature and quality of the debate in the General Assembly. The Declaration of Human Rights has directly influenced the new constitutions of Israel and Indonesia and the policies of French Somaliland. The right of the UN to censure violations has also been established. Maintaining a lively faith in fundamental human rights is a contribution which the Christian Church can make in all the nations in which it is active.[20]

The World Council of Churches has called upon its constituent members "to press for the adoption of an International Bill of Rights making provision for the recognition, and national and international enforcement, of all the essential freedoms of man, whether personal, political or social." [21] Despite widespread differences in theological viewpoints the World Council unitedly assigns to organized political authority the duty of condemning violations of human rights and guaranteeing religious liberty. At the Evanston Assembly in 1954 the call was judged as "all the more insistent in this age when, in various parts of the world, totalitarianism—based on ideologies sometimes atheistic and sometimes under the guise of religion—oppresses the freedom of men and of institutions." [22] The Commission of the Churches on International Affairs, sponsored jointly by the International Missionary Council and the World Council of Churches, continues a concern in the field of human rights and especially the freedom of religion and conscience as articulated at both the Oxford Conference in 1937 and the Madras Conference in 1938. Dr. O. Frederick Nolde, director of the CCIA, has noted the part played by the churches in the

[20] See Report of the Fourth National Study Conference on the Churches and World Order, *Christian Faith and International Responsibility*, October 27-30, 1953.

[21] Visser 't Hooft, *First Assembly of the World Council of Churches: The Official Report*, p. 96.

[22] Visser 't Hooft, *Evanston Report*, p. 140. Used by permission of Harper & Bros.

San Francisco Conference of 1945, stating that an "international Christian influence played a determining part in achieving the more extensive provision for human rights and fundamental freedoms which ultimately found their way into the charter." [23]

Since the idea of the responsible society includes the positive affirmation of basic human rights, it is well to recall that discussion of their theological foundation reflects diverse doctrinal convictions. Some would hold to views which reflect the political philosophy and heritage of the natural law tradition; some would argue for the coalescence of philosophical and theological perspectives in the sacredness of personality; some would insist that human rights are grounded in God's grace and that it is for secular authorities to recognize and protect them; some would base human rights on the fact of an individual's faith as a Christian; some would insist that the question of rights in the political order is of less interest than doctrinal purity and the independence of the church; some would ground the need for human rights in terms of religious freedom required by the mission of the church of Christ to evangelize the world, thus making a claim on the protection of the state to guarantee that liberty of preaching. But whatever the ultimate theological or philosophical ground, the ecumenical movement has supported the development of a Christian view of human rights which applies to all men and which can be used in approaching national and international political authorities. This functional personalistic approach has given both unity and strength to the work of the churches.

D. The Scientific Attitude

In addition to the explicit formulation of human rights and duties and the evangelical efforts of Christianity and other world religions, there is a subtle humanizing influence at work in the diffusion of scientific methods and attitudes. Scientific findings can be used and misused. The scientific spirit and discipline is a peacemaker among warring claimants regarding fact.

The expanding and widespread knowledge of scientific methods and technical skills throughout a whole population eventually will result in a revolutionary reassessment of traditional methods of thought and dogmas regarding nature, man, society, and man's relationship to ultimate values. Given a prolonged period of relative peace, it is not

[23] *The Church and International Disorder*, p. 151.

difficult to envisage a time when young people and adults from the remotest parts of the world will find one another in the most animated scientific conferences on an unlimited number of subjects and problems. The meeting of American and Soviet scientists in Geneva in 1955 and the work of UNESCO throughout the world are but heralds or harbingers of potentially unlimited communication. Science not only is a set of procedures or methods adapted to the solving of certain problems; it is an attitude in facing problems, a discipline before the facts, a humility, and a co-operative perspective.

At this point we must raise a caution about the world-wide significance of science. One of the great temptations of the West is to make too close an identification of its scientific and technological advancement with its assumptions about economic organization, political arrangements, and religious values. The non-Western world shows an uneven interest in these various aspects of our culture and is inclined to assume that one part of the Western world may be appropriated without taking the whole of the rest of it. This attitude is often difficult for Westerners, especially Americans, to appreciate. In this book I have stressed the interrelatedness of culture and the fact that a culture cannot be fully understood in its various institutional expressions until one has grasped the basic values and meanings which give it coherence and wholeness. Responsible action must rest on this premise. Such a thesis may be taken to imply that with Western science and technical know-how must go all the other aspects of its way of life. This implication would, however, be an error.

Countries as culturally different as Russia and Japan have drawn heavily from American and west-European scientific methodology and technology. Others are likely to do so in the future. Science and technology are instrumental and may be used in the interests of ulterior goals. They generally affect the means rather than the ends involved. Nuclear fission, as everyone knows, may serve the radically different purposes of destruction in military action or of peacetime production. The West must increasingly be prepared for non-Western nations to apply modern methodologies for the most diverse economic and political goals.

E. Drives in the New Nationalism

Many new nations have achieved independent statehood since 1945. Independence has bred a passionate nationalism which for historic reasons is imbued with anti-Western emotion. Some persons have erroneously inferred that the explosive expressions of criticism of Europe and the United States were a direct result of Soviet action. There are other and deeper sources that must be understood. Criticisms of America, for example, are not due simply or primarily to effective Communist propaganda and intrigue. They are not duplications of attitudes originally "made in Moscow." In New Delhi and Cairo, in Karachi and Jakarta and Nairobi, are men and women exhilarated with the wine of new nationalism, men and women who have never read a page from Marx, Lenin, or Stalin. These new non-Westerners desire what material achievements the Western nations have wrought, but theirs is what has been called the passion of the "revolution of rising expectations." Where national exhilaration runs high and there is restlessness to overcome poverty, retardation, disease, and ignorance, frustration in the face of serious difficulty is likely to produce hostility against the "haves" and against those whose colonial and imperialist policies failed to prepare the peoples for the day of their liberation. This explosive nationalism is combined with anticolonialism and independence. Far from being invented by the Soviets it represents a determination of the people to stand on their own feet, to govern themselves, to develop natural resources for their own welfare, and to prove that nonwhites have ended the long reign of legalized inferiority and can walk with dignity in newness of life. Though hostile for historical reasons to the West, the new nationalism is ideologically derived from it.[24]

It is not only against the West that anxiety and hostility are expressed in many new nations. Japan's aggressions between 1932 and 1945, the Arab states' invasion of Israel in 1947, the invasion of Communist China in Korea and Tibet, and the conflict between Pakistan and India over Kashmir indicate that the tensions of the present age are multidimensional. They are by no means only polarized between Washington and Moscow. The significance of the multiple focuses of national and international conflicts becomes more and more evident as the second decade following World War II reveals the racial, religious, economic, and geographic plurality of forces at work. No nation has ever had a monopoly of goodness or vice, of saintliness or cruelty, of wisdom or foolhardiness.

[24] See Adlai Stevenson, "The Support of Nationalism Helps Combat Imperialist Communism," *Western World*, No. 1 (May, 1957), pp. 34-38.

The nationalistic unrest, compounded with anticolonial feelings and an urgency to achieve the standards of material well-being of the most privileged nations, is bound to continue for a considerable period of time. Nationalism and anticolonialism have a strikingly different relationship to each other in the West from what obtains in non-Western countries. When Western nations give up colonialism or reflect on their own colonial periods, their sense of history is that an era has passed. But for the new nations of Asia and Africa, as Vera Micheles Dean so forcefully points out, "colonialism is not just a memory to be laid aside and forgotten, but a vivid reality which it will take at least another generation or more to erase." [25] The resentment which many feel is like the long heaving and laboring of the sea after a hurricane.

Nationalistic ferment of itself does not produce the constructive reorganization of political, economic, religious, and social life which must attend forward development in the postcolonial period. The drive for "national personality" and economic improvement may tempt a new nation to use shortcuts to achievement, such as Communism seems to offer in its spectacular material advancement since 1917 in the Soviet Union. It is important to grasp the time pressure on a new government today. It must try to telescope several revolutions into one. (1) There must be the transition from revolutionary action to responsible administration. (2) There is the problem of choosing between democratic processes among often politically unprepared peoples and authoritarian government in behalf of the people. (3) There is the problem of fulfilling the material expectations held out to the people during the preceding struggle. These three problems are part of the larger constructive revolution in uniting all the elements in the nation on a common basis and program in such a way that it can go forward. Western nations should be expected to empathize more fully than they have with the struggle in a postcolonial country to find the way of broadening the base of its political power, of encouraging free elections, of affording unchallenged protection for civil rights, and of fostering a sense of community responsibility and dedication on the part of each citizen to the welfare of his country.[26]

[25] Vera Micheles Dean, *The Nature of the Non-Western World* (New York: New American Library, 1957), p. 193. © 1957 by Vera Micheles Dean. Used by permission of the New American Library of World Literature, Inc.

[26] *Ibid.*, p. 215.

In the West the national developments have taken place over several centuries. Cultural changes could therefore be more gradually assimilated than in many parts of Asia and Africa. It is easy to forget that in the early days of the emergence of the nation states in Europe strong individual monarchs dominated the scene. Perhaps Henry VIII and Queen Elizabeth, Louis IX and Louis XIV, Peter the Great, and the like have counterparts in Nasser, Naguib, Peron, Tito, Sukarno, Lenin, Stalin, Mao Tsetung, and Kemal Ataturk. Miss Dean comments on this phenomenon as follows:

These leaders have one thing in common: each is a charismatic personality—a personality who, in the eyes of his people, has a more than human endowment, a touch of divine grace and special wisdom, which fits him in a way no one else in the country is fitted for the office to which God, or destiny, or the will of the people as he senses it has called him.[27]

When such a personality is the leader, the nation undergoes a real crisis. He can, and often does, develop the bases for what may eventually become a democratic government and society. On the other hand, he may betray the revolution. The form of democracy that India, China, Russia, Indonesia, or Burma may eventually produce may be markedly different from what emerged in the United States or Britain, but it may be nonetheless real. To make a real transition to democracy, or to any other basic new alignment, involves profound psychological adjustment in ways of thinking, habits of living, and relationships to changing institutional forms of government, religion, work groups, and family life. In the non-Western world these simultaneous revolutions put a strain on persons vastly greater than in those slower transitions of the West from the medieval world to the mid-twentieth century.

F. Economic Well-Being

The nationalistic drive to be free and independent is linked, as has been emphasized above, with the desire for economic well-being. This goal precipitates a number of difficult questions: How can the desired industrialization take place without first getting rid of the domination of landowners and redistributing the land? Since many identify economic plenty with urban industry, how may the leaders help youth to take the agricultural problems and challenges seriously? What are the

[27] *Ibid.*, p. 214.

sources of the new capital? How does the nation develop the technicians needed for the nuclear age? Can the time gap be closed between ancient agricultural and village economies and modern urban life? How maintain the mental health of people involved in purposive technical change? [28] How can population growth be controlled in the age of cultural transformation?

These problems must be realistically confronted both by the nations undergoing change and by the nations from whom assistance is expected. There must be self-knowledge of the interrelatedness of all cultural factors on the part of the people in transition and sympathetic understanding of their psychological and objective tensions by other nations.

Population and food, land reform and industrialization, capital formation and technical assistance, education and employment, the reconciliation of human welfare with the stability of the state, the role the new nation is to play in world affairs—all these problems which were once in the hands of native rulers or Western colonial powers cry simultaneously for answers. And at the pace at which mankind is moving in the nuclear age, these answers must be found not in some distant future, but today.[29]

Special attention must be given, in passing, to the relation of industry and agriculture. As the West developed, its peoples made advances in agriculture which permitted them to increase their output of food and hence to release manpower from the land for work in industry. In the U.S.A. 10 per cent of the population are able to provide ample food for the other 90 per cent, whereas in India 80 per cent of the poulation are engaged in quite primitive agriculture. The underdeveloped lands are compelled to develop their agriculture as rapidly as possible so as to expand their output of food, cut down on food imports, which divert resources of foreign currency from industrialization, and release manpower from farm labor for new industry. But under the pressure of revolutionary impatience there is often a tendency to overemphasize industry at the expense of agricultural reform. There is a widely held belief that agriculture and raw-material production—the principal occupations of colonial territories in the days of imperialism—are inferior to industrial pursuits, which are

[28] See Mead, *op. cit.*
[29] Dean, *op. cit.,* p. 220.

the unique attribute of the West and the basis of its success.[30] It is easy under these circumstances to forget that the forest must be planted all at once. There is a tendency to overlook the importance of modern techniques in the development not only of agriculture but of transportation, communication, and trade. They need co-ordinated improvement.

The revolution in agriculture requires not only a change in the form of land tenure, which is generally but the first phase. Immediately thereafter the problem of land use and the integration of agriculture has to be faced. Dividing up large estates into small land plots does not of itself pave the way to the most effective land use in the modern world. Russia, China, Israel, and Yugoslavia have all discovered this. When the great landed estates have been divided and given to the peasants, they resist vigorously the collectivization of their plots of ground. In Russia and currently in China the Communist governments are confronted with major political crises because of collectivization. In India a voluntary form of transition is employed.

Small plots of land farmed separately do not permit the modernization required for the general welfare. Beyond efficient land integration and use lies the further problem of cash crops to get the money to buy the machinery, fertilizer, and the like which are part and parcel of greater agricultural productivity. Cash crops for export involve the farmers in the fluctuations of world markets. We have seen in the chapter on agriculture that the gap between farm prices and manufacturing prices haunts all countries, America as well as India. World price fluctuations and the gap between industrial and agricultural income can be overcome only by co-ordinated global trade policies. It must be noted, in passing, that the U.S.A. has resisted such remedial action as would create international commodity agreements to stabilize world prices at a level that would assure the internal stability of national markets.

These crucial difficulties in agriculture tend to divert major attention and efforts to industrialization in a number of Asian countries. India, however, has shown that it is not necessary to take an "either-or" position on the relation of land reform to industry. It is quite

[30] *Ibid.*, p. 236. See World Council of Churches Department on Church and Society, *The Common Christian Responsibility Toward Areas of Rapid Social Change* (Geneva, 1957), No. 2, pp. 14-21.

possible to combine small-scale industries with village community developments. In such a program there is less disruption of family and social life than when vast urban industrialization mushrooms over night. The co-ordination of agricultural reform and village industries does not preclude large industrial developments in other centers.

The agricultural and industrial revolutions can well go forward side by side in a co-ordinated state policy. New governments have an opportunity to synchronize the modernization of agriculture with the creation of industry. In both spheres they can apply the short cuts devised by twentieth-century science and technology. Their people do not need to repeat the long and extreme hardships of the early modern English countryside with its slums and child labor. Neither do they have to repeat the cycle of emptying the rural areas into the cities and then seeking ways of diffusing the industrial population through decentralization. They can conceivably begin with the best that the welfare state has to offer by modernizing villages with electricity, water systems, schools, and hospitals, and they can provide more adequate housing accommodations for wholesome family life. Good planning can bring diversity of occupations to the village. Such a synthesis of the benefits of rural and urban life and such a synchronization of scientific and technological development require planning and general direction by the state. But this does not mean that many detailed operations may not be left to individual or corporate private enterprise both in agriculture and in industry.

In responding to world conditions Americans must understand the need for the non-Western governments to take vigorous economic leadership. It is quite impossible for them to respond adequately and quickly to Western financial help and know-how in any other way.

G. Response to the Appeal of Communism

If nationalism is the dominant dynamic in the non-Western world, then why, it may be asked, does Soviet Communism seem to have such an appeal? The answers to this question are many, but the most significant ones are aspects of the failure of the West to act with faith in the ideals that have made the West a liberating influence for mankind. First of all, Soviet Communism has in theory and in practice identified itself with anticolonialism. Lenin's doctrine of imperialism has been persuasive to some Asian and African nations ever since it was formulated forty years ago. Soviet policy has continually identified itself with colonially dependent and exploited peoples. The image it has created is anti-Western and pro-Asian. By way of contrast the contemporary role of the United States has been cast in defense of its Western allies who were major imperialist powers.[31]

America's fear of Communism has generated an anti-Communism that has placed its military policy and much of its political and economic policy in conflict with the expressive nationalism of newly created independent governments. By history and tradition the United States has been one of the most powerful anticolonial forces, but it has not followed through with a constructive program for a people's freedom —and by default has built up the prestige of the very system it rightly deprecates.

While for many Western powers Communism has been an object of fear and a threat to much that they hold dear, for many Asian and African powers it is a symbol of hope because of its material accomplishments through forty years. The drive to modernize agriculture and industry and to raise the standard of living on the part of postcolonial nations finds in the Soviet achievement an example of what can be quickly done. Russia's possession of nuclear weapons seems sufficient proof that with her methods a formerly "backward" nation can rapidly traverse the technological, power, and prestige-producing distance which Western powers have taken centuries to travel. Science and technology resolutely put to work, using methods that liquidate all "reactionary" elements, can apparently telescope centuries and hence overcome the time lag of the underdeveloped countries.

In many of the new nations there do not exist mores, customs, traditions, institutions, and the moral spirit which undergird democratic political process, freedom, and justice. Consequently the strong men who lead in the postrevolutionary era in their respective countries do not find readily at hand the spiritual resources in the social order for genuine parliamentary procedures. These must be slowly nurtured. They cannot be installed like a steel plant, an oil refinery, or a nuclear reactor. Social life is biological and cultural. It must be grown.

To encourage responsible governments and sound economic pro-

[31] United States policy on the invasion of Egypt has measurably aided in emphasizing America's true anti-colonialism.

grams means to emphasize certain elements in Western and especially American policy. First, it is not too late to reconstruct a policy of the people's freedom coherent with the idea of the responsible society. Second, it is quite possible to give assistance to nations undergoing rapid social change in forms which do not threaten internal stability. For example, Hermann J. Abs,[32] a proponent of the common market idea in Germany, has urged activization of the idea of a European Marshall Plan for bringing aid to underdeveloped countries. The underdeveloped countries urgently need the building up of basic resources and equipment in order to improve the soil, to develop large-scale transport, to exploit mineral resources, to build steam and water power plants, to erect schools, dwellings, and hospitals. Investments in these fields are not commercially very profitable. They must be provided by governments and private sources. But they must all be given in such a way as to maintain co-operation among the helping countries and self-respect and reasonable autonomy for the receiving country. It is urged that such a European Marshall Plan establish a central board for liaison with the International Bank for Reconstruction and Development. Indeed, it is often urged that capital-importing countries feel securer in their autonomy when they deal with international agencies rather than with powerful national governments.

The best response to Communism is to nourish the roots of freedom and to share the fruits of freedom with those who need it so badly. There are differences of opinion as to the best way of developing capital formation, the amounts that are needed, and the conditions in non-Western nations most favorable to effective use of the capital. In the context of the present volume we are not able to decide the relative merits of bilateral arrangements, arrangements through the United Nations and its specialized agencies, or programs of regional bodies, or the World Bank and the International Finance Corporation. Perhaps all these patterns and others yet to be invented will have to be used if the vast job of building the world economy is to be achieved. America's responsibility is great. The United States is the principal source of capital in the free world but has seemingly paid little attention to the foreign capital requirements of the non-Western nations.

[32] Abs is President of the Süd-Deutsche Bank in Frankfurt am Main. See "The Common Market and Aid to Underdeveloped Countries," *Western World*, No. 2 (June, 1957), pp. 59-62.

Miss Dean points out, for example, that in Southeast Asia with a population of more than 600 million the U.S.A. and the World Bank invested only 90 million dollars up to 1956 compared with the 16 billion in Marshall Plan funds in a decade in Europe.[33] There would be more than financial merit, for example, in a plan by which both the U.S.A. and the U.S.S.R. would jointly—through an international agency—divert money now going into the nuclear arms race into the economic development of the Bandung community.

H. Levels of Responsibility

Though the world is interdependent, its problems are not all equally general or universal. Some issues are easily categorized as national, some are regional, while others are clearly global in scope. Great progress in thinking about responsible world order will attend a clear recognition of what issues belong at what level. A. A. Berle, Jr., has pointed out that in the cultural and philosophical field nation-states will permit interference by no one. "Language, religion, culture, manner of life, organization of society, conceptions which give wholeness and personality to a people: these are national." [34] Changes in these areas must come about in ways that are not regarded as interference. Resentment to interference when it occurs may be illustrated by riots and revolts in Poland and Turkey.

Disputes of a border character, but which do not endanger world peace, are perhaps best handled in a regional context. But controversies which endanger world peace or involve great numbers of peoples must be settled at the world level. The United Nations must be made more effective to handle major transportation and natural resource matters, illustrated by Suez transit and the oil supplies by which whole economies are sustained. At this general level belong quite obviously the possibilities of atomic warfare, guided missiles, and the danger of poisoning air and food through atomic fall-out.

But if the United Nations is to be truly effective, it must in the crucial areas affecting world-wide interests be given a monopoly of jurisdiction and power. It must have a monopoly on certain kinds of force, and this means the transference of the corresponding aspect of

[33] Dean, *op. cit.*, p. 251.
[34] "The United States and the United Nations," *Western World*, No. 2 (June, 1957), p. 20.

national sovereignty to the authority of the world government. This shift is today an imperative of responsibility. The United Nations must be given the power to guarantee a stable equilibrium definable as peace. On the negative side this means that nation-states must surrender all nuclear bomb test privileges to the UN. On the positive side the charter provisions must be modified in accordance with this and other responsibilities to provide a greatly strengthened, though limited, world government.

"Massive retaliation" is a dubious—indeed immoral—policy. In the past it has been limited to a few great powers who possessed atomic weapons. But tomorrow such weapons in various forms can readily become a part of the arsenal of all nations, so that the smallest or least responsible country will be able to inflict indescribable damage on others. The power to destroy illimitably will have become universal. This possible situation makes it all the more urgent that the United Nations become the sole custodian of this kind of force.

Self-sufficient nationalism in the West comprises one of the chief blocks to responsible social institutions. The abrogation of complete national sovereignty at the world levels of trade, economic institutions, conventions on human rights, international law and the United Nations is required. At the economic level some initial steps have been taken, but the realities of the mid-twentieth century call for more radical steps. One such step would be to expand the supranationally controlled markets in Europe. It is often recognized that one of the main reasons why the European economy lags behind the American is that its national markets are shrinking and paralyzed by customs barriers. Eliminating the customs barriers would lower the price of merchandise and increase consumption. There is urgency to work out a program of gradual development through the harmonizing of social burdens and the co-ordination of economic and monetary policies. Centuries ago the nation abolished the taxes and tolls between cities and towns. Today a supranational region needs to live in one common market of more than 150 million people.

When account is taken of the social realities of atomic power and the requirements of its constructive peaceful use, it is evident that a progressive and stable economy in Europe is no longer thinkable within the framework of national self-sufficiency. To use nuclear energy effectively necessitates enormous investments of money and technical skill

279

in men. To marshall these successfully calls for co-operation not only of private and public financing but of international agencies. But there are such inherent limitations in the intergovernmental form of development that some have urged the setting up of a supranational organization with sufficient power and independence to guarantee the swift development of this new form of energy. Supranational organization in the peaceful development of atomic power need not necessarily be a part of the United Nations organization. But atomic weapons must be the monopoly of the UN. Intergovernmental control linked to national sovereignty is most likely to fail in either case. Supranational authority may assist greatly in providing the effective framework for a widening common market with freer institutions.

For Christians and the Christian Church the call to give leadership to a responsible society is inescapable. We are led to conclude that negatively speaking the church must completely repudiate the use and testing of H-bombs and that positively speaking all such power must be assigned to the UN. Though the vocation of the church may not embrace pacifism as a political ideology, its work of reconciling love must break through all nationalistic political alignments and the military impasse of our historical situation. By its words translated into deeds the church must become truly ecumenical and show forth the real fact of the reconciliation of all races, nationalities, and classes in the love of Christ. In this way it will demonstrate that the responsible society is not a transient "Christian ideology" but the work of God in the healing of the nations.

Bibliography

The following bibliography comprises books, pamphlets, and magazine articles used in the actual writing of this book.

Abs, Hermann J. "The Common Market and Aid to Underdeveloped Countries," *Western World*, No. 2, June, 1957.

Andrews, F. Emerson. *Philanthropic Giving*. New York: Russell Sage Foundation, 1950.

Anshen, Ruth Nanda, ed. *The Family: Its Function and Destiny*. New York: Harper & Bros., 1949.

Barth, Karl. *Against the Stream*. New York: Philosophical Library, 1954.

Bates, M. Searle. *Religious Liberty: An Inquiry*. New York: Harper & Bros., 1945.

Beach, W., and Niebuhr, H. R. *Christian Ethics*. New York: Ronald Press, 1955.

Beals, Ralph L., and Hoijer, Harry. *An Introduction to Anthropology*. New York: The Macmillan Co., 1953.

Beauvoir, Simone de. *The Second Sex*. Tr. and ed. H. M. Parshley. New York: Alfred A. Knopf, Inc., 1953.

Becker, Carl L. *Freedom and Responsibility in the American Way of Life*. New York: Alfred A. Knopf, Inc., 1945.

Bell, G. K. A. *The Kingship of Christ. The Story of the World Council of Churches*. Baltimore: Penguin Books, Inc., 1954.

Benda, Clemens. *Der Mensch im Zeitalter der Lieblosigkeit*. Stuttgart: Steingruben Verlag, 1956.

Bendix, Reinhard, and Lipset, Seymour M., eds. *Class, Status and Power*. Glencoe, Ill.: Free Press, 1953.

Benedict, Murray R., and others. *Can We Solve the Farm Problem?* New York: Twentieth Century Fund, 1955.

Bennett, John C. *The Christian as Citizen*. New York: Association Press, 1955.

——. *Christian Ethics and Social Policy*. New York: Charles Scribner's Sons, 1946.

——, and others. *Christian Values and Economic Life*. New York: Harper & Bros., 1954.

——. "The Responsible Society," *Social Action*, November, 1954.

Berger, Morroe. *Equality by Statute*. New York: Columbia University Press, 1952.

——, and others, eds. *Freedom and Control in Modern Society*. Princeton, N. J.: D. Van Nostrand Co., 1954.

Bergler, Edmund. *The Revolt of the Middle-aged Man*. Rev. ed. New York: Hill & Wang, Inc., 1957.

Berle, A. A., Jr. "The United States and the United Nations," *Western World*, No. 2, June, 1957.

Beyer, Clara M. "Youth Employment: Opportunity and Protection," *Social Action*, February, 1957.

Bidney, David. *Theoretical Anthropology*. New York: Columbia University Press, 1953.

Bienenfeld, F. R. *Rediscovery of Justice*. New York: Oxford University Press, 1947.

Bienert, Walther. *Die Arbeit Nach der Lehre der Bibel*. Stuttgart: Evangelisches Verlagswerk GMBH, 1954.

Bilheimer, R. S., ed. *Response to Evanston*. Geneva: World Council of Churches, 1957.

Blough, Roy. "Christian Perspectives for an Age of Abundance." New York: National Council of Churches, 1956.

Boodin, J. Elof. *The Social Mind*. New York: The Macmillan Co., 1939.

Bosley, Harold A. *What Did the World Council Say to You?* Nashville: Abingdon Press, 1955.

Boulding, Kenneth E. *The Organizational Revolution*. New York: Harper & Bros., 1953.

Bowen, Howard R. *Social Responsibilities of the Businessman*. New York: Harper & Bros., 1953.

Bowles, Chester. *The New Dimensions of Peace*. New York: Harper & Bros., 1955.

Braun, Konrad. *Justice and the Law of Love*. New York: Contemporary Books, 1951.

Brightman, E. S. *Moral Laws*. New York: Abingdon Press, 1933.

———. *Persons and Values*. Boston University Press, 1952.

Brownell, Baker. *The Human Community*. New York: Harper & Bros., 1950.

Brunner, Emil. *The Divine Imperative*. Philadelphia: Westminster Press, 1943.

———. *Justice and the Social Order*. New York: Harper & Bros., 1945.

Bryson, Lyman, and others, eds. *Approaches to World Peace*. New York: Harper & Bros., 1944.

———. *Freedom and Authority in Our Time*. New York: Harper & Bros., 1953.

———. *Perspectives on a Troubled Decade*. New York: Harper & Bros., 1950.

Bryson, Lyman, and Finkelstein, Louis. *Science, Philosophy and Religion: Second Symposium*. New York: Conference on Science, Philosophy and Religion, 1942.

Bryson, Lyman, and others, eds. *Symbols and Values: An Initial Study*. New York: Harper & Bros., 1954.

Buchanan, N. S., and Ellis, H. S. *Approaches to Economic Development*. New York: Twentieth Century Fund, 1955.

———, and Lutz, F. A. *Rebuilding the World Economy*. New York: Twentieth Century Fund, 1947.

Bullis, Harry A. "The Future Belongs to the Educated Man," *Saturday Review*, January 21, 1956.

Butterfield, Herbert. *Christianity, Diplomacy, and War*. Nashville: Abingdon Press, 1954.

Cadoux, C. J. *Christian Pacifism Re-examined*. Oxford, Eng.: Basil Blackwell & Mott, 1940.

Caplow, Theodore. *The Sociology of Work*. Minneapolis: University of Minnesota Press, 1954.

Cave, Sydney. *The Christian Way*. New York: Philosophical Library, 1951.

Cayton, Horace, and Nishi, Setsuko. ("Churches and Social Welfare," Vol. II.) *The Changing Scene: Current Trends and Issues*. New York: National Council of Churches, 1955.

Chafee, Zechariah, Jr. *The Blessings of Liberty*. Philadelphia: J. B. Lippincott Co., 1956.

Chakerian, Charles G. *The Churches and Social Welfare*. The Hartford Seminary Foundation, Bulletin No. 20, Fall, 1955.

Chandler, Lester V. *A Preface to Economics*. New York: Harper & Bros., 1947.

Church Peace Mission. "The Christian Conscience and War," Statement of a Commission of Theologians and Religious Leaders appointed by the Church Peace Mission, n.d.

Clark, John M. *The Ethical Basis of Economic Freedom*. Westport, Conn.: The Kazanjian Foundation, 1955.

Conference on Economic Progress. *Full Prosperity for Agriculture*. Washington, D.C.: Conference on Economic Progress, 1955.

Copeland, Melvin T. *The Executive at Work*. Cambridge, Mass.: Harvard University Press, 1951.

Cordiner, Ralph J. *New Frontiers for Professional Managers*. New York: McGraw-Hill Book Co., 1956.

Corson, John J., and others. *Economic Needs of Older People*. New York: Twentieth Century Fund, 1956.

Cripps, Sir Stafford. *Towards Christian Democracy*. New York: Philosophical Library, 1946.

Cronan, E. P. *The Dignity of the Human Person*. New York: Philosophical Library, 1955.

Cushman, Robert E. *Civil Liberties in the United States*. Ithaca, N.Y.: Cornell University Press, 1956.

David, Henry, and Ginsberg, Eli. *Womanpower*. New York: Columbia University Press, 1957.

Davidson, H. A. *Forensic Psychiatry*. New York: Ronald Press, 1952.

Dawson, J. M. *America's Way in Church, State, and Society*. New York: The Macmillan Co., 1953.

Dean, Vera Micheles. *The Nature of the Non-Western World*. New York: New American Library, 1957.

Demant, V. A. *Religion and the Decline of Capitalism*. New York: Charles Scribner's Sons, 1952.

D'Entreves, A. P. *Natural Law: An Introduction to Legal Philosophy*. New York: Rinehart & Co., 1951.

"Development of Agriculture's Human Resources." Washington: House Document No. 149 of the 84th Congress, 1st Session, 1955.

Dewey, John. *Freedom and Culture*. New York: G. P. Putnam's Sons, 1939.

Duff, Edward. *The Social Thought of the World Council of Churches*. New York: Association Press, 1956.

Ehler, S. Z., and Morrall, J. B., eds. *Church and State Through the Centuries*. Westminster, Md.: Newman Press, 1954.

Ehrenström, Nils. *Christian Faith and the Modern State*. Chicago: Willett, Clark & Co., 1937.

——, and others. "The Revelation in Christ and the Christian's Vocation" by H. H. Farmer. *Christian Faith and the Common Life*. New York: Willett, Clark & Co., 1938.

Evans, Joseph W., and Ward, Leo R. *The Social and Political Philosophy of Jacques Maritain*. New York: Charles Scribner's Sons, 1955.

Farnham, M. F. "Women's Opportunities and Responsibilities," *The Annals*, 251, May, 1947.

Federal Council of Churches. "Atomic Warfare and the Christian Faith," Report of the Commission on the Relation of the Church to the War in the Light of the Christian Faith, appointed by the Federal Council of Churches, March, 1946.

——. "The Christian Conscience and Weapons of Mass Destruction," Report of a Special Commission, 1950.

Fitch, John A. *Social Responsibility of Organized Labor*. New York: Harper & Bros., 1957.

Fletcher, Joseph F., ed. *Christianity and Property*. Philadelphia: Westminster Press, 1947.

——. *Morals and Medicine*. Princeton, N. J.: Princeton University Press, 1954.

Galbraith, John K. *American Capitalism*. Boston: Houghton Mifflin Co., 1956.

Galloway, G. B. "The Operation of the Legislative Reorganization Act of 1946," *American Political Science Review*, March, 1951.

Gerhart, Eugene C. *American Liberty and "Natural Law."* Boston: Beacon Press, 1953.

Golden, Clinton Strong, and Parker, Virginia, eds. *Causes of Industrial Peace Under Collective Bargaining*. Fourteen case studies. New York: Harper & Bros., 1955.

Goldschmidt, Walter. *As You Sow*. New York: Harcourt, Brace & Co., 1947.

Graham, G. A. *Morality in American Politics*. New York: Random House, 1952.

Groves, Ernest R. and Gladys H. *The Contemporary American Family*. Philadelphia: J. B. Lippincott Co., 1947.

Gurian, W., and Fitzsimons, M. A., eds. *The Catholic Church in World Affairs*. Notre Dame, Ind: University of Notre Dame Press, 1954.

Guttmacher, Manfred S., and Weihofen, Henry. *Psychiatry and the Law*. New York: W. W. Norton & Co., 1952.

Haas, F. J. *Man and Society*, New York: Appleton-Crofts, Inc., 1952.

Harding, A. L., and others. *Religion, Morality, and Law*. Dallas: S.M.U. Press, 1956.

Harsch, Joseph C. "The Supreme Court and Leadership," *The Christian Science Monitor*, June 12, 1957.

Havighurst, Robert J., and Albrecht, Ruth. *Older People*. New York: Longmans, Green & Co., 1953.

Heard, Gerald A., and others. *The Kingdom Without God*. San Jacinto, Calif.: Foundation for Social Research, 1956.

Heering, G. J. *The Fall of Christianity*. Tr. J. W. Thompson. London: George Allen & Unwin, 1930.

Heimann, Edward. "The Economy of Abundance," *Social Action*, January, 1957.

————. *Vernunftglaube und Religion in der Modernen Gesellsehaft.* Tübingen, 1956.

Herskovits, Melville J. *Man and His Works.* New York: Alfred A. Knopf, Inc., 1948.

Hoch, Paul H., and Zubin, Joseph, eds. *Psychiatry and the Law.* New York: Grune & Stratton, Inc., 1955.

Holloway, R. J. *A City Is More Than People.* Minneapolis: University of Minnesota Press, 1954.

Hordern, William. *Christianity, Communism, and History.* Nashville: Abingdon Press, 1954.

Hoyt, Elizabeth E., and others. *American Income and Its Use.* New York: Harper & Bros., 1954.

Huber, Raphael M. *Our Bishops Speak.* Milwaukee: Bruce Publishing Co., 1951.

Hunt, Robert N. Carew. *Marxism: Past and Present.* New York: The Macmillan Co., 1955.

————. *The Theory and Practice of Communism.* New and rev. ed. New York: The Macmillan Co., 1951.

Hunter, Leslie Stannard. *Church Strategy in a Changing World.* London: Hodder & Stoughton, 1950.

Husslein, Joseph. *Social Wellsprings.* Milwaukee: Bruce Publishing Co., 1940, 1942. Vol. I, Leo XII; Vol. II, Pius XI.

Hutchison, John A., ed. *Christian Faith and Social Action.* New York: Charles Scribner's Sons, 1953.

International Development Advisory Board. *Partners in Progress.* (Report to President Truman.) New York: Simon & Shuster, Inc., 1951.

Jenkins, Daniel T. *The Strangeness of the Church.* Garden City, N. Y.: Doubleday & Co., 1955.

Jones, Rufus M., ed. *The Church, the Gospel and War,* New York: Harper & Bros., 1948.

Kahin, George McTurnan. *Asian-African Conference, Bandung, Indonesia, April, 1955.* Ithaca, New York: Cornell University Press, 1956.

Kaighn, Raymond P. *How to Retire and Like It.* 2nd ed. rev. New York: Association Press, 1951.

Karrenberg, F. "Church and Social Questions in Germany" in Study Department of World Council of Churches, "The Responsible Society in a World Perspective," n.d.

Kegley, Charles W., and Bretall, Robert W., eds. *Reinhold Niebuhr: His Religious, Social and Political Thought.* New York: The Macmillan Co., 1956.

Kelsen, Hans. *General Theory of Law and State.* Cambridge: Harvard University Press, 1945.

Kluckhohn, Clyde. *Mirror for Man.* New York: McGraw-Hill Book Co., 1949.

Knudson, A. C. *The Philosophy of War and Peace.* Nashville: Abingdon-Cokesbury Press, 1947.

————. *The Principles of Christian Ethics.* Nashville: Abingdon Press, 1943.

Kvaraceus, William C. *The Community and the Delinquent.* Yonkers, New York: World Book Co., 1954.

Lawton, George, ed. *New Goals for Old Age.* New York: Columbia University Press, 1943.

Lenin, Nikolai. *The State and Revolution.* New York: Vanguard Press, 1926.

Ligutti, the Right Rev. Msgr., Davidson, Gabriel, and Landis, Benson Y. "Man's

Relation to the Land," a statement published by the Committee on Town and Country, 297 Fourth Ave., New York City.

Linebarger, Paul M. A., and others. *Far Eastern Governments and Politics.* Rev. ed. Princeton, N. J.: D. Van Nostrand Co., 1956.

Linton, Ralph. *The Tree of Culture.* New York: Alfred A. Knopf, Inc., 1955.

Lippmann, Walter. *Essays in the Public Philosophy.* Boston: Little, Brown & Co., 1955.

Long, Edward LeRoy, Jr. "A Prolegomena to Discussions Between Pacifist and Non-Pacifist Christians," *Christianity and Society,* Winter, 1951-52.

Loos, A. William, ed. *Religious Faith and World Culture.* Englewood Cliffs, N. J.: Prentice-Hall, Inc., 1951.

McConnell, Grant. *The Decline of Agrarian Democracy.* Berkeley, Calif.: University of California Press, 1953.

McIlwain, C. H. *The Growth of Political Thought in the West.* New York: The Macmillan Co., 1932.

MacIver, R. M. *The More Perfect Union.* New York: The Macmillan Co., 1948.

———. *The Web of Government.* New York: The Macmillan Co., 1947.

MacKinnon, D. M., ed. *Christian Faith and Communist Faith.* New York: St. Martin's Press, 1953.

Madden, Ward. *Religious Values in Education.* New York: Harper & Bros., 1951.

Mannheim, Karl. *Freedom, Power and Democratic Planning.* New York: Oxford University Press, 1950.

Maritain, Jacques. *The Rights of Man and Natural Law.* Tr. Doris C. Anson. New York: Scribner's Sons, 1943.

Maston, T. B. *Christianity and World Issues.* New York: The Macmillan Co., 1957.

Maynard, Donald M. *Your Home Can Be Christian.* Nashville: Abingdon Press, 1952.

Mead, Margaret, ed. *Cultural Patterns and Technical Change.* New York: Columbia University Press, 1953.

———, and Métraux, Rhoda, eds. *The Study of Culture at a Distance.* University of Chicago Press, 1953.

Mercier, C. A. *Criminal Responsibility.* New York: Physicians & Surgeons Book Co., 1926.

Mills, C. Wright. *The Power Elite.* New York: Oxford University Press, 1956.

Muelder, Walter G. *In Every Place a Voice.* Cincinnati, Ohio: Woman's Division of Christian Service, Board of Missions, The Methodist Church, 1957.

———. "Institutional Factors Affecting Unity and Disunity," *The Ecumenical Review,* VIII (January, 1956), 113-26.

———. *Religion and Economic Responsibility.* New York: Charles Scribner's Sons, 1953.

———. "Walter Rauschenbusch and the Contemporary Scene," *The City Church,* April-May, 1957.

Myers, Sir John. "The Influence of Anthropology on the Course of Political Science," *University of California Publications in History,* 4 (1916), No. 1.

Myrdal, Alva, and others. *America's Role in International Social Welfare.* New York: Columbia University Press, 1955.

Myrdal, Gunnar. *An American Dilemma.* New York: Harper & Bros., 1944.

———. *An International Economy: Problems and Prospects.* New York: Harper & Bros. 1956.

286

———. *The Political Element in the Development of Economic Theory.* Cambridge, Mass.: Harvard University Press, 1954.

Naftalin, Arthur, and others. *An Introduction to Social Science.* Philadelphia: J. B. Lippincott Co., 1953.

National Council of Churches. *Christian Faith and International Responsibility.* Report of the Fourth National Study Conference on the Churches and World Order, October 23, 1953.

———. "Christian Responsibility Toward Some Ethical Problems in Inflation," 1952.

———. *Reference Manual on U. S. Diplomatic Representation at the Vatican.* New York: National Council of Churches, 1951.

Nelson, Claud D. "Church and State." New York: National Council of Churches, 1953.

Newcomb, T. M. *Social Psychology.* New York: Dryden Press, 1950.

Nichols, James Hastings. *Democracy and the Churches.* Philadelphia: Westminster Press, 1951.

Niebuhr, H. Richard. *Christ and Culture.* New York: Harper & Bros., 1951.

Niebuhr, Reinhold. *The Children of Light and the Children of Darkness.* New York: Charles Scribner's Sons, 1944.

———. *Christian Realism and Political Problems.* New York: Charles Scribner's Sons, 1953.

———. *Christianity and Power Politics.* New York: Charles Scribner's Sons, 1940.

———. *Faith and History.* New York: Charles Scribner's Sons, 1949.

———. *An Interpretation of Christian Ethics.* New York: Harper & Bros., 1935.

———. *The Self and the Dramas of History.* New York: Charles Scribner's Sons, 1955.

Nimkoff, Myer F. *Marriage and the Family.* Boston: Houghton Mifflin Co., 1947.

Oldham, J. H., ed. *The Oxford Conference: Official Report.* Chicago: Willett, Clark & Co., 1937.

———. *Work in Modern Society.* New York: Morehouse-Gorham Co., 1950.

O'Neill, J. M. *Religion and Education Under the Constitution.* New York: Harper & Bros., 1949.

Opitz, E. A. *The Powers That Be.* San Jacinto, Calif.: Foundation for Social Research, 1956.

Opler, Morris E. "Themes as Dynamic Forces in Culture," *American Journal of Sociology,* November, 1945.

Parsons, Talcott, and Bales, Robert F. *Family, Socialization and Interaction Process.* Glencoe, Ill.: Free Press, 1955.

Peck, William G. A. *A Christian Economy.* New York: The Macmillan Co., 1954.

Pfeffer, Leo. *Church, State, and Freedom.* Boston: Beacon Press, 1953.

Pound, Roscoe. *Criminal Justice in the American City.* Cleveland: Cleveland Foundation, 1922.

———. *Social Control Through Law.* New Haven, Conn.: Yale University Press, 1942.

Public Advisory Board for Mutual Security. *A Trade and Tariff Policy in the National Interest* (the Bell Report). Washington, 1953.

Ramsey, Paul. *Basic Christian Ethics.* New York: Charles Scribner's Sons, 1950.

Rasmussen, A. T. *Christian Social Ethics.* Englewood Cliffs, N. J.: Prentice-Hall, Inc., 1956.

287

Raven, Charles E. *The Theological Basis of Christian Pacifism*. New York: Fellowship of Reconciliation, 1951.

Report of Ecumenical Christian Conference. *A Socialistic Pattern of Society*. Bombay: The National Christian Council of India and The Christian Institute for the Study of Society, 1956.

Riesman, David. *The Lonely Crowd*. New Haven, Conn.: Yale University Press, 1950.

Rommen, Heinrich A. *The State in Catholic Thought*. St. Louis: B. Herder Book Co., 1945.

Rose, Arnold M., ed. *Race Prejudice and Discrimination*. New York: Alfred A. Knopf, Inc., 1951.

Rouse, Ruth, and Neill, Stephen Charles. *A History of the Ecumenical Movement: 1517-1948*. Philadelphia: Westminster Press, 1954.

Rubenstein, I. H. *A Treatise on Contemporary Religious Jurisprudence*. Chicago: The Waldain Press, 1948.

Rutenber, Culbert G. *The Dagger and the Cross*. New York: Fellowship of Reconciliation, 1950.

Sabine, G. H. *A History of Political Theory*. Rev. ed. New York: Henry Holt & Co., 1950.

Sait, E. M. *Political Institutions: A Preface*. New York: Appleton-Century-Crofts, Inc., 1938.

Sax, Karl. *Standing Room Only: The Challenge of Overpopulation*. Boston: Beacon Press, 1955.

Schermerhorn, Richard A. *These Our People*. Boston: D. C. Heath & Co., 1949.

Schiffer, Walter B. *The Legal Community of Mankind*. New York: Columbia University Press, 1954.

Schnucker, Calvin. *How to Plan the Rural Church Program*. Philadelphia: The Westminster Press, 1954.

Schrey, H. H. "Die Wiedergeburt des Naturrechts," *Theologische Rundschau*. 19 (1951), Nos. 1, 2, 3.

———. "Naturrecht und Gottesgerechtigkeit," *Universitas*. 5 (1950).

Schuster, Sir George. *Christianity and Human Relations in Industry*. New York: British Book Center, 1952.

Shaull, M. Richard. *Encounter with Revolution*. New York: Association Press, 1955.

Shott, John G. "How 'Right-to-Work' Laws Are Passed: Florida Sets the Pattern." Washington: The Public Affairs Institute, 1956.

Simpson, G. E., and Yinger, J. Milton. *Racial and Cultural Minorities*. New York: Harper & Bros., 1953.

Sleeman, John F. *Basic Economic Problems*. London: S.C.M. Press, 1953.

Smith, Rockwell C. *The Church in Our Town*. Nashville: Abingdon Press, 1945.

———. *Rural Church Administration*. Nashville: Abingdon Press, 1953.

Smith, Stanley Hugh. *Freedom to Work*. New York: Vantage Press, 1955.

Smith, T. V. "The Happiness of Pursuit," *Western World*, No. 1, May, 1957.

Søe, Niels Hansen. *Christliche Ethik*. München: C. Kaiser, 1949.

Spann, J. Richard, ed. *The Church and Social Responsibility*. Nashville: Abingdon Press, 1953.

Staley, Eugene. *The Future of Underdeveloped Countries*. Harper & Bros., 1954.

Stalin, Joseph. *Foundations of Leninism*. New York: International Publishers, 1932. Vol. I.

Stevenson, Adlai. "The Support of Nationalism Helps Combat Imperialist Communism," *Western World*, No. 1, May, 1957.

Stokes, Anson Phelps. *Church and State in the United States*. New York: Harper & Bros., 1950. 3 vols.

Stouffer, Samuel A. *Communism, Conformity, and Civil Liberties*. Garden City, N. Y.: Doubleday & Co., 1955.

Study Department of World Council of Churches. "Christian Action in Society" by the Oxford Study Group, Study SIE/328, June, 1951.

———. "Social Questions: Responsible Society in a World Perspective," No. 53 E/353, July, 1953.

Tawney, R. H. *Equality*. New York: Harcourt, Brace & Co., 1931.

Temple, William. *Christianity and the State*. New York: The Macmillan Co., 1928.

———. *The Church Looks Forward*. New York: The Macmillan Co., 1944.

———. *Mens Creatrix*. New York: The Macmillan Co., 1917.

———. *Social Witness and Evangelism*. London: Epworth Press, 1943.

———. *Thoughts in War-Time*. New York: The Macmillan Co., 1940.

Thielicke, Helmut. *Theologische Ethik*. Tübingen: J. C. B. Mohr, 1951.

Thomas, George F. *Christian Ethics and Moral Philosophy*. New York: Charles Scribner's Sons, 1955.

Tillich, Paul. *Love, Power, and Justice*. New York: Oxford University Press, 1954.

———. *The Protestant Era*. University of Chicago Press, 1948.

Thomas, M. M. "The Responsible Society in India," *Indian Journal of Theology*, November, 1952.

Thompson, Samuel H. "Unemployment, Income, and Age," *The Personnel and Guidance Journal*, XXXV (Feb., 1957), 377-83.

Troeltsch, Ernst. *Der Historismus und Seine Probleme*. Tübingen: J. C. B. Mohr, 1922.

United Nations Department of Economic Affairs. *Commodity Trade and Economic Development*. New York: United Nations, 1953. Publication Sales No.: 1954, II. B. 1.

Visser 't Hooft, W. A., ed. *Bulletin of the Ecumenical Commission on European Cooperation*, No. 1, February 18, 1953.

———, ed. *The Evanston Report*. The Second Assembly of the World Council of Churches, 1954. New York: Harper & Bros., 1955.

———. *The Kingship of Christ*. New York: Harper & Bros., 1948.

———, *Official Report of the First Assembly of the World Council of Churches: Man's Disorder and God's Design*. New York: Harper & Bros., 1948.

———, and Oldham, J. H. *The Church and Its Function in Society*. New York: Willett, Clark & Co., 1937.

Vorspan, Albert, and Lipman, Eugene J. *Justice and Judaism. The Work of Social Action*. New York: Union of American Hebrew Congregations, 1956.

Vyshinskii, Andrei I., ed. *The Law of the Soviet State*. Tr. H. W. Babb. New York: The Macmillan Co., 1948.

Ward, A. Dudley, ed. *Goals of Economic Life*. New York: Harper & Bros., 1953.

Warner, W. Lloyd, and others. *Social Class in America*. Chicago: Science Research Associates, 1949.

Weber, Max. *The Theory of Social and Economic Organization*. Ed. A. M. Henderson and Talcott Parsons. New York: Oxford University Press, 1947.

Wendland, H. D. "Social Humanism and Christian Care," *The Ecumenical Review*, VIII (January, 1956), 127-42.

Whyte, William H., Jr. *The Organization Man*. New York: Simon & Shuster, Inc., 1956.

Wilcox, Walter W. *Social Responsibility in Farm Leadership*. New York: Harper & Bros., 1956.

Wirth, Louis. "The Urban Way of Life," *The American Journal of Sociology*, July, 1938.

World Council of Churches. "The Common Christian Responsibility Toward Areas of Rapid Social Change," Second Statement, World Council of Churches, October, 1956.

———. *Ecumenical Documents on Church and Society*. Geneva: World Council of Churches, 1954.

———. *Six Ecumenical Surveys*. Preparatory Material for the Second Assembly, Evanston, Ill. New York: Harper & Bros., 1954.

———. "Statement on Totalitarianism" by Central Committee, Chichester, July 9-15, 1949.

Wright, G. Ernest. *The Biblical Doctrine of Man in Society*. London: S.C.M. Press, 1954.

Wright, Quincy, ed. *The World Community*. University of Chicago Press, 1948.

Zinkin, Maurice. *Problems of Economic Development in Asia*. Rev. ed. New York: Institute of Pacific Relations, 1954.

Index